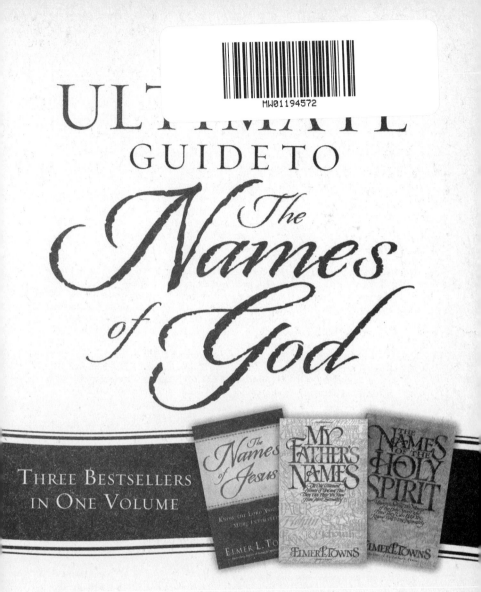

ULTIMATE
GUIDE TO
The Names of God

THREE BESTSELLERS
IN ONE VOLUME

The Names of Jesus

MY FATHER'S NAMES

THE NAMES OF THE HOLY SPIRIT

ELMER L. TOWNS

Regal

For more information and
special offers from Regal Books, email us at
subscribe@regalbooks.com

Published by Regal
From Gospel Light
Ventura, California, U.S.A.
www.regalbooks.com
Printed in the U.S.A.

This work is a compilation of the following titles:
My Father's Names © 1991 by Elmer L. Towns
The Names of Jesus © 1987 by Elmer L. Towns, previously printed by Accent Publications
(ISBN 0-89636-243-4)
The Names of the Holy Spirit © 1994 by Elmer L. Towns

Library of Congress Cataloging-in-Publication Data
Towns, Elmer L.
The ultimate guide to the names of God : three bestsellers in one / Elmer L. Towns.
pages cm
ISBN 978-0-8307-6967-4 (trade paper)
1. God (Christianity)—Name. 2. Jesus Christ—Name. 3. Holy Spirit—Name. I. Towns,
Elmer L. My Father's names. II. Towns, Elmer L. Names of Jesus. III. Towns, Elmer L.
Names of the Holy Spirit. IV. Title.
BT180.N2T69 2014
231—dc23
2014003793

Rights for publishing this book outside the U.S.A. or in non-English languages are
administered by Gospel Light Worldwide, an international not-for-profit ministry.
For additional information, please visit www.glww.org, email info@glww.org, or write to
Gospel Light Worldwide, 1957 Eastman Avenue, Ventura, CA 93003, U.S.A.

To order copies of this book and other Regal products in bulk quantities,
please contact us at 1-800-446-7735.

Contents

BOOK ONE

My Father's Names

BOOK TWO

The Names of Jesus

PART 1:
OUR LORD JESUS CHRIST

PART 2:
GROUPINGS OF THE NAMES OF JESUS CHRIST

when it comes to understanding who Jesus is: Jesus called Himself Son of Man, but He was also the Son of God and the only begotten Son.

Several names and titles of Jesus express the uniqueness of His nature and have important theological implications in the study of Christology. These include "the Image of God," "the Firstborn," "the Beloved," "the Alpha and Omega" and "the Logos" (the Word).

The name "Jehovah" was so revered by the Jews that they never uttered it. It was the name of the One who had introduced Himself to Moses as I AM THAT I AM. The proof that Jesus was Jehovah is seen in the fact that He used that divine title for Himself in eight ways in the Gospel of John.

Jesus promised that He would build His Church, so one would expect to find Him closely identified with that Church. Several names of Christ have special significance in that they reveal His relation to His Church. These titles include "Bridegroom," "Shepherd," "Head," "Vine," "Stone," "Temple" and "Gardener."

The final book of the New Testament offers the fullest revelation of Jesus Christ in Scripture. It is not surprising, then, that John uses at least 72 different names of Jesus to describe important truths about the Lord. This chapter takes a closer look at several of the more significant names in the book of Revelation.

BOOK THREE

The Names of the Holy Spirit

PART 1:
JESUS AND THE HOLY SPIRIT

Jesus used the term Paraclete, meaning "Helper," to describe the Holy Spirit to His disciples. Perhaps more than any other, this name consistently describes the character of the Holy Spirit in His relationship to us prior to our conversion, at the time of our conversion and following our conversion.

PART 2:
THE MINISTRY OF THE HOLY SPIRIT IN THE BELIEVER

PART 3:
THE NATURE OF THE HOLY SPIRIT

names include "the Gift of God," "the Helper," "the Spirit of Christ," "the Spirit of Jesus," "the Spirit of Jesus Christ," "the Spirit of His Son" and "the Spirit of Truth."

   Certain attributes ascribed to the Holy Spirit in Scripture tend to describe His character, and they answer the question "What is the Holy Spirit like?" These terms make specific references to life, eternity, generosity, goodness, holiness, graciousness, judgment, knowledge, love, might, power, truth, understanding, wisdom and steadfastness.

PART 4:
THE GENERAL WORK OF THE HOLY SPIRIT

   Certain traits ascribed to the Holy Spirit tend to emphasize the Holy Spirit's role in the inspiration and preservation of Scripture. These authorship names include "the Anointing," "the Fullness of God," "the Helper," "the Spirit of the Holy God," "the Spirit of Prophecy," "the Spirit of the Prophets," "the Spirit of Revelation," "the Spirit of Truth" and "the Wind."

   Certain names ascribed to the Holy Spirit emphasize His role in the creation and sustaining of life on Earth. These creative names include the Breath names, "the Finger of God," the Life names and the Voice names of the Holy Spirit.

   In what may be the apostle Paul's most complete discussion of the ministry of the Holy Spirit, a number of descriptive names for the Holy Spirit are stated or implied in the Epistle to the Ephesians to describe the balanced ministry of the Holy Spirit. These names include "the Spirit of Promise," "the Spirit of Wisdom," "the Spirit of Access," "the Spirit of Indwelling," "the Spirit of Revelation," "the Spirit of Power," "the Spirit of Unity," "the Spirit of Feeling," "the Spirit of Sealing," "the Spirit of Fruitfulness," "the Spirit of Fullness," "the Spirit of Victory" and "the Spirit of Prayer."

   Certain names or titles for the Holy Spirit describe His work in revival. These terms include "the Anointing," "My Blessing," "the Breath of Life," "the Dew," "the Enduement [clothing] of Power," "the Finger of God," "Floods on the Dry Ground," "the Fullness of God," "the Glory of the Lord," "the Oil of Gladness," "the Power of the Highest," "Rain," "Rivers of Living Water," "Showers that Water the Earth," "the Spirit of Glory," "the Spirit of Life," "the Spirit of Power" and "Water."

A number of the names or titles of the Holy Spirit may be viewed as emblems that portray various aspects of who the Holy Spirit is and what He does. Among these portraits of the Holy Spirit are "the Anointing," "My Blessing," "a Deposit," "the Dew," "the Doorkeeper," "a Dove," "an Enduement" (clothing), "the Finger of God," "Fire," "Fountain," "the Guarantee," "the Oil," "Rain," "Rivers," "Water" and "the Wind."

BOOK ONE

My Father's Names

THE OLD TESTAMENT NAMES OF GOD AND HOW THEY CAN HELP YOU KNOW HIM MORE INTIMATELY

ELMER L. TOWNS

Introduction

Can you imagine two persons really getting to know and love each other without knowing each other's names? Somehow, our name becomes so intertwined with our personality that only those who know our name can truly love and understand us.

This is no less true in our relationship with God. Yet many of us have not taken the time to get to know and love God by becoming familiar with the many names by which He is known in Scripture. This book is therefore a guide for those who want to come to know Him more intimately.

There are three primary names of God in the Old Testament: "God" (*Elohim*), "Lord" (*Jehovah*, or *Yahweh*) and "Lord/Master" (*Adonai*). Beyond these, God is called by over 80 other compound names or descriptive titles. The names are studied here in the order in which they first appear in Scripture.

In chapter 1 these primary names are examined, and this becomes a foundation for the rest of the book. In the next chapter eight important names of God are surveyed through the structure of Psalm 23 under the general title "The Lord Is My Shepherd." Then other names of God are surveyed, one name in each chapter (chapters 3-8), corresponding roughly to the time when the name was introduced to God's people in the Old Testament.

The final chapters are climactic, studying the primary names of God in depth, building on what has gone before. Chapter 9 examines our slave relationship to *Adonai*, the Lord/Master. Chapter 10 looks at the name *Elohim* and answers the question "Who is God?" by defining His nature. Chapter 11 answers the question "What is God like?" by examining the name *Jehovah* and describing Jehovah's attributes. The last chapter is the capstone. It looks at the name "Father," the New Testament name for God. All the Old Testament meanings of the names of God are wrapped up in the New Testament name "Father."

Although not every name of God is discussed in these 12 chapters, the names of God that have been chosen for study in this book are those most discussed in the history of the Church and those that give the most significant insights into the Person and nature of God.

This book was originally a series of Sunday School lessons that I taught in the Pastor's Bible Class at Thomas Road Baptist Church in Lynchburg, Virginia. Senior pastor Jerry Falwell said that this is the largest Sunday School in America because of the thousands who attend in person and the almost one million who view it on television. Class members were caught up in the content of this series because it contained so much material that was new to them. Theirs was not an infatuation with secret knowledge but a yearning to know and approach God in prayer. Their response encouraged me to put the lessons into print so that others could have this information and teach it in their classes. May this book help you understand God better and, as a result, may you become more dedicated to Him.

Elmer L. Towns
Lynchburg, Virginia

1

Hallowed Be Thy Names

One evening I visited Mount Rushmore National Monument in South Dakota—and almost missed it. I had spoken at an evening meeting for pastors some 30 miles away, and after my message I asked one of the ministers to drive me to the monument. I did not know that the floodlights that illuminate the gigantic sculptures of Washington, Jefferson, Lincoln and Roosevelt were turned off at 11 o'clock. We arrived at the base of Mount Rushmore at 11:10 P.M.— 10 minutes late. The spectacular carvings were veiled in darkness. As a result of an imminent storm, there wasn't even any moonlight.

But what I thought was a barrier became a blessing. Flashes of lightning accompanied the thunderstorm, and with each flash I got a quick glance at the great sculptures. I had certain preconceived images in mind from photographs, and I strained to compare each statue with the likeness in my mind's eye. The more I watched, the more I realized that I was appreciating their magnificence and grandeur even more than I would have if the storm had not forced me to view them more intensely.

In the same way, we struggle to understand God. We know He is there, but in the darkness of this life, we cannot see Him. Then come flashes of light that reveal Him: the creation—the miracles— the Ten Commandments—His presence in our conscience.

But there is another flash of illumination that is often overlooked. We can come to know God through His names. The many descriptive titles and names given in Scripture are like lightning flashes on a summer night revealing His nature and works. We can get to know God better through His names.

Why does God have so many names? Just as white light is made up of seven different rays or colors, so too God is made up of different attributes that are illuminated by different names. Just as a person can examine each of the seven different colors to understand the nature of light, so too we can examine each of God's attributes in order to better understand Him. Put together, the seven hues of light become white light, with the individual colors obscured to the unaided eye. The unity of light is its diversity, and only thus do we understand it. In much the same way, God's names combine to reveal the One God, divine in all His attributes.

Why Study the Names of God?

We come to understand people by their names and titles. David, the man after God's heart, is better understood by a study of his various names or titles. Knowing that David is described as a shepherd, warrior, king, poet and musician helps us understand his character and gives us insight into David the man. He was the son of Jesse and a great grandson of Boaz. David was from the line of Judah, the royal line from which many of Israel's kings came and from which Jesus Christ was born.

In a similar way, studying God's names reveals His character to us more intimately. Among other names, for example, we know God as Creator, Judge, Savior and Sustainer. By reflecting on His names, we can gain insight into His nature and understand more about how He works in our lives. While mortals cannot fathom His nature completely, God has revealed Himself through His Scriptures and has given us the Holy Spirit as a guide in knowing Him. While we remain human, we can only "know in part" (1 Cor. 13:12), and with our limited understanding we will never fully grasp all that an unlimited God is and does. But as we come to understand God's names, we approach further in our understanding of God Himself.

A second reason for studying the names of God is in order to understand the different relationships that we can have with Him. A young man calls his girlfriend sweetheart, but after he marries her, the two of them have a new relationship signified by a new name: wife. She may have been Mary Jones, but after the marriage ceremony, if she follows the usual custom, she has a new name—perhaps Mary Livingston. Her new name tells everyone that she has a new relationship with her husband.

The names of God become meaningful as we adjust to new or growing relationships with Him. Usually God revealed a new name to people at a fork in their road of life. He would help people through a difficulty by allowing them to experience Him in a different way, through a new name.

Abraham seems to have learned more of the different names of God than any other person in Scripture. Why? Because Abraham was pioneering new trails in the walk of faith. Each time God wanted Abraham to reach higher, He revealed to him a new name. Abraham had known God as "the LORD" (*Jehovah*, or *Yahweh*, Gen. 13:4); but when he tithed to Melchizedek, Abraham learned a new name: *El Elyon*, "the most high God, possessor of heaven and earth" (14:18-19).

When Abraham complained to God in prayer that he did not have an heir for the promised inheritance, God revealed to him another of His names: *Adonai*, meaning "Master" or "Lord" (15:2). The eternal LORD God of heaven would care for Abraham in a Master-slave relationship. Later Abraham learned that God would nurture and powerfully sustain him as *El Shaddai* (17:1), that the secret name of God is *El Olam* (21:33), and that God would provide for him as *Jehovah Jireh* (22:14). Each time Abraham entered into a deeper relationship with God, he learned a new attribute of God through a new divine name.

A third reason for studying the names of God is that through His names God reveals that He is the source and solution to our problems. When Israel fought Amalek, they learned the name *Jehovah Nissi*, "the LORD Our Banner," meaning that God would and could protect them (Exod. 17:15). As each name of God is unfolded, a new source of strength is revealed to His people. Moses learned the name *Jehovah Rophe* (from *rapha*, "to heal"), meaning that God would provide healing for the people (15:26). Later, Gideon learned of God as *Jehovah Shalom*, revealing a God of peace to a young man who was fearful and unsure of himself (Judg. 6:24).

Finally, the various names of God teach us to look to Him in our crises. God revealed His different names in times of crisis to reveal how He would help His servants.

Christians sometimes seem to think that they are immune to problems—that salvation solves them all. Of course this is shown to be untrue when problems or crises arise and we find ourselves crying out, "Why me? Why now? Why this?"

God allows people to have problems for a number of reasons. Sometimes He wants to test us, to see if we will handle problems by faith or in our own strength. At other times He allows problems to overwhelm us so that we will turn to Him. In our crises God reveals Himself anew, just as He originally revealed Himself through His names when His people needed help. If we know God's names, we can more freely turn to Him in the name that fits our situation. The following chart shows some facts about the three primary names or titles of God revealed in the Old Testament.

The Three Primary Names of God

Hebrew	English	First Reference	Root	Meaning
Elohim	God	Genesis 1:1	*Alah*—to swear, or to bind with an oath	Strong Creator
Jehovah	LORD	Genesis 2:4	*Hayah*—to become, or to continue to be	Self-existent One who reveals Himself
Adonai	Lord	Genesis 15:2	to be master	The master of a slave

Beyond these primary names, there are many compound names that also refer to God. As we have noted, God has different names to show us different aspects of His nature, or different ways in which He relates to us. Names and titles function this way among us, as well. When Ruth Forbes became my wife, her name became Ruth Towns. The new name reflected new duties and a new and intimate relationship to me. We became one flesh. Then Ruth Towns became a mother. My new baby daughter called her "Mother," a different name with new responsibilities and new intimacies.

The people of God first began using *Elohim* as a primary name for God the Creator. As they walked with God, they learned that He was also "LORD," or *Jehovah*, the Self-existent One. Later they learned that He was *Adonai*, their Master. (Some scholars believe that *Jehovah* or *Yahweh* ["the LORD"] is actually the only proper, personal name for God and that all other names are just descriptive titles.) A brief overview of all three names will introduce all that will follow in this book.

Elohim, the All-Powerful Creator

The first reference to God in Scripture uses the name *Elohim*: "In the beginning God [*Elohim*] created . . ." (Gen. 1:1). This name for God is a reference to the supreme Being, the original Creator, the perfect Being, the eternal One. Just as most religions describe their divinities in terms of ultimate power (that is, God), *Elohim* focuses on several aspects of power, strength or creativity. The Hebrew word *Elohim* is from *El*, the strong One, or the Creator, or *alah*, to swear or to bind oneself with an oath (implying faithfulness). Therefore, when we call the Creator God, we are referring to His strength or omnipotence. He is all-powerful, more powerful than any person in the universe. Nothing is equal to Him in power.

Elohim appears 31 times in the first chapter of Genesis, because there God's creative power is emphasized. "God saw" (1:4), "God called" (1:5), "God said" (1:6), "God made" (1:7), "God blessed" (1:22) and "God created man in his own image" (1:27).

The names of God in the Bible indicate that He has personality, that He is a Being with intellect, emotion and will. To many people God is not personal. Plato thought that God is eternal mind, the cause of all good in nature. Aristotle considered God the ground of all being. The German philosopher Hegel said that God is an impersonal being, like a picture on the wall or a plate on the table. Spinoza, a pantheist, called God "the absolute universal substance," which means that He is the same thing as matter. Others have said that God is influence, power or energy. Some say that God is just an idea, with no real existence. But by revealing the names of God, the Old Testament presents God as a powerful Person who thinks, feels and makes decisions—He has the attributes of personality.

Jehovah, the Self-Existent One

The term "LORD" (spelled with a capital and small capitals in many translations) indicates the name *Jehovah* (or *Yahweh*), meaning "the Self-existent One." The root word is *hayah*, "to become." In Exodus 3:14 this root appears twice, as God identifies Himself as "I AM THAT I AM." Thus God signifies that He alone is that Being who is self-existing—His existence depends on no other. The word *hayah* also implies that God is that Being who is continuously revealing Himself.

The name "LORD" or *Jehovah* is the most frequently used term for God in the Old Testament, appearing 6,823 times. The name "I AM" is always appropriate for God, since He has always existed in the past and will always exist in the future.

The LORD Our Master

The third primary name for God is "Lord" (with only the first letter capitalized, to distinguish it from "LORD"), which is translated from the Hebrew word *Adonai*. This word comes from *adon*, which refers to the master of a slave. Hence *Adonai* indicates headship. When a person truly believes in God, that person also becomes a slave in service to his Lord, who has done so much for him. This title for God implies a twofold relationship: the Master can expect implicit obedience from the slave, and the slave can expect the Master to give him orders and to provide for his needs.

Jesus said, "Ye call me Master and Lord: and ye say well; for so I am" (John 13:13). Thus the believer is the slave of Christ, who has redeemed him. Since service is the issue in the master-slave relationship, the name *Adonai* is used in Scripture to indicate that believers are to minister for God.

Compound Names for God

These three primary names of God are often joined together, or compounded, to communicate further insight into the Person of God and how He cares for His people. Three of these are illustrated by the following expansion of the previously displayed chart.

Primary Names

Elohim	God	Genesis 1:1
Jehovah	LORD	Genesis 2:4
Adonai	Lord/Master	Genesis 15:2

Compound Names

	Jehovah Elohim	Genesis 2:4
Lord GOD	Adonai Jehovah	Genesis 15:2
Lord God	Adonai Elohim	Daniel 9:3

The name "LORD God" (*Jehovah Elohim*), which blends two major names of the Deity, is used distinctively in Scripture to indicate (1) the relationship of God to man in creation (see Gen. 2:7-15), (2) the moral authority of God over man (see vv. 16-17), (3) the One who controls man's earthly relationships (see vv. 18-24), and (4) the One who redeems man (see 3:8-15,21).

The name "Lord GOD" (*Adonai Jehovah*) emphasizes the *Adonai* or lordship characteristics of God rather than His *Jehovah* traits. While He is still Creator, of course, the expression "the Lord GOD" indicates that God is Master of His people as well.

The third compound name, "Lord God" (*Adonai Elohim*), refers to God as Master and Creator. This name means that God is the Master over all the false gods of other religions. When Daniel prays, "I set my face unto the Lord God" (Dan. 9:3), he is affirming that his Master (*Adonai*) is the God (*Elohim*) of false deities who claim to be God.

How the Jews Used God's Name

A study of the Hebrew proper names of God is more than a study of God's titles. It is also a history of Israel's view of God. Since a people's view of God is a commentary on their view of their own life and culture, a study of the emerging Jewish use of the names for God is really a study of the Jews.

The various names of God represent a theology of God from the perspective of the Hebrew mind. According to the various Jewish encyclopedias, of all the names of God recorded in the Old Testament, the name *Jehovah* (or *Yahweh*) is God's distinctive personal name. The other names for God are actually titles, descriptions or reflections of His attributes.

In Old Testament times the Jews felt that the divine name was equivalent to God's divine presence or power. The name of the LORD (*Jehovah*) was specially connected with the altar or the holy of holies, because that was the localized presence of God on Earth. Instead of looking to pagan altars, the Israelites were to look to "the place which the LORD your God shall choose out of all your tribes to put his name there, even unto his habitation" (Deut. 12:5). Subdued enemies of God would eventually be brought to "the place of the name of the LORD of hosts, the mount Zion" (Isa. 18:7). So precious was the name of *Jehovah* that the people were not even to take the names of false gods upon their lips lest they blaspheme the name of *Jehovah* by allowing both names to come out of the same mouth (see Exod. 23:13; Josh. 23:7).

According to early Jewish custom, the name *Jehovah* was used in personal greetings, as "The LORD be with you" and "The LORD bless thee" (Ruth 2:4). But with time, the idolatry around the Jews became a temptation. To reinforce their belief in monotheism, the rabbis came to recognize *Jehovah* as the only proper name for God, rather than *Elohim* or *Adonai*, which were considered only descriptive appellations of divinity.

Eventually, the name *Jehovah* was considered too holy to pronounce, and the rabbis simply referred to it as "the Name." Others called it the "extraordinary name," the "distinguished name" or the "quadrilateral name" (or Tetragrammaton), for the four letters, YHWH. With the passing of time, the name *Jehovah* was pronounced only by the priests in the Temple when blessing the people (see Num. 6:23-27). Outside the Temple, they used the word *Adonai*.

The high priest also mentioned the name *Jehovah* on *Yom Kippur*, the Day of Atonement, 10 times, so that its pronunciation would not be lost. Also, older teachers repeated this name to their disciples once during every sabbatical year. They would repeat Jehovah's words: "This is my name for ever, and this is my memorial unto all generations" (Exod. 3:15). In teaching young theological students, the rabbis would write "for ever" (*olam*) defectively, rendering it *alam*, "to conceal," thus teaching their students that the name of God was to be concealed.

During the Maccabean uprising in the second century B.C., the Temple in Jerusalem was destroyed, and the priests ceased to pronounce the name altogether. Also because of the Maccabean revolt, occupying forces prohibited the utterance of "the Name." Later, when the Jews won relative independence from Rome, the rabbis decreed that the name could be used in certain formal notes and documents. Thus *Jehovah* was identified regularly in everyday life. This practice, however, was soon discontinued, because the rabbis thought that the name would be defiled when their notes were cancelled or thrown away, especially if they were found by someone who would profane or blaspheme the name. Consequently, the pronunciation of the name YHWH passed off the scene.

According to tradition, when the Jews wanted to distinguish Israelites from Samaritans and later from Christians, they taught that the faithful would not pronounce the name. Slowly the doctrine arose that those who pronounced it were excluded from a share of the world to come. One rabbi said that whosoever explicitly pronounced the name would be guilty of a capital offense.

Since the name of God was synonymous with holiness, to profane the name was a heinous sin. Another rabbi said that he who was guilty of profaning the name could not rely on repentance or upon the power of the Day of Atonement to gain him expiation or upon sufferings to wipe it out; death alone could wipe it out. Yet another rabbi was even stricter, saying that the profaner of the name was classed among the five types of sinners for whom there is no forgiveness.

All kinds of practices grew up about writing the name *Jehovah*. When a scribe copying the Scriptures came to the sacred name, he would lay aside his quill and get a new one with which to write *Jehovah*. Then he would break the new pen so that no other name would ever flow from it, ensuring that the scribe could not be charged with blaspheming the name.

When Jesus came, He taught the multitudes to call on the name of the LORD God by addressing their prayers to the first Person of the Trinity. He taught people to use the intimate introduction in prayer, as in "Our Father which art in heaven, hallowed be thy name" (Luke 11:2).

Hallowing the Name Today

Several practical Christian applications flow from knowing the name of the LORD.

Prohibition Against Cursing

Commandments prohibit a person from taking God's name in vain. When a person lightly uses the name of God, he is speaking lightly of God. When a person blasphemes God's name, he blasphemes God. When a person curses by using God's name, he is either trying to take the place or authority of God, or he is rejecting God's authority in his life. Because God's name represents His Person, He said, "Thou shalt not take the name of the LORD thy God in vain" (Exod. 20:7).

Seeking God by His Name

The Bible clearly commands us, "Be still, and know that I am God" (Ps. 46:10). Knowing God's name is a good way to know God, for it reveals to us the nature of His Person and His work. As we are searching to know God, however, we should remember that He is also searching us and examining us. As David gave his son Solomon the plans for the Temple, he said, "Know thou the God of thy father, and serve him with a perfect heart . . . : for the LORD searcheth all hearts, and understandeth all the imaginations of the thoughts: if thou seek him, he will be found of thee; but if thou forsake him, he will cast thee off for ever" (1 Chron. 28:9).

A person comes to God through Jesus Christ His Son, but even then God's name becomes important, for "as many as received him, to them gave he power to become the sons of God, even to them that believe on his name" (John 1:12). Later in the same Gospel, John says that he writes "that ye might believe, . . . and that believing ye might have life through His name" (20:31).

Gaining Knowledge of Ourselves

The Bible teaches that we are created in the image of God: "God created man in his own image, in the image of God created he him; male and female created he them" (Gen. 1:27). The more we learn about God, therefore, the more we learn about ourselves. Because we are created in God's image, we have a subconscious idea of God. But instead of recognizing God as our Master and submitting to Him, we strive subconsciously to take His place. That was the sin of Lucifer in wanting to be like the Most High (see Isa. 14:13-14). Since we have God's nature, the more we learn about Him, the more we learn about ourselves.

Knowing God and Eternal Life

When Jesus prayed in the garden the night before His death, He said, "This is life eternal, that they might know thee the only true God, and Jesus Christ, whom thou has sent" (John 17:3). It is impossible to know God without being saved. "Neither is there salvation in any other: for there is none other name under heaven given among men, whereby we must be saved" (Acts 4:12).

2

The Lord Is My Shepherd: Jehovah Roi

THE CARING NAME OF GOD

When the Bible says "All we like sheep have gone astray" (Isa. 53:6), it compares us to dumb animals. Sheep never perform in a circus, because, as the animal trainer will tell people, it is almost impossible to train them to do tricks. Sheep were not given protection like the quills of a porcupine, the scent of a skunk, the claws of a cat or the teeth of a lion. Of all the animals, sheep are characteristically the least protected. In water their wool gets so soaked and heavy that it pulls them under, and they easily drown. They have little instinct of danger and are susceptible to poisonous snake bites and infectious insect bites. They only lie down when they are full, and then if someone doesn't turn them over, they may suffocate.

The total dependence of sheep upon the shepherd is the reason sheep are used as an illustration for the relationship between the Lord and believers. When Psalm 23:1 says "The LORD is my shepherd," it is speaking of *Jehovah Roi*, the faithful God who watches over us and cares for us. Notice that it is "the LORD" (*Jehovah*) who is our shepherd, not God. The use of the personal name *Jehovah* keys on God's intimacy with His people. *Jehovah* signifies the covenant-keeping God, and *Roi* refers to the way He tenderly cares for us.

Some have supposed that the Old Testament portrays God only in His awesome majesty, not as a God with the love and concern of a Father, as in the New Testament. But the picture of *Jehovah*

Roi in Psalm 23 is of God as an intimate Father who cares for His own.

The two words *Jehovah Roi* are not a phrase consisting of the LORD'S name attached to a noun or an adjective, indicating an actual title for God. The two words comprise a sentence indicating a function of God, or a description of what He does: "The LORD is my shepherd" (Ps. 23:1). As a matter of fact, Psalm 23 has several other descriptions that show God's care for His people. Each trait also appears elsewhere in Scripture, with a descriptive phrase or implied title for *Jehovah*, as the following chart shows.

Traits of God in Psalm 23

Functions in Psalm 23	Implied Name or Trait	Reference
The LORD is my shepherd (v.1)	*Jehovah Roi*	Psalm 23:1
I shall not want (v. 2)	*Jehovah Jireh* (the LORD Shall Provide)	Genesis 22:14
He leadeth me beside the still waters (v. 2)	*Jehovah Shalom* (the LORD [Our] Peace)	Judges 6:24
He restoreth my soul (v. 3)	*Jehovah Rophe* (the LORD [Our] Healer)	Exodus 15:26
He leadeth me in the paths of righteousness (v. 3)	*Jehovah Tsidkenu* (the LORD Our Righteousness)	Jeremiah 23:6
I will fear no evil (v. 4)	*Jehovah Nissi* (the LORD My Banner)	Exodus 17:15
Thou art with me (v. 4)	*Jehovah Shammah* (the LORD Is There)	Ezekiel 48:35
Thou anointest my head with oil (v. 5)	*Jehovah Mekaddishkhem* (the LORD Who Sanctifies You)	Exodus 31:13

Notice that each divine function corresponds to a deep human need. Psalm 23 is structured to show that our needs are matched by the caring response of God. Taking each of the above human needs and its corresponding divine trait in order, let us see what they tell us of the caring God of Psalm 23 and how He meets our needs.

The God Who Meets Our Needs

Protection: *Jehovah Roi*

The Bible's first reference to God as a shepherd is in a statement made by Jacob in Genesis 48:15, in which he speaks of "the God which fed [shepherded] me all my life long." Even though Jacob had wandered far from God, as a sheep wanders from the pasture or the shepherd, God had been Jacob's shepherd all along. As an older man, Jacob realized that he had experienced *Jehovah Roi*.

What are sheep like? When Isaiah said that "All we like sheep have gone astray; we have turned every one to his own way" (53:6), he referred first to the fact that they are directionless, with no sense of where home is. Second, sheep have little sense of danger and are generally ignorant in matters of self-preservation. A sheep will wander too close to the den of a wolf or get caught in a thicket of briars or wander out into swift water where its fluffy fleece will first float it away, then weigh it down to be drowned. Because we, like sheep, do not know how to protect ourselves, we need *Jehovah Roi*, the divine Shepherd.

This threefold nature of sheep means that a shepherd has a threefold task. Under the leadership of *Jehovah Roi*, the Good Shepherd, earthly shepherds or pastors also help fulfill this function. First, they lead the sheep by example. The power of a godly role model is great. Good pastors lead the flock "beside the still waters" (Ps. 23:2) so that the sheep can "drink" of Jesus Christ, have fellowship with Him and build up their spirituality. Shepherds also lead the sheep "in the paths of righteousness for his name's sake" (v. 3). This is leadership away from sin and to-ward true godliness.

Second, a shepherd feeds his sheep by guiding them into green pastures or by picking clover and feeding them by hand. Earthly pastors feed the flock by teaching and explaining the Word to the people. Jesus reminded Peter of his responsibility in this area three times (see John 21:15-17). He was to be an example to the flock, to teach and preach the Word of God, and to tend the sheep.

Third, the shepherd tends his flock by protecting the sheep. Earthly shepherds protect the sheep by rebuke, warning and counsel, helping them guard against sin.

Bread: *Jehovah Jireh*

"I shall not want" (Ps. 23:1). Life's basic needs are provided by *Jehovah Jireh*, "the LORD Shall Provide."

When Jesus taught His disciples to pray, "Give us this day our daily bread" (Matt. 6:11), He was including all our daily needs. "Bread" meant food, water, clothing, a roof over our heads, strength for the journey and anything else needed to keep body and soul together. These provisions are from *Jehovah Jireh*.

God also provides us with what we need to offer Him in the way of sacrifice. In this context we can note that the phrase *Jehovah Jireh* is one of the few names for God that is given by man rather than revealed by God Himself. Abraham had been commanded to take his son Isaac to Mount Moriah and to sacrifice him to the LORD (see Gen. 22). In obedience and as an act of faith, Abraham took his son to the point of death, even lifting the knife for the ultimate sacrifice. But *Jehovah Jireh* stopped him and provided "a ram caught in a thicket by his horns" (v. 13). Abraham took the ram and offered it to God. Then "Abraham called the name of the place, The-LORD-Will-Provide [*Jehovah Jireh*]; as it is said to this day, 'In the Mount of the LORD it shall be provided'" (v. 14, *NKJV*).

When young Isaac had asked about the lamb for the sacrifice, his father, Abraham, had promised him, "Son, God will provide himself a lamb for a burnt offering" (v. 8). Some translators place the comma differently and translate this verse, "God will provide himself, [as] a lamb for a burnt offering." Although the Hebrew literally says "God will provide for *Himself* the lamb for a burnt offering," the fact is true that God did give Himself through His Son, Jesus Christ, as the offering for the sins of the world (see Zech. 12:10; John 1:29; 3:16). In this sense, Jesus Christ was the ultimate provision of *Jehovah Jireh*, the God who supplies both our physical and our spiritual needs.

Emotional Upsets: *Jehovah Shalom*

"He leadeth me beside the still waters" (Ps. 23:2). This is a function of *Jehovah Shalom*, "the LORD [Our] Peace." The LORD takes care of us in times of discouragement and in the emotional storms of life. Believers who are tormented by their feelings need to know *Jehovah Shalom*, the LORD [Our] Peace. In the midst of difficult and pressure-filled situations, "He maketh [us] to lie down" (v. 2) inside, in our hearts, resting in His solution.

The phrase *Jehovah Shalom* was revealed when Gideon faced a task that was too great for him. The LORD came to Gideon and told him that he was to lead his people in victory over the Midianites. Gideon felt that he was too small for the task. He complained that he was the youngest son in his father's family and that theirs was the least family in the tribe of Manasseh, which was the least of the 12 tribes of Israel. But God revealed Himself to Gideon, which is always enough to get the task done. Because of that revelation, Gideon said, "Alas, O Lord GOD! For I have seen the Angel of the LORD face to face" (Judg. 6:22, *NKJV*).

God responded to Gideon, "Peace be with you; do not fear, you shall not die" (v. 23, *NKJV*). Then "Gideon built an altar there unto the LORD, and called it Jehovah-shalom" (v. 24), which means "Jehovah [Is Our] Peace." Again, a man gave a new name to *Jehovah* to explain His help in the face of a crisis. Gideon learned that when he faced a task that was fearful or threatening, *Jehovah Shalom* could bring peace to his heart.

When Gideon built an altar before gathering an army or forming a battle plan, he was exercising faith. The only way a person can have the peace of *Jehovah Shalom* is by faith: "Therefore being justified by faith, we have peace with God through our Lord Jesus Christ" (Rom. 5:1). Then, as we attempt to live for God after we are saved, the Bible says, "The God of peace shall be with you" (Phil. 4:9; compare to *Jehovah Shalom*).

A shepherd once observed that sheep only lie down when they are full. And, as we have noted, they cannot be left lying down by themselves too long lest they roll over and suffocate in their own wool or be attacked and infected by poisonous insects or snakes. *Jehovah Shalom* enables the sheep to lie down in safety. And since they are afraid of swiftly running water, He makes them lie down by still water.

Healing: *Jehovah Rophe*

"He restoreth my soul" (Ps. 23:3). The LORD who is a Shepherd heals His sick sheep, restoring them to wholeness. In this work He is *Jehovah Rophe*, "the LORD [Our] Healer." Whereas some animals have self-protective instincts, sheep have little or none. Most are not aware of the fact that they have been hurt or that they are sick. It takes a shepherd to know that they need healing and to care for them.

The phrase *Jehovah Rophe*, "the LORD [Our] Healer" ("the LORD that healeth thee"), occurs in Exodus 15:26. Moses, God's shepherd for Israel, led the multitude through the Red Sea into the wilderness. For three days the people found no water. This was likely a terrifying and life-threatening experience. Finally the people came to a pool of water called Marah, but its waters were bitter, and they complained.

"Bitter water" can mean water that is not acceptable to the taste but is not harmful, or it can mean water that is contaminated and dangerous. Apparently both are implied here. Upon God's instructions, Moses found a tree, cut it down and threw it into the water. God often works through symbols as He did in this case, using that which is visible to accomplish His inner workings. The tree could have had an agent that actually sweetened the water, or it could have been a visible symbol of the miracle of God that made the waters fit to drink. In either case, God used the incident to teach a lesson: the LORD can heal.

From this healing of the waters, *Jehovah Rophe* teaches of His power over illness. First, He "heals" through preventative medicine. "I will put none of these diseases upon thee" (15:26), He promises, meaning that if the Israelites follow Him, He will keep them from the plagues inflicted upon the Egyptians. The condition was "If thou wilt diligently hearken to the voice of the LORD thy God" (v. 26).

Many Christians have enjoyed the results of *Jehovah Rophe*'s preventative medicine by simply living self-controlled lives. They have not smoked, which has been proven dangerous to health. They have not given themselves to drugs, alcohol or other substances that can shorten one's life span. Demonstrating temperance in many other areas of practice has contributed to the good health of Christians.

A second element of the healing of *Jehovah Rophe* is corrective medicine. Just as God healed the bitter waters of Marah, He can heal those with disease. Within a few years of this promise to Moses, his sister Miriam was healed of leprosy (see Num. 12:11-16). Today, *Jehovah Rophe* still heals—physically, mentally, socially and spiritually.

The tree cast into the waters at Marah may be taken as a symbol of the cross of Jesus Christ, which in turn symbolizes God's ultimate healing power. While physical healing may not immediately come to everyone who embraces the atonement (in some cases it may not be realized until the Resurrection; see 1 Cor. 15:42), the Cross stands for any healing relationship God has with man. The apostle Paul reminds us, "Cursed is every one that hangeth on a tree" (Gal. 3:13), indicating that Christ took the curse of human infirmities upon Himself.

The miracles of modern science have not yet invented a cure for the common cold. Yet the mother who bundles up her children before sending them out into the snow is exercising preventative medicine. If they do catch cold, or the flu, she gives them corrective medicine, such as cough syrup or aspirin. In much the same way, *Jehovah Rophe* bundles us up in His love and tells us how to live a righteous life, thus giving us preventative measures to keep us physically and spiritually healthy. And when we do fall into sickness or sin, He has corrective medicine. Sometimes this is in the form of the forgiveness of sins. At other times He grants miraculous physical healing. At still other times He restores a relationship or heals a psychological problem. He is *Jehovah Rophe*, the LORD [Our] Healer.

Righteousness: *Jehovah Tsidkenu*

God is also *Jehovah Tsidkenu*, "the LORD Our Righteousness," meeting our desperate need to have the guilt of sin removed. It is *Jehovah Tsidkenu* who "leadeth [us] in the paths of righteousness" (Ps. 23:3).

Sin is many things, among them seeking our own way or straying like wayward sheep from the right path. "We have turned every one to his own way" (Isa. 53:6). When our ways are the ways of sin, we are guilty of transgression. We deserve the judgment or punishment of hell. But *Jehovah Roi*, our Shepherd who guides us, is also *Jehovah Tsidkenu*, the LORD Our Righteousness, who in mercy will give us a new standing before Him.

The phrase *Jehovah Tsidkenu* is found in Jeremiah 23:6. When the Lord returns at the end of the age, the Jews who have rejected Jesus Christ will recognize Him as their Messiah and turn to Him as their Savior. Jeremiah predicts that they will then come to know God by the name "the LORD Our Righteousness." It is through His righteousness that the Jews will come to know the justification that Christians already experience.

Justification is not being made inherently righteous but being *declared* righteous through the righteousness of Christ. A right standing before God is not something we can gain for ourselves. God must declare us righteous. Therefore it is *Jehovah Tsidkenu* who "leadeth [us] in the paths of righteousness" (Ps. 23:3). He declares His own to be righteous not because of what we have done but "for his name's sake" (v. 3).

Courage: *Jehovah Nissi*

"Though I walk through the valley of the shadow of death, I will fear no evil" (Ps. 23:4). This courage that conquers our fears comes from *Jehovah Nissi*, "the LORD My Banner."

Fear often comes when we face the unknown or feel overwhelmed by opposing forces. The small boy, afraid of the dark, wants his mother to go upstairs with him when he goes to bed. A man walking down a dark road at night wants a companion. Many other fears beset us. But when we know *Jehovah Nissi*, the LORD My Banner, we can walk with courage and in the confidence of victory.

The phrase *Jehovah Nissi* was a battle term. The soldier who became separated from his outfit in conflict needed to be able to find his army's battle staff or flag flying above the conflict. He could rally to the flag and not have to fight alone. Hence, *Jehovah Nissi*, the LORD My Banner.

This title was revealed when Israel went to battle with Amalek. This was Israel's first fight after escaping from Egypt. Throughout the Old Testament, Israel had a continuing war with Amalek.

Joshua led the troops into battle at Rephidim, while Moses stood on top of a hill with the rod of God in his hand. As long as Moses held up his hands (in prayer?), Israel prevailed; but "when he let down his hand, Amalek prevailed" (Exod. 17:11). When Moses' hands became tired, Aaron and Hur held his hands up so he could continue to intercede. As a result, Joshua won the day. "And Moses built an altar, and called the name of it Jehovah-nissi" (v. 15). This is another name given to God by man. "The LORD My Banner" means "the LORD that prevaileth." Even though men fought the battle, God gave the victory.

Amalek serves as a symbol for the flesh in the Old Testament. Even today Christians battle the flesh, struggling with our old nature. It is God who gives us the victory in this battle too—a victory that is already guaranteed because of the death of Jesus Christ on the cross. Yet the Bible teaches that the Christian must wrestle, run and fight. The Christian can serve the Lord with complete confidence about the outcome of the battle, because *Jehovah Nissi*, the LORD My Banner, will prevail.

Loneliness: *Jehovah Shammah*

When the psalmist says, "Thou art with me" (Ps. 23:4), he is affirming the presence of *Jehovah Shammah*, "the LORD Is There."

One of our greatest gifts, along with salvation, is the presence of God in our lives. God promised Moses His presence when He charged Moses to lead Israel out of Egypt: "Certainly I will be with thee" (Exod. 3:12). When Jesus gave His disciples the Great Commission, He promised, "Lo, I am with you always, even unto the end of the world" (Matt. 28:20).

The name *Jehovah Shammah* is found in Ezekiel 48:35. At the end of his prophecy, Ezekiel described the eternal city and said that even in heaven "the LORD is there" (*Jehovah Shammah*).

When the Shepherd who is with us comforts us with His rod and His staff (see Ps. 23:4), He is protecting us from the enemy. The shepherd used the rod as a club to beat off wild animals. His staff was a crook that assisted sheep in trouble. With it the shepherd could lift a sheep from the water or from a pit. Technically, the word for "comfort" means "to lead." *Jehovah Shammah* will lead or guide His sheep by using His rod against attackers or His crook to rescue us from trouble.

Sanctification: *Jehovah Mekaddishkhem*

"Thou anointest my head with oil" (Ps. 23:5). Throughout Scripture oil is used to sanctify things, people and places for God's special use. The basic meaning of the word "sanctify" is "set apart." In the wilderness, after He delivered Israel from Egypt, God gave instructions regarding the building of the Tabernacle and the keeping of the Sabbath. The question might arise: are the people of God sanctified or holy enough for God to live among them and meet with them? *Jehovah* answers, "Verily my sabbaths ye shall keep: for it is a sign between me and you throughout your generations; that ye may know that I am the LORD that doth sanctify you" (Exod. 31:13).

"The LORD That Sanctifies You" is *Jehovah Mekaddishkhem*. Since we have no holiness by which to sanctify ourselves, God Himself sets us apart in order that we may dwell in His presence. *Jehovah Mekaddishkhem* alone is able to sanctify.

Oil was used in various ways in Bible times. The shepherd would anoint the heads of the sheep with oil for several reasons. First, it was a cleansing agent. When a sheep had a filthy sore, the shepherd used oil to clean dirt or filth from the wound. Similarly, when we sin and receive a wound in our soul, *Jehovah Mekaddishkhem* cleanses it with the oil of His Spirit.

Medicinal oil also heals, just as God anoints us with the healing flow of the blood of Christ in the forgiveness of sins. And oil soothes. When we are sunburned, we put oil or lotion on to take away the burning. Oil replenishes the natural body oils burned away by the sun. When a shepherd anoints the sheep with oil, he replenishes their bodies' natural system.

Oil is a symbol of the Holy Spirit (see 1 Sam. 16:13; Isa. 61:1; Acts 10:38). In the heat of life, *Jehovah Mekaddishkhem* sends the third Person of the Trinity to restore, cleanse, soothe and heal.

Jesus Is *Jehovah Roi*

Jesus Gives a Shepherd's Care

Just as the shepherd gives the sheep his total care and concern, so too Jesus promised that as the Good Shepherd, He "giveth His life for the sheep" (John 10:11). Because of His dedication to our care, Jesus could say, "I am the good shepherd" (v. 11).

As the Good Shepherd, Jesus knows His "own sheep" so personally that "He calleth his own sheep by name" (v. 3). "He putteth forth his own sheep, he goeth before them, and the sheep follow him" (v. 4). The intimate relationship between shepherd and sheep is a reflection of the relationship between Jesus and the believer. Once a believer enters into the shepherd-sheep relationship, he has eternal life. There he is promised "life . . . more abundantly" (v. 10).

Shepherding Ministries Under Christ
The word for "pastor" in the New Testament also means "shepherd." A pastor shepherds the souls of those under his care. As a shepherd, the pastor leads the sheep—by example, in decision making and in problem solving. He feeds the sheep by instruction, counsel and educational administration. He tends the sheep by discipleship, warning and inspection.

If the pastor is a shepherd, the Sunday School teacher and group leader are extensions of the pastoral ministry into the lives of those in the Sunday School class and small-group study. In this way the Sunday School teacher and group leader are also shepherds. Everything the pastor-shepherd is to the larger flock, the teacher and leader are to the Sunday School and small-group flocks.

Although Jesus is the Good Shepherd, He communicates His intimate care to us through human shepherds who minister in His name (see John 21:15-17; Acts 20:32; 1 Pet. 5:1-5).

3

Almighty God: El Shaddai

GOD WHO SUPPLIES MY NEEDS

Sometimes we let a problem become a giant crisis. Only later in life do we see how small the original problem really was, especially to the Lord who solves our problems. He is *El Shaddai*, the One who is strong enough to help and sensitive enough to care.

When I graduated from Dallas Theological Seminary in May 1958, I was pastoring Faith Bible Church in Dallas at the same time. While I was preaching on the Sunday morning of my Baccalaureate service, someone broke into my house and stole my suits, my shirts and my graduation cap and gown. Since the gown was in a suit box, they probably thought it was another suit.

I discovered my loss at about 12:30 P.M. I realized that I couldn't march in the Baccalaureate procession that afternoon. When I phoned the seminary's registrar, he told me that I would graduate, of course, but that I couldn't have the honor of marching across the platform. It was a crushing loss to me at the time. I prayed. The registrar phoned me back with an idea. I was able to borrow a graduation cap and gown from Southern Methodist University, which had them on hand.

God of Nourishment and Power

This scene is typical of the nature of *El Shaddai*. God was sensitive to my cry, and He was strong enough to supply the answer to my problem.

When the patriarch Abraham was 99 years old, he needed reassurance of what God had promised: that his descendants would become a great nation, that he would inherit the Promised Land and that from him all the nations of the world would be blessed. Abraham had not sought these promises from God. The LORD had appeared to Abraham and given him these promises when he was 75 years old. But now, in their old age, Abraham and his wife Sarah were past the age to bear children.

A New Name Revealed

God was sensitive to Abraham's need and strong enough to do something about it. The LORD appeared to Abraham and said, "I am the Almighty God [El Shaddai]; walk before me, and be thou perfect" (Gen. 17:1). This is the first time that the name "Almighty" is used in the Bible. It is a compound name consisting of El, a shortened form of Elohim, "the strong Creator," and Shaddai, the Hebrew word for "Almighty." Even though Shaddai and the Hebrew word for shad, meaning "breast" (as in Gen. 49:25; Job 3:12; Ps. 22:9), are two different words, they sound alike. The wordplay reminds us that God tenderly provides for us. God does not come to Abraham as the Creator alone but as the God who can supply Abraham's need as a woman satisfies the need of a child at her breast.

Thus two divine qualities are implied in the name El Shaddai. God is both the strong One who is able to deliver and the tender One who nourishes and satisfies. Unfortunately, the English word "Almighty" tends to communicate only the aspect of God's strength and power. Some feel that the term "All-sufficient" would be a better translation.

How can we communicate both strength and tenderness? It is a picture of blue jeans (toughness) and lace (delicate fabric "tatted" with tenderness). When we have financial needs, we pray to the Almighty, the God who is strong to supply our needs, but we may also cry out to the tender God who weeps with us in our need. God is both blue denim and lace.

When the term "Almighty" was first used, God wanted to communicate a new side of His nature to Abraham. For 24 years Abraham had obeyed God and dwelt in the Promised Land. This new name was given to reveal a new aspect of how the God he had been serving works. The same is true of relationships today. The girlfriend may quickly be called a sweetheart, a term of endearment. After marriage she is called a wife. Later she may be called "Mother."

A New Promise Given

God not only revealed to Abraham a new name, Almighty God; He gave Abraham a new promise: "I will make my covenant between me and thee, and will multiply thee exceedingly" (Gen. 17:2). When God promises His blessings to us, we must claim them and act on them. Abraham was no different. "And Abram fell on his face: and God talked with him" (v. 3). Abraham had to pray, intercede and trust the Almighty for the promise.

God said to Abraham, "As for Sarai thy wife, thou shalt not call her name Sarai, but Sarah shall her name be. And I will bless her, and give thee a son also of her: yea, I will bless her, and she shall be a mother of nations; kings of people shall be of her" (vv. 15-16).

This too was a promise of the Almighty God (*El Shaddai*). Abraham and Sarah would supernaturally have a son when they were past ordinary childbearing age. The twofold aspect of the name "Almighty God" is *strength* and *satisfaction*. Abraham and Sarah would have strength to conceive a son, and this would bring them satisfaction at the fulfillment of God's promise.

The Promise Passed On

Abraham passed his knowledge of *El Shaddai* on to Isaac, the son of promise. For when Isaac was old, he sent his own son Jacob to the land of his ancestors to get a wife, saying, "God Almighty [*El Shaddai*] bless thee, and make thee fruitful, and multiply thee" (28:3).

The name *El Shaddai* continued to be handed down in the family. When Jacob grew to be an old man, he in turn blessed his own son Joseph in the name of "the Almighty, who shall bless thee with blessings" (49:25).

The name "Almighty God" occurs 48 times in the Old Testament. Of these occurrences, 31 are in the book of Job. Job lost all his earthly possessions, including his family. He lost his health and ended up sitting on an ash heap and scraping the boils on his body with broken pottery. Job and his friends knew that it was the tough-but-tender

Almighty God who could deliver him from his distress, and he was counseled, "Happy is the man whom God correcteth: therefore despise not thou the chastening of the Almighty" (5:17).

From the book of Job we learn that the tender, caring Almighty God also has a stern aspect to His personality. Even though a mother loves her children, she will correct and spank them if necessary, because she loves them. A loving mother will put soothing ointment on a burn, but she will also spank a child who plays near the fire. She doesn't spank because she is angry but because she loves her child and wants the child to learn not to lie near the fire. In the same manner, the Almighty may chasten His children both as the strong One and as tender Father. In love He will soothe our wounds, but also in love He may allow us to be wounded if necessary for our discipline.

In the New Testament, the name "Almighty" (Greek *pantokrator*) occurs twelve times, nine of them in the book of Revelation. The same tough and tender sides of God's nature are revealed here in the use of the name "Almighty." The Almighty will faithfully reward the believer for good works—and He will pour out judgment on the willful unbeliever. He is eternal: "I am Alpha and Omega, the beginning and the ending, saith the Lord, which is, and which was, and which is to come, the Almighty" (Rev. 1:8).

El Shaddai, the Almighty God, is a name that believers should know and trust. When we face problems or dangers, we can call on the Almighty for help. He will not always take away our problems or remove us from life's storms, but He will give us the strength to endure them. We should remember three things about problems: (1) We can't run from them; (2) we can't prevent their coming into our lives; and (3) we can't always solve all of them. Yet *El Shaddai* strengthens us in the midst of problems.

James counseled, "Count it all joy when you fall into various trials" (1:2, *NKJV*). He explains that trials or tests are inevitable, they are "various" or different, and they need not defeat us but can actually be met with joy. As children of God face trouble, they must remember that the world is not coming to an end because they can't solve all problems. Nor are they a failure. All God's children have problems.

Application

Six guidelines, each one related to the character of *El Shaddai*, will help believers face and overcome problems:

1. *Separate yourself from sin (negative holiness)*. Many of our problems come because of sin in our lives. It is the nature of sin to defeat, destroy, disrupt, dilute and damage the child of God. Therefore, the Almighty insists on the principle of separation from sin: "Come out from among them, and be ye separate . . . and touch not the unclean thing . . . and ye shall be my sons and daughters, saith the Lord Almighty" (2 Cor. 6:17-18). *El Shaddai* is still both strong to save and tender to help. But if we harbor sin in our lives, He cannot be merely tender and kind; He must judge.

2. *Seek* El Shaddai*'s presence (positive holiness)*. The Almighty is tender and wants to help His children, but He wants us to actively seek Him. I sometimes see a ministerial student struggling in seminary with finances. He works a job, goes to seminary where he struggles to learn Hebrew and Greek, and preaches at every opportunity. When he prays for help, especially for financial relief, usually God does not send a rich benefactor to pay the student's way. If the seminarian had an easy life, he would probably not seek help from the Almighty, and his effectiveness as a minister would be hampered. *El Shaddai* asks him to work hard, to actively pursue His presence in order to have an effective ministry.

When we reach heaven and stand around the throne, we will sing, "Holy, holy, holy, Lord God Almighty" (Rev. 4:8). Then we will experience the all-sufficient, holy God of strength and satisfaction—all of which is attached to Him in the name *El Shaddai*.

3. *Rest in the presence of* El Shaddai. God is not just a powerful Creator who is far removed from believers. He is as close to His people as a mother is to her children or a shepherd is to his flock. Once there was a wayward sheep who kept wandering from the flock. The shepherd knew the dangers. The wayward sheep might fall off a ledge or drown in a swift current. But no matter how many times the shepherd tenderly brought back the sheep, it would stray again. Finally, for the sheep's own good, it was time for toughness. The shepherd broke one of the sheep's legs, and the animal was forced to stay near the shepherd in safety. "He that dwelleth in the

secret place of the most High shall abide under the shadow of the Almighty [*Shaddai*]" (Ps. 91:1).

4. *Follow the directions of* El Shaddai. A child cannot dwell in the favor of his parents without obeying each parent's voice. Because we are born in sin, it is difficult for us to obey. We like to do things our own way. A mother tried to get her young son to sit down, but he would not. Finally, she forcibly made him sit. He said, "I may be sitting down on the outside, but inside I'm standing up."

The boy is a picture of too many believers. Instead of obeying from the heart, we rebel inside. When God came to Abraham, He had to remind him, "I am the Almighty God [*El Shaddai*]; walk before me, and be thou perfect" (Gen. 17:1).

5. *Evaluate your spiritual health.* If you do not sense that God is using hardships in your life to move you closer to Him or to reveal unconfessed sin, it may indicate that you aren't really His child. The writer of Hebrews says, "If ye endure chastening, God dealeth with you as with sons; for what son is he whom the father chasteneth not?" (12:7; see also vv. 5-11). It is the nature of *El Shaddai* to lovingly discipline those who are really His children. Hence, "My son, despise not thou the chastening of the Lord, . . . for whom the Lord loveth he chasteneth, and scourgeth every son whom he receiveth" (vv. 5-6).

In the book of Ruth, we read of Naomi and her husband Elimelech. Both disobeyed God and left Israel, where there was a famine, to live in Moab, which was prospering. They made their choice with an eye on *things* rather than with the eye of faith. They prospered in Moab, but Elimelech died. Then both of Naomi's sons died. Finally, when everything was stripped from her, Naomi returned to Israel and her hometown. She told her friends, "Call me not Naomi [pleasant], call me Mara [bitterness] . . . , seeing the LORD hath testified against me, and the Almighty [*Shaddai*] hath afflicted me" (Ruth 1:20-21).

The Almighty disciplines His disobedient children. If you have ever been punished by a loving parent, you know that there can be comfort even in the pain of judgment. In the same way, you can take comfort in the midst of discipline from the fact that you are a child of God. If you will obey the Almighty, He will be your *Shaddai*—your strength and satisfaction.

6. *Claim the provision of* El Shaddai. Because God is faithful and strong to save, He will take care of you. When ministerial students come to seminary, I always challenge them with the promise, "Faithful is he that calleth you, who also will do it" (1 Thess. 5:24). I point out to students that if God has called them, they can endure the problems of seminary, such as time pressure, heavy studies, Greek and Hebrew, financial needs, and others. "God will do it," I promise the students. And some students have told me 20 years afterward that it was this promise that got them through seminary and into the ministry. He who calls us in His divine tenderness will hear our cry in His divine strength.

When old Jacob was facing death, he wanted to bless his grandsons, and he wanted them to walk in obedience to God. So he gave them the promise of *El Shaddai*, "the Almighty, who shall bless thee with blessings" (Gen. 49:25). Jacob, who had experienced both the blessings and the punishment of *El Shaddai*, knew that these two aspects of God's nature would guide his grandchildren as they followed the LORD.

4

Most High God: El Elyon

POSSESSOR OF HEAVEN AND EARTH

A wife may call her husband "Honey," usually reflecting their intimate relationship. An enemy, however, would use an entirely different name. What names would the enemies of God use when addressing Him?

When Satan and his demons, God's prime enemies, address Him, they usually use the term *El Elyon*, which means Most High God. They do not use this name to curse God or to impugn His character. Rather, they call Him Most High God because that title reflects the attributes of God that they lust after.

The Superlative God

As we have seen, the prefix *El* comes from *Elohim*, "strong Creator." *Elyon* is "highest" or "most." It is the superlative degree, as in high, higher and highest. *Elyon* means that the Lord is "God of gods" or "the ultimate God."

The superlative word *elyon* is used in the book of Ezekiel to speak of the highest pool, the highest gate, the highest porch and the highest house. The heavens are higher than the earth (comparative), but God is highest (superlative). The term reveals that God is the highest and that everyone else is below Him. Because God is *Elyon*, He has the power to rule and the right to receive worship from all below Him.

When the title *El Elyon* first appears in Scripture (see heading "Melchizedek Served *El Elyon*"), the *King James Version* identifies it with Him who is "possessor of heaven and earth" (Gen. 14:19).

One Church father translated this phrase "founder of heaven and earth," and the *New International Version* speaks of the "Creator of heaven and earth." *El Elyon* is a name for God that is often associated with His creation, revealing that He is both sovereign and owner of the heaven and the earth.

The word translated "possessor" in Genesis 14:19 is a derivative of a verb from which the *King James Version* on other occasions has rendered the words "possess" or "contain." Another form means "whole." Therefore to possess heaven and Earth is to have a rightful claim to the ownership of all there is. When Abraham tells the king of Sodom, "I have lifted up mine hand unto . . . the most high God [*El Elyon*], the possessor of heaven and earth" (14:22), he is telling this Gentile leader that God is the king's leader and that the king is God's servant. Abraham is declaring that the king had received everything from God and would give everything back to God.

In the New Testament, Stephen's sermon to the unbelieving Jews proclaimed that God was not limited to their Jewish Temple: "The most High dwelleth not in temples made with hands" (Acts 7:48). Stephen's point was that God did not always limit Himself to a man-made temple, so the newly emerging Church would not be limited to the Old Testament Temple. If Stephen had used the name *Jehovah*, he would have linked God to the Temple; but the name *El Elyon* identified the Church with the world, which was the target of the Great Commission.

The name *El Elyon* is also often identified with the Gentiles (that is, the earth) rather than the Jews (that is, the Promised Land). This usage appears in the book of Deuteronomy: "The Most High divided to the nations [that is, the Gentiles] their inheritance, when he separated the sons of Adam" (32:8).

Satan Knows of *El Elyon*'s Power

Satan knows that there are armies on this earth and armies in heaven. These armies are made up of angels called "sons of God" or God's "ministers." Angels are beings with intellect, emotion and will. These beings rejoiced at creation (see Job 38:7). They appeared before the presence of God (see 1:6; 2:1). Angels are higher than man (comparative), but God is the highest being (superlative), greater than both angels and people.

Satan knows and lusts after power. He knows that there are powers on the earth, that the powers of angels in heaven are higher (comparative), and that the power of God is highest (superlative). Satan and his demons are great in power too (see Eph. 6:12), but God's power is the greatest of all. He is *El Elyon*. Whereas evil men on this earth are blinded to the existence and power of God, evil angels and Satan know God as the Most High God. Thus, *El Elyon* is the "God of gods" (Ps. 136:2), the "King of kings" and the "Lord of lords" (Rev. 19:16).

Before the fall of Adam and Eve, Lucifer (Satan or the devil) referred to God as "the most High" (Isa. 14:14). Lucifer, the first created angel, was in rebellion against God. He was not just trying to destroy God but to take God's place. In Isaiah 14:12-14, Satan, who is prefigured in the king of Babylon (see v. 4), exercises his self-will in assaulting the authority of God and attempting to take His place. Satan said,

1. "I will ascend into heaven."
2. "I will exalt my throne."
3. "I will sit also upon the mount of the congregation."
4. "I will ascend above the heights of the clouds."
5. "I will be like the most High [*El Elyon*]."

As Satan climbed these five steps toward the place of God, his ultimate passion was to be like God and to sit in God's place. When Satan surveyed the heavens created by God, he wanted them. But more than wanting to possess things, he wanted to be God. Therefore, Satan called God the Most High God, the position he desired for himself.

In the New Testament, the name "Most High God" is used by fallen angels (demons) when addressing Jesus Christ.

Legion, the fallen angel who had possessed the man of Gadara, said, "Jesus, thou Son of the most high God" (Mark 5:7). The demon recognized what the New Testament teaches: "All things were made by him [Jesus]; and without him was not any thing made that was made" (John 1:3). And again, "All things were created by him, and for him: and he is before all things, and by him all things consist" (Col. 1:16-17).

Demons recognized Paul as a preacher of Jesus Christ. A demon-possessed servant girl followed Paul and his company throughout Philippi, crying out, "These men are the servants of the Most High God" (Acts 16:17, *NKJV*). When a demon recognizes the presence of Jesus Christ, he cannot help but confess His deity. What a shame that, in comparison, many Christians are tongue-tied or mute when it comes to confessing Jesus Christ!

On other occasions demons recognized Christ as "the Holy One of God" (Mark 1:24), even though they did not link Him to the Most High. Again in the book of Acts, there was an exorcist service in which a person attempted to cast out a demon. The evil spirit answered and said, "Jesus I know, and Paul I know; but who are ye?" (19:15). Again, demons indicated that they knew Christ. This is reinforced by James, who said, "Thou believest that there is one God; thou doest well: the devils also believe, and tremble" (Jas. 2:19).

Why do demons and Satan recognize the Most High God and Jesus? Because they want to be who He is (the Founder or Creator), and they want to possess what is His (the heavens and the earth).

Melchizedek Served *El Elyon*

Although Satan was the first to use the name *El Elyon*, before the creation of the world (see Isa. 14:12-14), the first reference to this name in the Scriptures as we have them is by Abraham in Genesis 14:17-24. Abraham, the man of faith, pursued a band, or army, of raiders to Damascus to rescue his nephew, Lot. Abraham divided his 318 servants and attacked the enemy by night. The Bible describes the victory as "the slaughter of Chedorlaomer" (v. 17). Abraham not only brought back Lot but the goods and the people who were with him as well. Abraham apparently was a fierce and skillful warrior, but it was the sovereign God and His intervention that gave Abraham the victory.

On his return from the battle, Abraham came near the ancient city of Salem, which later would be called Jerusalem. He met two kings in the "valley of Shaveh," which was also called "the king's dale" (v. 17), apparently a place where the king met dignitaries for certain ceremonies. This is probably the brook Kidron, between Gethsemane and the Golden Gate that leads to the Temple.

The two kings approached Abraham in this cool, green valley. They were kings of city-states, meaning each man was like the mayor of a great city, ruling over those within his walled city as well as those in the immediately surrounding area.

The first king was from Sodom, which had been plundered in the raid in which Lot was captured. This was the evil city known for its sodomy that God would later destroy. When Abraham and Lot had divided up the land, Lot had gone to live in Sodom, choosing the well-watered plains that surrounded the city (see 13:8-12). He had chosen with the outward eye, not the inward voice of God. He did not recognize that he had made himself vulnerable to an attack from marauding armies as they plundered the Jordan valley, and the attack of Satan, who would attempt to destroy his morality through sodomy.

Now the king of Sodom wanted to strike a bargain with Abraham. The rules of war said that Abraham, the victor, could keep the people and possessions that he had captured. But the king of Sodom said, "Give me the persons, and take the goods to thyself" (14:21). The deal was simple. The king of Sodom, with the worldly man's practical eye to the value of material goods, would make Abraham a rich man with the goods from Sodom.

But the second king, Melchizedek, king of Salem ("King of peace" [Heb. 7:2]), had a different set of values. Melchizedek was not only a king; he was also a priest of *El Elyon* (see Gen. 14:18-19). It is natural that this priest-king would call God by this name, since it was associated with the Gentiles. The remarkable thing about the story is that Abraham, father of the chosen people, actually paid tithes of the booty he had won to Melchizedek the Gentile (see v. 20).

Some have thought that this is a Christophany—an appearance of Christ—and that Melchizedek was in fact Jesus. The writer of the book of Hebrews does compare Melchizedek to Christ, who is said to be a priest "after the order of Melchizedek" (see Heb. 5:6;

Ps. 110:4). But it is likely that the biblical writers were only drawing an analogy between the two figures.

What is more likely is that in this story two great men meet—a weary Abraham returning from a long trip and a hard battle, and a dignified Gentile king who is also a believer in *El Elyon*. Melchizedek served bread and wine to Abraham in gratitude for protecting his city, Salem, and for any possessions that were returned to him. In exchange, Abraham gave Melchizedek a tithe of what he had gained, just as today tithes are given to churches for God's use. Note that Abraham did not worship Melchizedek but rather Melchizedek's God, *El Elyon*. As Abraham himself said, "I have lift up mine hand unto the LORD, the most high God, the possessor of heaven and earth" (Gen. 14:22).

Daniel and the Power of God Most High

The next extensive use of the name *El Elyon* is found in the book of Daniel (see 3:26; 4:17,24-25,32). Because *El Elyon* is identified with the Gentiles, it was only natural for Daniel, a young Hebrew boy who had been taken captive into Babylon, to pray to God who possessed the heavens and the earth.

In fact, it is interesting that Daniel did not rely heavily on Jewish-related names for God. Besides *El Elyon*, Daniel's next favorite name for deity was "the God of heaven" (2:19). Why did he use these names? Because he was outside the Promised Land, he realized that the Temple was destroyed, Gentiles controlled Israel, and Gentiles controlled Daniel's own circumstances. Therefore Daniel prayed to the One who possessed heaven and Earth—the God who is Lord over Babylon as well as Israel and who is greater than any earthly circumstance.

When Nebuchadnezzar, king of Babylon, had a terrible dream and no one could interpret it, Daniel came to the palace and through the power of *El Elyon* was able to give the interpretation (see 2:1-45). As a result, the heathen king of Babylon recognized *El Elyon* as Daniel's God. But since He was not the king's God, Nebuchadnezzar made an idol of gold approximately 90 feet tall and commanded everyone to bow down and worship it (see 3:1-7;

many think the idol was Nebuchadnezzar himself and that people were worshiping him as an expression of deity).

Shadrach, Meshach and Abednego, three other Jews in Babylon, refused to worship the idol. King Nebuchadnezzar cast them into a fiery brick kiln, called a furnace in the Bible (see vv. 8-23). When Nebuchadnezzar looked into the mouth of the brick kiln to see their fate, he saw four men walking—Shadrach, Meshach and Abednego and a fourth Person who is described thus: "The form of the fourth is like the Son of God" (v. 25).

Nebuchadnezzar shouted into the mouth of the fiery brick kiln, "Ye servants of the most high God [*El Elyon*] come forth, and come hither" (v. 26). It is remarkable that this Gentile king, who was the most powerful man in the world and who might be expected to identify *himself* as the possessor of the earth, identified God by that title, using His Gentile name.

But even though Nebuchadnezzar *recognized* God, he did not worship Him. In fact, in the next chapter, the king walked through his city boasting and taking credit for all the grandeur of ancient Babylon (see 4:29-30). Nebuchadnezzar put himself in the place of God.

Daniel saw in a vision what was coming. He predicted the fall of Nebuchadnezzar from power, as a result of his arrogance, "till thou know that the most High [*El Elyon*] ruleth in the kingdom of men, and giveth it to whomsoever he will" (v. 25). He delivered the bad news to King Nebuchadnezzar in the name of *El Elyon*: "This is the interpretation, O king, and this is the decree of the most High, which is come upon my lord the king" (v. 24).

The decree happened just as Daniel said. Nebuchadnezzar's mind was taken from him. He was apparently struck with lycanthropy—commonly called the wolf-man disease. He went out into the fields and behaved like an animal. He ate grass like an ox, and his hair grew to look like a beast's. He lost his mind for seven years, and in the process, he lost his authority over his realm (see vv. 25-26,28,31-33). The possessor of heaven and Earth does not share His glory with anyone—even the king of Babylon.

At the end of seven years, Nebuchadnezzar came to his senses. He regained his throne, and his life returned to normal (see v.

36). After his experience he could finally confess, "I blessed the most High, and I praised and honoured him that liveth for ever, whose dominion is an everlasting dominion, and his kingdom is from generation to generation" (v. 34; see also v. 37).

Daniel also used the name "Most High God" (*El Elyon*) when dealing with the next heathen ruler of Babylon, King Belshazzar (see 5:18). It was King Belshazzar who took the gold vessels that had been captured from Solomon's Temple and used them in a drunken feast (see vv. 1-4). Suddenly a hand came and wrote upon the wall, "Mene, mene, tekel, upharsin" (5:25; see also 5:5).

Upon seeing the hand, Belshazzar cried out, fearing for his life. The queen mother (the wife of Nebuchadnezzar) was called to the palace. She indicated that Daniel could interpret what Belshazzar had seen (see vv. 10-14). When Daniel came to confront Belshazzar, he reminded him, "O thou king, the most high God [*El Elyon*] gave Nebuchadnezzar thy father a kingdom, and majesty, and glory, and honour" (v. 18).

The Most High God once again showed that it is He alone who possesses the heavens and the earth. That very night Belshazzar was slain, and power was transferred to Darius the Mede (see vv. 30-31).

Other Glimpses of *El Elyon*

Toward the end of his life, Moses ascribes to *El Elyon* the sovereign power to set the boundaries of the nations, as we have seen. "When the Most High divided to the nations their inheritance, when he separated the sons of Adam, he set the bounds of the people according to the number of the children of Israel" (Deut. 32:8). Again, we see that it is *El Elyon*, not mere man, who really possesses the heavens and the earth.

On several occasions David prayed to *El Elyon*, the Most High God. In Psalm 9:2 David exulted, "I will sing praise to thy name, O thou most High." The writer of Psalm 91 gives testimony, "He that dwelleth in the secret place of the most High shall abide under the shadow of the Almighty" (v. 1).

Applications of *El Elyon*

What lessons can Christians draw from the way the name *El Elyon* is used in Scripture?

The Satanic Substitute

Satan has a twofold desire: (1) to rebel against everything that is holy and godly, and (2) to substitute himself in the place of God as "possessor of heaven and earth." This is in accordance with the New Testament picture of the Antichrist, who not only opposes Christ but wants to be a substitute Christ. Satan regrets that he cannot be the founder of heaven and Earth; the world is already created. So he wants to be the possessor of all that is and to have people worship him instead of *El Elyon*.

When Satan tempted Jesus Christ to fall down and worship him, he offered Him the kingdoms of this world in exchange (see Matt. 4:8-9). As the god of this world (see Eph. 2:2-3; 6:11-12), Satan wants to possess it. And he wanted Jesus to recognize his claim.

The Process Principle

As we have seen, demons recognize *El Elyon* and are forced to cry out this name in acknowledgment of who He is (see Mark 5:7). Demons want to possess the world, and they want to possess people. But how do demons possess a person as they possessed Legion and the young girl who told fortunes (see Mark 5:9; Acts 16:16-18)? Demon possession comes slowly. Just as God wants to fill a person with the Holy Spirit (see Eph. 5:18), so too Satan wants to fill a person. The *New International Version* of the Bible calls this "demon possession" (see Matt. 15:22), but the term is actually "demonization" in the original language.

People are demonized in the same way in which they are filled with the Spirit: in a gradual process. First, they yield to the influence. Then, the more they yield and seek, the more they become filled or possessed. Whether the Holy Spirit or an evil spirit, the presence usually fills them gradually, according to the level of the person's learning and commitment. Some people are more filled or possessed than others. And both filling and possession are for the purpose of causing the person to honor and serve one's master.

The Holy Spirit does not fill a person who is rebellious toward God. He comes only to those who are yielding to and seeking Him. In the same way, demons do not invade a person who is not seeking the occult and yielded to satanic powers.

The Jesus Answer
The solution to demon possession is the name "Jesus." Demons already recognize His name and His Person. The only power with which we can cast out demons is "in the name of Jesus." Jesus' blood is the power that repels demons (Acts 20:28; Rev. 1:5). The solution to gradual demon possession is increasing dependence on the name of Jesus.

The Tithing Principle
The tithe was first given when Abraham gave a tenth of his spoils to a Gentile, Melchizedek, king of Salem and priest of *El Elyon*. The tithe is usually a gift to deity. Inasmuch as God possesses heaven and Earth, we must surrender everything we have to the control of God. The tithe is only a token of what we possess. Giving a tithe to God is not buying God or bribing Him. A tithe is an outward symbol of the inward gift of oneself to God.

Many claim that tithing was only for God's people under the Old Covenant. They say it is a principle of the Law and should not be used under grace. But inasmuch as the tithe is suggested and used to bless the Lord, why should anyone do less today? However, God, who possesses all things, not only wants our tithe; He wants everything that we have. We give Him all our love, our hearts, our bodies and our possessions. He controls everything. A tithe is given to God to indicate that all the rest of what we have belongs to Him.

The Possession Principle
The Most High God possesses heaven and Earth. All creation belongs to Him because He is its Creator. However, the Most High God wants most to possess our hearts. This includes our will, our feelings and our mind. The proper response to this claim on our lives is to yield to Him, to seek His blessing, and to obey His command.

Neither Satan nor man should expect to possess that which is God's by His divine right. The psalmist said, "When I consider thy heavens, . . . what is man, that thou art mindful of him?" (Ps. 8:3-4). Looking at creation should only bring us to acknowledge the greatness of *El Elyon*, not create a desire in us to possess it as our own. The same thing is true of life itself. James asked the question, "What is your life? It is even a vapour, that . . . vanisheth away" (Jas. 4:14). Because we are only here for a short time, we realize that we are not our own. The high and holy *El Elyon* has created us for His own pleasure.

El Elyon and the Name of Jesus

Because God is three in one, Jesus Christ is *El Elyon*. He is the Creator, Sustainer and Possessor of heaven and Earth. As glorious as is the name *El Elyon*, it is the name of Jesus that will be the final name, for "at the name of Jesus every knee should bow, of things in heaven, and things in earth, and things under the earth; and that every tongue should confess that Jesus Christ is Lord, to the glory of God the Father" (Phil. 2:10-11).

El Elyon and *El Shaddai*

The titles *El Elyon* (Most High God) and *El Shaddai* (the Almighty) are linked together in Psalm 91:1: "He that dwelleth in the secret place of the most High shall abide under the shadow of the Almighty." These two titles are in juxtaposition, revealing two sides of God at the same. The powerful *El Elyon*, who is supreme and omnipotent, is also the personal God who is the Fountainhead of all grace. *El Elyon* is able to do what He wishes because He is powerful; *El Shaddai* gives grace and mercy. *El Elyon* causes us to fear and tremble before His greatness; *El Shaddai* invites us to come for comfort under His wings.

Mighty and gracious—*El Elyon* and *El Shaddai* are One God. He is able to do exceeding abundantly above all that we can ask or think because He is *El Elyon*. He is able to present us faultless before the divine throne because He is *El Shaddai*.

5

Everlasting God: El Olam

THE SECRET NAME OF GOD

Why do we keep secrets? There are many reasons to conceal information. Sometimes secrets are good, and sometimes they are harmful. A parent keeps a Christmas gift hidden to surprise the children and make Christmas more enjoyable. A poverty-stricken mother doesn't tell her children that there isn't enough food for the next day in order to keep them from worrying. Sometimes, when people are not able to handle the burden of knowledge, it's kind not to tell them everything.

God keeps secrets for many reasons too. But He never hides things to harm us or out of selfishness. He doesn't let us know how we will die, or when. It might devastate us. He doesn't tell us all the good things that He will do lest we let up and not work as hard as we should.

God doesn't tell us everything about Himself. Some things about His justice might depress us. Some things about His goodness we could not understand because we are not God. Only God can fully understand God.

God the Eternal and Mysterious

El Olam, the Everlasting God, is a secret name for God, hinting at His mysterious nature. The prefix *El*, we have noted, is from *Elohim* ("strong Creator"). *Olam* means time, or age. With a tiny change in the vowel signs in Hebrew, the ancient rabbis spelled it *alam*, "hidden" (see chapter 1), underscoring the mysterious nature of God. God's everlasting or timeless nature—without beginning or end—is one of the most profound mysteries of His nature.

In Psalm 90:2 the psalmist exalts God by saying that "from ever-lasting [*olam*] to everlasting, thou art God." The Hebrew word *olam* is a synonym for the Greek word *aion*, meaning age or dispensation. And in Psalm 10:1 the meaning of *alam*, "secret" or "hidden," is illustrated. The psalmist feels estranged from God and asks, "Why hidest thou thyself in times of trouble?" (see also Lev. 5:2; 2 Kings 4:27).

Beersheba: Place of Revelation

The title "Everlasting God" was first revealed to Abraham at the desert oasis Beersheba. The only water at Beersheba was a well that Abraham had dug. It was the last well a traveler would pass before entering the desolate Sinai Peninsula, making Beersheba a strategically located oasis. It had been taken from Abraham violently by the servants of Abimelech, the tribal chieftain of the Philistines. Abraham reproved Abimelech, and out of this confrontation came a covenant of peace. The agreement between Abraham and Abimelech was symbolized by animal sacrifice and accompanied by an oath. Abraham also "planted a grove in Beersheba, and called there on the name of the LORD, the everlasting God" (*El Olam*, Gen. 21:33).

Scholars have attempted to determine why the name *El Olam* was revealed at this particular time and place. Why was God called the Everlasting God at Beersheba instead of somewhere else? Some have suggested that this is the place where Abraham first exercised squatter's rights in the Promised Land. Giving Abraham and his descendants the land of Palestine was a part of the "everlasting [*olam*] covenant" that God had made with Abraham (17:7). When Abraham dug a well and possessed Beersheba, it was an act of faith in God's eternal promise. In calling *Jehovah El Olam*, Everlasting God, Abraham was expressing faith in the God of the everlasting covenant. There is mystery or hiddenness (*alam*) here too: it is a mystery that Abraham had faith enough to see the well of Beersheba as a down payment on the future Kingdom.

Place of Availability

By calling on God as *El Olam*, Abraham was calling on the One who is always and eternally available to us. To use modern theological language, he called upon the omniscient, omnipresent and omnipotent God—the God who is eternally changeless. People today need just such a God as the eternal, unchangeable Lord, *El Olam*. We call on Him because His "tender mercies and [His] lovingkindnesses . . . have been ever [*olam*] of old" (Ps. 25:6). David also said that "the LORD is good; his mercy is everlasting; and his truth endureth to all generations" (100:5). *El Olam* means "the mercy of the LORD is from everlasting to everlasting upon them that fear him, and his righteousness unto children's children" (103:17).

Place of Protection

Thus, when Abraham called upon *El Olam* at Beersheba, he was asking God to protect his well not only as long as Abimelech lived; he sought long-term protection as well. Prior to this event, God had given Abraham immediate help according to his daily need. When he needed protection, wisdom or peace, God was there. But when Abraham called on *El Olam*, he was calling for God to protect the Promised Land from the enemies of Abraham's descendants after he died. Abraham wanted Beersheba and the Promised Land to be his family inheritance forever.

Place of Mystery

Others see the hidden (*alam*) God at Beersheba. They point out that since the future was hidden (*alam*) from Abraham, he called on the name of the God who can mysteriously see into future ages (*olam*). As the apostle Paul teaches, these Old Testament events were shadows or types of what was to come in Christ. For example, the birth of Isaac of a "free woman" and Abraham's rejection of the "son of the bondmaid" is a picture of God's dealing with the Jews and later with the Gentiles (see Gal. 4:22-30). Since these things are done in mystery—that is, their fulfillment awaits a dispensation (*olam*) yet to be revealed—they are in the hands of *El Olam*, the God of secrets and mysteries.

This connection between eternity, or age, and mystery is seen in the way Paul related the idea of a dispensation to mystery:

If ye have heard of the dispensation of the grace of God which is given me to you-ward: how that by revelation he made known unto me the mystery . . . which in other ages was not made known unto the sons of men, as it is now revealed unto his holy apostles and prophets by the Spirit (Eph. 3:2-3,5).

"Forever" and "hiddenness" are also linked in the Old Testament laws of bondservants. If a slave who was about to go free loved his master and wanted to stay in his service, the law provided that the servant's ear could be pierced with an awl as a symbol of his choice. It was a sign that he should serve his master "for ever" (*olam*, Exod. 21:6; Lev. 25:46 indicates that the servitude was only until the year of Jubilee, showing that *olam* can mean a specific period as well as "everlasting"). In such cases, perhaps God had a secret plan for the slave who made this special commitment.

Similarly, when Hannah gave her child Samuel to the Lord, she said, "I will not go up until the child be weaned, and then I will bring him, that he may appear before the LORD, and there abide for ever" (1 Sam. 1:22). By this she meant, "As long as he liveth he shall be lent to the LORD" (v. 28). As it turned out, God had a secret plan for Samuel to carry out in leading Israel to greatness.

The word *olam* is also used to describe a former time. Joshua told his people, "Your fathers dwelt on the other side of the flood in old time" (*olam*, Josh. 24:2). He did not mean that they had dwelt there forever but for a certain time within God's purpose. The word can also refer to this present world, as when the psalmist says, "These are the ungodly, who prosper in the world" (*olam*, Ps. 73:12), meaning that they prospered in this present age or in this lifetime. In these references, *olam* simply expresses the purpose of God in time and does not mean time without limits. It shows that God has a purpose in time that is not yet known—it is a mystery. *El Olam* is "God who has His own purpose in time," or the "God of this time." It implies that God is working His will behind the scenes and that His purpose will eventually be completed.

We have seen that the name *Jehovah* is taken from the verb *Hayah*, which means "I am that I am." *Jehovah* is the God of the present tense. *El Olam* is the everlasting God, the God of the future, who "will be what I will be."

The New Testament application of *El Olam* is found in Ephesians 3:8, where Paul speaks of "the unsearchable riches of Christ." God has a secret purpose that we do not know, but it is rich and full of grace. Paul describes how this secret is revealed: "To the intent that now unto the principalities and powers in heavenly places might be known by the church the manifold wisdom of God" (v. 10). Only in the New Testament do we see the full explanation of the eternal plan of *El Olam* "according to the eternal purpose which he purposed in Christ Jesus our Lord" (v. 11).

There are many complex things in the Bible that transcend our understanding. For example, God seems to have a law respecting the firstborn and the firstfruits. In His mysterious wisdom, He chose Jacob instead of Esau through whom to fulfill His promise to Abraham (see Rom. 9:13). He chose Ephraim over Manasseh (see Gen. 48:14-17). When we are left to ask why, we can only look to *El Olam*.

As we study the Scriptures, we see the mysterious periods of time that are often repeated: seven days, seven weeks, seven months, seven years and seven times seven (see Lev. 25:8-9). We read of the seven years of tribulation and the coming periods of time, and we do not understand why time is divided into sevens. Yet *El Olam* understands the reasons.

Under the Law, a person works six days and then rests one. In the new dispensation, most believers rest on the first day and work for six. Why? This is a secret known to *El Olam*.

We do not know why the Melchizedekian priesthood came first or why God then turned to the Aaronic priesthood after the order of Levi. Later God re-implements the Melchizedekian priesthood, with Christ the priest after the order of Melchizedek. Why? Again, *El Olam*, the Everlasting God whose name is secret, has His own purpose.

Application

Several applications can be drawn from the revelation of the name *El Olam*, the Everlasting God whose name is secret.

1. *The secret of God gives new meaning to trusting.* Since believers must walk by faith, we must understand the nature of faith. Faith is affirming what God has said in the Bible. To walk by faith is to

obey the principles of the Word of God. Hence, the better a person knows the Scriptures, the better opportunity he has for a successful life of faith. But what about obeying what is unknown? Can we guide our lives by what is secret? This is a tough question.

"The secret things belong unto the LORD our God: but those things which are revealed belong unto us and to our children for ever, that we may do all the words of this law" (Deut. 29:29). This verse establishes that God has withheld some secret things from us. Obviously, God would not harm us or treat us unmercifully. He would not withhold something to punish us. Yet the secrets of God challenge us to trust Him all the more.

What grounds do we have for trusting the secrets of God? First, the nature of God. He will always act rightly and judge rightly. God cannot go against His righteous nature. Second, the way God has dealt with secrets in the past. The things God withheld in the Old Testament but then revealed in the New Testament were for our good and for the glory of God. Therefore, we can now trust God even in the areas that are hidden from us. Because we have established a positive relationship with Him on what we know, we should proceed to trust Him for the things we do not know.

2. *The silence of God gives new meaning to the voice of God.* The believer learns when God speaks, but he also learns when God does not speak. We hear the voice of God in three ways: First, He speaks through His Word: "God, who at sundry times and in divers manners spake in time past unto the fathers by the prophets, hath in these last days spoken unto us by his Son" (Heb. 1:1-2). Second, God speaks through nature; He reveals His power and His personality (Godhead) through the creation (see Rom. 1:18-20). And third, God speaks through the conscience to tell us of our wrong actions. Like a thermometer, the conscience reveals our condition when we go against God's moral law: "their conscience also bearing witness, and their thoughts the mean while accusing or else excusing one another" (Rom. 2:15).

But what about God's silence? What does this say to us? Sometimes we act as though we expect God to speak when He has already spoken. When people commit adultery, they don't need God to speak and tell them that their sexual actions are wrong.

God has already told them it is wrong. Some even expect God to strike them dead on the spot when they sin. But God has already judged sin on Calvary, and He will not do it again. If you sin and know better, the silence of God ought to frighten you.

Some Christians want God to make an exception for them in special situations or to tell them what to do. But God has spoken in His word; now the Christian must seek the principles in God's Word to find out God's will for his life. Since God has spoken in the Word, and the normal voice of God is in the Word, do not seek an abnormal voice of God.

3. *What God withholds gives new meaning to the revelation of God.* God's nature is to reveal Himself, just as the nature of light is to shine. When we speak of the revelation of God, we mean the "self-revelation" of God. Revealing Himself is something He does. There is no possibility that any person can uncover God or discover something about God if He does not choose to reveal it.

We know much about God from the Bible. We know that He has moral attributes of holiness, love and goodness. He has revealed these to us. But there may be other things about God that He has not revealed. Why? Because we cannot understand them. Since God is so majestic, we can only know those things about Him that a human person can know. We cannot know the things that only deity can know. And what we do know, we know only by the Holy Spirit:

> But as it is written, Eye hath not seen, nor ear heard, neither have entered into the heart of man, the things which God hath prepared for them that love Him. But God hath revealed them unto us by His Spirit: for the Spirit searcheth all things, yea, the deep things of God (1 Cor. 2:9-10).

4. *We are only responsible for what we know about God.* What we know about God is revealed to us by the Holy Spirit:

> Now we have received, not the spirit of the world, but the spirit which is of God; that we might know the things that are freely given to us of God. Which things also we speak,

not in the words which man's wisdom teacheth, but which the Holy Ghost teacheth; comparing spiritual things with spiritual. But the natural man receiveth not the things of the Spirit of God: for they are foolishness unto him: neither can he know them, because they are spiritually discerned (2:12-14).

We are not responsible for what we do not know. But the principle of the burden of knowledge tells us that we must respond to God as we know Him, acting on the commands we have received, and that we will be judged by the light that we have (our understanding).

A great man's statement could be paraphrased, "It is not the things about the Bible I do not understand that bother me—it is the things I understand."

6

Mighty God: El Gibbor

AND THE STRONG NAMES OF GOD

During my college days I led singing for a revival meeting at a small country Presbyterian church outside Savannah, Georgia. A fierce thunderstorm swept over the area during the service. Suddenly the power line to the church was snapped by a falling limb, and the lights went out. The piano stopped since the accompanist couldn't see the music. Everyone stopped singing.

At first I panicked, but then realized that I had to take control of the situation. "This reminds me of a story," I said, speaking loudly over the sound of the rain. The crowd grew still, and the pastor went to get an electrician to fix the wire while I continued my story.

"Augustus Toplady walked through a storm like this years ago. The lightning illuminated the sky like tonight, and the thunder rumbled." I didn't need to establish the mood for the story. The little white-frame church was whipped by sheets of rain. The people listened to me.

"Can you imagine being on a lonely mountain road in a storm like this one?" I asked. The congregation didn't respond. I continued, "Augustus Toplady was terrified, thinking that he would be stranded in the cold rain and maybe even die from exposure.

"Up ahead, in a flash of lightning, Toplady saw a massive rock. He knew that he could find protection from the rain on the leeward side of the rock. When he got there, he found that the huge boulder had been split by lightning. By crawling into a cleft of the rock, he was protected from both wind and rain. It was as though the rock had been split just for him.

"Toplady began to think of the spiritual applications: *Jesus is the Rock—firm, strong and protective. Yet Jesus was crucified for me, and a spear split open His side. He was the Rock cleft for me. In Jesus a person is safe from the storms of sin and strife.*

"As the storm passed, Toplady got paper and pencil and wrote these words: 'Rock of Ages, cleft for me, let me hide myself in Thee.'"

After I finished telling the story to the audience at that revival meeting, I had them sing the words of the song from memory. We sang without the piano. Other songs followed, and we sang for over 45 minutes. The preacher returned, unable to get the lights repaired at the moment, but he went ahead and preached in the darkened auditorium. I don't remember how many were saved that night, but the lights didn't come back on until after the meeting was over.

Afterward, everyone in the community talked about the story of the rock in the storm. People remembered how the crowd sang. That was the event that drew them back every evening during the rest of the revival meeting.

A God for the Storms of Life

The name "Rock" is only one of several strength names for God in the Old Testament. He is also called "Mighty God," "Strong One," "Fortress" and "the LORD My Strength," among other titles.

These names were not used by the people of God when they needed might in battle. When they faced a powerful enemy or were in danger of being defeated in battle, they were more likely to call on *Jehovah Sabaoth*, the LORD of Hosts, a name referring to God as Lord of the fighting angels. Rather, they would use the strength names of God in the spiritual storms of life when they were weak, discouraged or in need of emotional strength.

Perhaps the best-known strength name of God is *El Gibbor*, "Mighty God," and the best-known passage in which it appears is a messianic prophecy in the book of Isaiah. Israel was discouraged at the prospects of losing a military conflict. But the nation really needed spiritual revival. God promised them that a Messiah would come and save them, coming as a child through a virgin birth (see Isa. 7:14). Then Isaiah exults,

For unto us a Child is born, unto us a Son is given; and the government will be upon His shoulder. And His name will be called Wonderful, Counselor, Mighty God [*El Gibbor*], Everlasting Father, Prince of Peace (Isa. 9:6, *NKJV*).

The term *Gibbor* was first applied to God by Moses when he said, "For the LORD your God is God of gods, and Lord of lords, a great God, a mighty [*gibbor*], and a terrible" (Deut. 10:17).

David speaks of God as "the LORD strong and mighty, the LORD mighty in battle" in Psalm 24:8, a song celebrating military victory. *Gibbor* appears in this verse as an adjective. It is a term that implies exceptional physical strength and agility, and it is used frequently of men mighty in battle. *El Gibbor* speaks of God's might and power.

Another Hebrew word for "mighty One" is *Abir*, a term that blends the words for "mighty" and "strong." Interestingly, *Abir* is used only in conjunction with the names "Jacob" and "Israel." Jacob used the term on his deathbed, referring to the strength of his son Joseph, whose "bow abode in strength, and [whose] arms of his hands were made strong by the hands of the mighty [*Abir*] God of Jacob" (Gen. 49:24; see also Ps. 132:2). Isaiah spoke of "the mighty One of Israel" (1:24).

It is also interesting that Jacob should refer to himself by the name "Jacob" instead of "Israel," the new name that God had given to him (see Gen. 35:10). The name "Jacob" means "supplanter" (see 27:36), while "Israel" means "prince with God." Apparently Jacob was referring in Genesis 49:24 to his old deceitful ways when he had supplanted his brother Esau. But even when he was living after the flesh, "the mighty God of Jacob" kept him from falling. He may have been implying that God had been faithful to bring him through the valley of temptation into the place of God's blessing.

Another of the strong names of God is *Tsur*, or "Rock." For those in the Near East traveling near the desert, a rock was noted as a fortress or a place of protection. Five times in the song of Moses, God is referred to as a Rock (see Deut. 32:4,15,18,30-31). The large rocks in Palestine were so unassailable and enduring that they have impressed man from the beginning of history. When a person was attacked by wild beasts, a rock could be a place of protection and refuge. A rock might provide protection in a storm and shade from the scorching Middle Eastern sun—a need little understood by many Westerners until their soldiers took up posts in the Arabian Desert in 1990. The Bible constantly describes the refuge offered by *El Gibbor* as offering the rest and protection and shade of a great Rock.

Application

Several lessons are apparent when we think of the strong names of God, especially as we compare His strength with ours.

1. *God cannot protect what we won't give Him.* We naturally protect what belongs to us—our "turf," our kids, our job, our homes, our reputation. We don't give nearly so much energy to protecting something that belongs to another. We may try to some degree to help protect someone else's job, and at times we may even go the second mile to defend someone else's property. But we will fight to the death when our own jobs or our own property is threatened. We work harder, we make twice as many calls, we study—and we even appeal to a federal fair-employment agency if necessary.

Why do we go to such lengths to protect what is ours? First, because our lives are wrapped up in our work, our relatives, our material possessions. These things actually become a part of us. They are an extension of our personality. Second, we are selfish by nature, and we want (lust after) things, people and position. While this is negative motivation, there is also a positive aspect to it: people and things are the objects of our love. We defend our friends and relatives because we love them. If a schoolteacher mistreats a child, she usually stirs up the wrath of the mother, who will figuratively (and in some cases literally!) claw the eyes out of anyone who threatens her child.

God loves us and protects us so much that He gave His Son for us. But sometimes we don't seem to experience that protection. The enemy attacks us like a roaring lion (see 1 Pet. 5:8), and we seem helpless to protect ourselves. We fall into trouble, and God seems to stand by. He doesn't rush in to defend us. Why? Because we think that we can protect ourselves, that we are in control of our own lives and property. But God can't protect us when we won't let Him.

The shepherd can protect the sheep that sleeps closest to him. But if a rebellious lamb insists on straying away from the fold at night, it is beyond the shepherd's protection. By removing itself from the fold, the rebellious lamb is prey to predators and other dangers. In the case of the Good Shepherd, such sheep make it difficult for the Mighty God to exercise His power in protecting His own.

God's sheep also make it difficult for Him to protect them in less intentional ways. Some Christians simply fail to surrender their lives to God. They don't deliberately rebel or engage in sins that are visibly outrageous. They just never commit their lives to Jesus Christ. But when troubles come—for example, financial difficulties—they want the protection of the Mighty God. It is fair to ask, "Should God protect the finances of believers who never surrender their time, talent or treasures to Him?"

Since we are selfish and often blinded to our selfishness, we may be ignorant of the blessings and protection offered by the Mighty God. The child of God may never have surrendered his finances to God and thus never experienced His protection in an economic sense. He may not know that God doesn't just want his tithe; He wants everything—not to take it away but to enable the believer to act as His agent and steward, managing his or her finances according to divine principles.

2. *God can't work His way in our lives while we work out our ways.* Too often the child of God is fighting battles his or her own way. To get victory, the child of God must surrender. This doesn't mean that we become passive. Surrendering is just the first step in ceasing our self-centered activity. The second step is to fight according to divine principles. God can't protect us with His biblical principles when we stubbornly insist on protecting ourselves with self-seeking principles.

Taking an example from our finances again, a Christian often tries to solve an economic crisis in his own self-seeking determination. He may moonlight a second job, push for a raise, put his wife to work, borrow his way out of debt, or try some get-rich-quick scheme. When such measures are tried in our own strength, and when biblical principles are ignored, we are going our own way; there is no room for God to protect us in His way.

3. *Protection begins with a relationship, not a rabbit's foot.* Many people treat God like a good-luck charm. When facing a difficulty, they use their Bibles like a person rubbing a rabbit's foot—letting it fall open at what he or she hopes will be a lucky passage. But Bible promises are for those who establish a relationship with the God of the Bible. Those who just use it as a lucky charm cannot claim its promises.

God has protected some soldiers on the battlefield who claimed the aid of the Mighty God, but other Christian soldiers have died. What is the difference? The promise of protection must be claimed within the will of God (see Jas. 4:14-15), must be within the realm of what God has promised to protect, and is dependent upon the believer's walk with God. In some cases, believers are not living spiritually in ways that enable them to claim biblical protection.

There are ways to keep ourselves close to the Shepherd so that we can expect His protection. First, those who know God's Word can better interpret it and apply it than those who are ignorant of it. Second, those who have a lifelong walk with God are better protected because they have not exposed themselves to danger. For example, the chances of getting lung cancer for practicing Christians who refrain from smoking are greatly reduced. Also, those who maintain sexual purity will not acquire AIDS from sexual misconduct. An obedient Christian will not go to prison for fraud for falsely reporting their income to the IRS. Salvation does not automatically guarantee healing for the new Christian who is dying from cirrhosis of the liver after being an alcoholic for 30 years.

Those who are living in constant obedience have better reasons to trust in the protection of *El Gibbor*, the Mighty God. Obviously, the new believer can expect God's immediate acceptance, regardless of his emotional, physical or social condition—just as the prodigal son received the robe, the ring, the welcome-home banquet and the kiss (see Luke 15:11-24). But the new believer cannot expect to avoid the consequences of his or her former rebellion against God's laws.

The thief on the cross experienced the consequences of his sins—death on a cross—even though he also enjoyed salvation and the immediate acceptance from Jesus: "Today shalt thou be with me in paradise" (23:43).

7

King: Jehovah Melek

THE THRONE NAME OF GOD

I had a friend who once had an audience with the king of Denmark. He told me that when the king entered the room, everyone stopped talking and stood up. "Everyone was aware of his presence," my friend said.

Even though the word "King" (*melek*) is not actually a personal name of God, it is truly one of His titles. God is the King. The psalmist uses "King" as a synonym for God: "my King, and my God" (Pss. 5:2; 84:3), equating God with the position and the person of King. When the psalmist says, "God is my King" (74:12), he is describing God in the function of a ruler. In Psalm 10:16 the psalmist says, "The LORD is King for ever and ever," giving the Lord the title of King.

Isaiah's Vision of the King

The prophet Isaiah was called into service after an experience of seeing the Lord as king: "Mine eyes have seen the King, the LORD of hosts" (Isa. 6:5). This call to Isaiah came to him the year that King Uzziah died (see v. 1). Historians believe that Isaiah was a close friend of King Uzziah and that the earthly king had even been Isaiah's hero. King Uzziah had defeated the Philistines, had expanded the kingdom, and had obviously been successful. But when he reached the zenith of power, he had apparently felt that he could tell God what to do. He had intruded into the office of the priesthood, and God had struck him with leprosy. Uzziah had been rejected from being king, lived in a house separated from everyone and died a leper (see 2 Chron. 26:16-21). With his death, Isaiah's hopes and dreams apparently were dashed. In Isaiah's despondency, God called him to service through a vision of the heavenly King.

Isaiah cried out, "I saw the Lord sitting on a throne, high and lifted up, and the train of his robe filled the temple" (Isa. 6:1, *NKJV*). In this vision, the Lord (*Adonai*, or Master) was enthroned in the heavenly throne room, which was apparently a temple rather than a royal residence like that from which an earthly king might reign. While some commentators believe that Isaiah saw the Lord sitting in the earthly Temple, a careful examination reveals that He was more likely sitting in the temple of heaven, the dwelling place of God. His royal robes extended from heaven into the Temple on Earth. This was probably a reference to the Shekinah glory cloud that extended from heaven into the holy of holies.

God the King is also identified as "the LORD of hosts, which dwelleth between the cherubims" (1 Sam. 4:4). This was the name used to describe God sitting in the holy of holies on the mercy seat above the Ark of the Covenant. The Lord is the King, but His reign begins in the Temple where there is redemption rather than from a human throne that is characterized by authority and might. The Lord's righteous reign begins with salvation.

Around the throne of God were seraphim (angels), who are associated with the protection and glory of God. In Isaiah's vision they cried, "Holy, holy, holy, is the LORD of hosts: the whole earth is full of his glory" (Isa. 6:3). As a result of their adoration, "the house was filled with smoke" (v. 4). This smoke was the Shekinah glory cloud that extended from heaven to Earth and filled the holy of holies.

Isaiah repented, "Woe is me! for I am undone; because I am a man of unclean lips, and I dwell in the midst of a people of unclean lips" (v. 5). He was overwhelmed because "mine eyes have seen the King, the LORD of hosts" (v. 5) and God had said, "there shall no man see me, and live" (Exod. 33:20). Earlier the phrase "the LORD of hosts" (*Jehovah Sabaoth*) was seen as a militant term describing *Jehovah*, who led the heavenly armies into battle. The earthly parallel is of the king of Israel, who led his armies against the enemies.

The Role of the King

Kingship had a twofold significance in Israel. First, the king was functional, that is, he provided legislative, judicial and executive services for the people. Second, the king was symbolic, that is, he was God's representative on Earth. As such, the king took the place of God for the people. This is called ritual kingship, or divine kingship. (When Jesus comes for the millennial Kingdom, He will fulfill both functions inasmuch as He will rule the earth from Jerusalem and also be the divine King who symbolizes the role of God in a theocracy.)

The functional king has several responsibilities. First, he has legislative power; he enacts laws. Earlier, on his deathbed, Jacob had predicted that Israel's king would come through the tribe of Judah: "The sceptre shall not depart from Judah, nor a lawgiver from between his feet, until Shiloh come" (Gen. 49:10). This prophecy has three aspects: First, it promised that there would be a king of Israel. Second, the king would have legislative power to establish laws. And third, the king of Israel would come from the tribe of Judah. The psalmist reinforces this prediction: "Judah is my lawgiver" (Ps. 60:7).

The king's role as lawgiver would be similar to that of the Congress of the United States (the House and the Senate), which establishes laws for the good of the people. Beyond the human king, God is the King-Lawmaker: "The LORD is our judge, the LORD is our lawgiver, the LORD is our king; he will save us" (Isa. 33:22).

The second function of the king is to interpret the laws. This function is parallel to the judicial branch of the United States government. On some occasions the king served as judge, as did Solomon when two prostitutes both claimed the same baby. During the night one prostitute slept on her baby, and it died. As king, Solomon interpreted the law. He decreed that the baby should be cut in half and each prostitute receive half of the dead body (see 1 Kings 3:16-28). Obviously, the legitimate mother refused to allow the baby to be killed. "And all Israel heard of the judgment which the king had judged; and they feared the king: for they saw that the wisdom of God was in him, to do judgment" (v. 28).

A third function of the king was to provide services for the people, such as building roads and creating valid currency. This is the executive branch of government, or the aspect of the government of the United States represented by the president. In this capacity, the king would facilitate the civil functions of the government. The superior organizational ability of Solomon is seen in 1 Kings 4, in which we see that he established managers to oversee every aspect of his kingdom. This function was another reason why the people followed Solomon: "God gave Solomon wisdom and understanding exceeding much, and largeness of heart" (v. 29).

Other Kingly Terms

Reign
The word "reign" is used interchangeably with "king" on many occasions in the Old Testament. It sometimes refers to the authority and power of the king, as in "The LORD reigneth" (Pss. 93:1; 97:1; 99:1). The fact that the LORD reigns is to be announced to the heathen (96:10). This may refer to the direct rulership of God that is similar to the theocracy of the judges. It also may refer to the fact that all kings actually reign only by the power delegated to them by the Lord, as in Proverbs 21:1: "The king's heart is in the hand of the LORD, as the rivers of water: he turneth it whithersoever he will."

Throne
The word "throne" is also used interchangeably with the words "reign" and "king." The throne is the place where the king functions, or sits as the divine representative. God does not sit upon a throne on the earth. "The LORD is in his holy temple, the LORD's throne is in heaven" (Ps. 11:4). God Himself enforced this truth: "Thus saith the LORD, The heaven is my throne, and the earth is my footstool" (Isa. 66:1). This reference to the localized presence of God is a figurative description, since God is omnipresent, meaning He is everywhere equally present at all times. The heaven where God reigns was thought of by the Jews as "the third heaven" (2 Cor. 12:2)—the first heaven being the atmosphere and the second the

stratosphere, or the stars. God's throne was spoken of as being in the third heaven, from whence He rules the universe.

There seemed to be more than one throne in Israel. The psalmist notes, "For there are set thrones of judgment, the thrones of the house of David" (Ps. 122:5), apparently meaning that other bureaucrats or officials of the king sat on subordinate thrones or places of authority. These officials sat upon a lesser throne and functioned with delegated power from the king.

The psalmist also refers to a "throne of iniquity" in Psalm 94:20—probably a reference to a position of authority usurped by demons. The apostle Paul recognized thrones of spiritual authority—"whether they be thrones" (Col. 1:16)—suggesting angels who sit on lesser thrones than God, who are responsible for His work and who carry out God's delegated authority.

The throne was important because of its symbolic power. The Bible describes Solomon's throne in elaborate detail:

> Moreover the king made a great throne of ivory, and over-laid it with the best gold. The throne had six steps, and the top of the throne was round behind: and there were stays on either side on the place of the seat, and two lions stood beside the stays. And twelve lions stood there on the one side and on the other upon the six steps: there was not the like made in any kingdom (1 Kings 10:18-20).

The human throne had to be beautiful, impressive and authoritative since it was the place where judgments were made and orders were given. More importantly, it was the place where the king sat as the divine representative of God.

The throne of God in heaven is described in even more awesome terms. John describes it in the book of Revelation:

> And, behold, a throne was set in heaven. . . . And round about the throne were four and twenty seats: and upon the seats I saw four and twenty elders sitting, clothed in white raiment; and they had on their heads crowns of gold (4:2-4).

These elders apparently had delegated power from God. John saw angels ministering to God, a beautiful glass-like sea in front of the throne and the rainbow of God surrounding the throne. The beauty of the throne in heaven reflects the majesty of God who sits upon it. At this beautiful scene the angels can only say, "Thou art worthy, O Lord, to receive glory and honour and power: for thou hast created all things, and for thy pleasure they are and were created" (v. 11).

Application

1. *Although God is as intimate as a father, as King He has sovereignty over our lives.* In the Lord's Prayer, Jesus taught us to pray, "Our Father which art in heaven . . ." (Matt. 6:9). God is a Father who receives us as intimately as if we were little children crawling into His lap. Hence, the believer can come into His presence anytime, anyplace and under any conditions. On the other hand, we must recognize the sovereignty of the King. Just as Queen Esther had to wait for the extended scepter that gave her permission to approach the king, so too we must come reverently and carefully into God's throne room (see Esther 5:2).

After Jesus taught us to pray to God as Father, He then immediately told us also to pray, "Thy kingdom come, thy will be done" (Matt. 6:10), tying the sovereignty of God to our intimate relationship with Him. Is it not interesting that we pray to our heavenly Father but that He is referred to as having a *kingdom*, not a family? Both the intimacy of fatherhood and the power, majesty and grandeur of a kingdom are seen here. And at the end of the prayer, Jesus taught His disciples to pray, "For thine is the kingdom, and the power, and the glory, for ever" (v. 13).

Because God is our Father, the believer can presume upon His goodness. Because God is our King, the believer must submit to His sovereignty and control. In this analogy we see two sides of God, like two poles of a battery, brought together in the nature of God. Our heavenly Father is also the King of the universe.

When John F. Kennedy was president of the United States, he had the controlling power over one of the greatest nations in the world. Yet in many cabinet meetings, his young son, John, would run into the room, interrupting the cabinet members to climb up into the lap of his father. Should we do any less than young John did in presuming that he would be accepted by his father when we approach our heavenly Father?

2. Jehovah Melek *(the LORD Our King) deserves reverence and worship.* Often those who attend church forget to worship God. They learn from the Bible, they get caught up in the singing, or they are aware of their needs in prayer. But most believers are too concerned with their own desires, protection and self-will. Worshipers get wrapped in their own world and forget to center their thoughts on God.

We ask what we can get out of a worship service; it can also be asked of the typical church service, "What did God get out of it?"

Worship is not a nice addition for our church services; worship is a mandate. Jesus said, "The Father seeketh such to worship him" (John 4:23). As one person said, "Worship is when the worth-ship that is due to God is given to Him." Worship centers on God; worship is when the reverence and honor that are due to God are actually given to Him.

And how should we worship? Jesus reminded the woman at the well of Samaria, "God is a Spirit: and they that worship him must worship him in spirit and in truth" (v. 24). In saying that worship involves our spirit, Jesus indicated that worship involves all three aspects of man's personality: emotion, intellect and will. Worshiping in spirit involves pouring out adoration to God through such emotions as love, joy, praise and other deep feelings. Worshiping in truth involves worship based on the revelation of God. True worship must be based intellectually in cognitive knowledge of His Word. If we do not have a true understanding of God or correct knowledge about Him, we cannot properly worship Him.

Much of modern worship is coined in a phrase using the word "celebration." A worship leader may say, "Let us celebrate our salvation" or "Let us celebrate the holiness of God." As good as this is, it may make mankind the center of worship. A person may celebrate for the wrong reason—for what he or she can get out of it. Some make celebration like a Fourth of July picnic or like gift giving at Christmas—the significance of the event is often lost in the way we celebrate it. Celebration may be man centered, but worship is God centered.

3. *A person enters the Kingdom by the new birth.* Jesus had at least two major revelations in His teaching: first, the divine fatherhood of God, and second, the kingdom of God, or the kingdom of heaven. The doctrine of the fatherhood of God set forth that the individual could have intimate relationship with God. The doctrine of the Kingdom defines the collective and social responsibility of Christians as determined by the rule of the King.

Interestingly enough, the titles "God the King" and "God the Father" can be used interchangeably in many places. Jesus adapted the Old Testament idea of *Jehovah* as King to an inner and spiritual principle. He dealt with attitudes, motives and character. Those who live by the principles of the kingdom of God live personal lives of godliness.

Jesus eliminated the exclusivism of the Jews in the Old Testament. Under His teaching, any person could enter the kingdom of God. Still, there is a requirement: "Except a man be born again, he cannot see the kingdom of God" (John 3:3). To be born again, a person believes in the name of Jesus, which is receiving Him as Savior. Jesus went on to indicate that the virtues of the Kingdom were to hunger and thirst after righteousness, love, mercy, purity and peace (see Matt. 5:3-10). Therefore, the Kingdom has an inner dimension— there is love and grace to all who enter by faith. And it has an outward dimension—God as King governs the behavior of those who enter the Kingdom by the Word of God and by the leading of the Holy Spirit.

4. *The present kingdom of God is different from the future kingdom of Israel.* There is a second Kingdom, the Millennium (1,000-year reign), which is future in time. This is the time when Jesus will return physically and reign from Jerusalem. That Kingdom is in fulfillment of the promises of the Old Testament to the nation of Israel. That Kingdom shall be national and coercive. No one will live there by sin or selfishness. Jesus shall rule this Kingdom with a rod of iron, and everyone will obey. This Kingdom is coming in the future when men shall see "the Son of man coming in his kingdom" (16:28).

The two kingdoms, the inner Kingdom and the coming Kingdom, will be joined together in the future under the one King Jesus Christ.

Jesus rejected the multitude when they came "by force, to make him a king" (John 6:15). Pilate humiliated Jesus Christ before a howling mob and proclaimed, "Behold your King!" (19:14). Pilate did not understand the future fulfillment of the Kingdom.

Under the present kingship of Jesus Christ, Paul honored the Lord, in his writing to Timothy, as "the King eternal" (1 Tim. 1:17). As Paul ended the epistle, he called Jesus "the King of kings, and Lord of lords" (6:15). At His return, Jesus shall have "on his thigh a name written, KING OF KINGS, AND LORD OF LORDS" (Rev. 19:16).

5. *Today the King rules His subjects by yieldedness.* A person enters the Kingdom by doing the Father's will (see Matt. 7:21). "For it is your Father's good pleasure to give you the kingdom" (Luke 12:32). Obedience is more than outward acquiescence; it is complete devotion to Jesus Christ and a serious attempt to please Him. This truth is described by Jesus: "Seek ye first the kingdom of God, and his righteousness; and all these things shall be added unto you" (Matt. 6:33).

We should pray for the Kingdom to come and manifest itself in our lives. Jesus taught His disciples to pray, "Our Father which art in heaven, . . . thy kingdom come" (Matt. 6:9-10). While this prayer relates to the coming millennial Kingdom, it does not rule out the rule of God in our hearts at the present time. The prayer for the Kingdom to come is more than intercession. This prayer involves conforming our desires to God's will, so much so that we are willing to conform our present life with the demands of the Kingdom. As we wait for Christ's coming with anticipation, we conform our inner life to *Kingdom life*, hence preparing for the future Kingdom on Earth.

8

The Lord of Hosts: Jehovah Sabaoth

THE MILITANT NAME OF GOD

The title *Jehovah Sabaoth* means "the LORD of Hosts." This is another way of saying "God of the Angels."

The term "host" means army or other organized group, and the term "angels" means messengers. Thus, when God is described as the "LORD of the Angels," it implies that He carries out His will by means of angels or messengers. *Jehovah Sabaoth* is the God of angelic hosts, who carry out His will.

The Work of the LORD of Hosts

One task of angels is to transport people into the presence of God at death. To be "absent from the body" is to be "present with the Lord" (2 Cor. 5:8), and God uses angels to usher the dead into His presence (see Luke 16:22). We should not fear death, because God is *Jehovah Sabaoth*, the God of the angels who accompany the dead to His bosom.

Another task of angels is to serve as guardians to protect us from physical harm: "For he shall give his angels charge over thee, to keep thee in all thy ways. They shall bear thee up in their hands, lest thou dash thy foot against a stone" (Ps. 91:11-12). (The indwelling Holy Spirit protects us from spiritual harm.) We can trust *Jehovah Sabaoth*, because He sends guardian angels to protect us from harm.

The phrase *Jehovah Sabaoth* occurs 281 times in the Old Testament and denotes that the God of Israel brought heavenly powers to the aid of His needy people. As we shall see, the title first occurs in the book of Samuel when Israel was fighting for her political and spiritual life. Since the term "host" can mean heavenly host, as in angels or heavenly messengers, "the LORD of Hosts" could be interpreted as "the God of angels who fight for us." But the term can also refer to the armies of Israel (see 1 Sam. 17:45).

This compound name "the LORD" ("the self-existing and self-revealing One") and *Sabaoth*, or "hosts" (multitudes in the service of God), told Israel that the God whose existence cannot be threatened by mere man was a militant God who would help them prevail against their enemies. David taught the people, "The LORD of hosts, he is the King of glory" (Ps. 24:10). As a heathen nation looked to its king to lead them into battle, God's people followed the LORD of Hosts.

The Use of *Jehovah Sabaoth*

The name "the LORD of Hosts" (*Jehovah Sabaoth*) is never found in the Pentateuch, Joshua or Judges. It rarely occurs in the books of Kings or Chronicles, and not many times in the book of Psalms. It is a phrase mostly related to the prophets. The name is prominently used 80 times in Jeremiah, the prophet who wept over the destruction of Jerusalem. It occurs 14 times in Haggai, 50 times in Zechariah and 25 times in Malachi, the last book of the Old Testament. Why is the name so prominent at the end of the Old Testament? To answer this question, it is helpful to recall Israel's experience after the Exodus from Egypt.

When Israel was a fledgling nation coming out of Egypt, the people had a vision of capturing the land. Coming through 40 years in the wilderness, Israel rallied behind *Jehovah* and conquered the land of promise. Once the land was theirs, however, their lack of faith caused them to waver. At the point of wavering, the name *Jehovah Sabaoth*, or "the LORD of Hosts," is first used to rally the people to battle and victory.

God's people had begun to capture the land in the book of Joshua, but they did not drive out all their enemies. The next period proved to be disastrous, as the book of Judges shows. The people constantly returned to their sins and turned to the worship of the gods of the Canaanites. When the name *Jehovah Sabaoth* was introduced, faithful Israelites were worshiping God at Shiloh, where the Tabernacle and the Ark were located. Old Elkanah and his wife Hannah, the parents of Samuel, who would be the last judge, were among the faithful: "This man went up out of his city yearly to worship and to sacrifice unto the LORD of hosts in Shiloh" (1 Sam. 1:3).

The book of 1 Samuel is a transitional book, and Samuel is a transitional leader. Prior to Samuel, Israel was led by different judges who were military, political and spiritual leaders. When Israel followed the LORD, they were victorious. When they returned to their sin, God allowed them to be defeated. At their lowest level of depression and bondage, God raised up Samuel, the transition man, to lead Israel from a theocracy into an earthly kingdom, from leadership by judges to leadership by kings.

Israel had grown dissatisfied with its judges and had begun to ask for a king like the nations around them—a strong military leader who could go before them in battle (see 1 Sam. 8:1-22). The problem was that their desire for an earthly king was really a rejection of God, their heavenly King. The Lord told Samuel, "They have not rejected thee, but they have rejected me, that I should not reign over them" (v. 7).

To Secure Victory or Judgment
The name "LORD Sabaoth" first appears to Israel as a nation in the context of this rejection of the God whose armies fleshly Israel could not see. In a battle with the Philistines, Israel was beaten, and approximately 4,000 men were killed. The leaders questioned, "Wherefore hath the LORD smitten us to day before the Philistines? Let us fetch the ark of the covenant of the LORD out of Shiloh unto us, that, when it cometh among us, it may save us out of the hand of our enemies" (4:3).

The people put more trust in a piece of furniture than in God. They knew that the LORD of Hosts was their militant Leader, because the Ark is described as "the ark of the covenant of the LORD of hosts [*Jehovah Sabaoth*], which dwelleth between the cherubims" (v. 4). They took the Ark into battle, thinking that with it they could not lose; but their faith was in a *thing* rather than in the LORD of Hosts. Israel was defeated, and the Ark was captured.

Later, young David became the champion of Israel because he recognized the LORD of Hosts. When Goliath challenged Israel to battle, no one dared fight against him. Finally, David came to him with only a sling and five smooth stones. But David was not fighting with a man's strength; he was fighting "in the name of the LORD of hosts, the God of the armies of Israel, whom thou hast defied" (17:45).

Throughout the period of the kings, God raised up prophets to call the people back from their sinful ways and idolatrous worship. As Israel began to lose her faith, she lost her battles too, because *Jehovah Sabaoth* did not fight for her or with her. Perhaps the prophets used the name "LORD of Hosts" so frequently because they felt the defeat of Israel so keenly. Late in this period Israel was a captive people and needed hope. Perhaps the name "LORD of Hosts" would reinforce optimism. Although the armies of Israel were defeated, God and His angels were not. Implied in the name is the promise of victory—if only Israel would repent, the LORD of Hosts would fight for her again.

Even though Israel had lost her battles and the city of Jerusalem was destroyed, God still had His fighting angels. He remained *Jehovah Sabaoth*, the LORD of the angels. This name pointed the people to a new and higher spiritual relationship to God as individuals, not just to a return to the former corporate relationship that *Jehovah* had with the nation.

As we saw in chapter 7, Uzziah, a king who had been victorious for Israel, died during the days of Isaiah.

The young prophet of God had put all his dreams into the reign of King Uzziah. After the king was dead, Isaiah saw a vision of the Lord and His angels. "And one cried unto another, and said, Holy, holy, holy, is the LORD of hosts [*Jehovah Sabaoth*]" (Isa. 6:3). The angels who were part of God's hosts spoke the name *Jehovah Sabaoth*.

Isaiah was commissioned to go preach but was told the people would reject his message. He was told Israel would be spiritually blinded and then punished. Hence, they learned that the LORD of Hosts (*Jehovah Sabaoth*) could lead His people into victory when He was followed, and He could punish when Israel rejected His leadership.

The punishment from the LORD of Hosts—on both Israel and her tormentors—is a recurring theme of the later prophets. "Therefore thus saith the Lord GOD of hosts, O my people that dwellest in Zion, be not afraid of the Assyrian: he shall smite thee with a rod, and shall lift up his staff against thee, . . . and the LORD of hosts shall stir up a scourge for him" (Isa. 10:24,26).

After Israel was taken into captivity, God came to His people with words of both rebuke and encouragement. Earlier it was mentioned that Haggai constantly used the phrase "the LORD of hosts." It appears nine times in the following passage, emphasizing hope in what God would do:

> Yet now be strong, O Zerubbabel, saith the LORD; and be strong, O Joshua, son of Josedech, the high priest; and be strong, all ye people of the land, saith the LORD, and work: for I am with you, saith the LORD of hosts. . . . For thus saith the LORD of hosts; Yet once, it is a little while, . . . and I will fill this house with glory, saith the LORD of hosts. The silver is mine, and the gold is mine, saith the LORD of hosts. The glory of this latter house shall be greater than of the former, saith the LORD of hosts: and in this place will I give peace, saith the LORD of hosts. . . . Thus saith the LORD of hosts. . . . In that day, saith the LORD of hosts, will I take thee, O Zerubbabel, . . . for I have chosen thee, saith the LORD of hosts (Hag. 2:4-9,11,23).

To Secure Blessing or Judgment

At the very end of the Old Testament, the verse usually associated with storehouse tithing also linked the LORD of Hosts with either blessing or judgment:

> Bring ye all the tithes into the storehouse, that there may be meat in mine house, and prove me now herewith, saith

the LORD of hosts [*Jehovah Sabaoth*], if I will not open you the windows of heaven, and pour you out a blessing, that there shall not be room enough to receive it (Mal. 3:10).

If Israel would obey and bring tithes to God, the LORD of Hosts promised,

I will rebuke the devourer for your sakes, and he shall not destroy the fruits of your ground; neither shall your vine cast her fruit before the time in the field, saith the LORD of hosts [*Jehovah Sabaoth*] (v. 11).

"Devourer" is the translation of the Hebrew word for "eater," which is a reference to insects that in time of plagues completely ate all the green vegetation. It is also another word for Satan (see 1 Pet. 5:8). The LORD of Hosts will protect both physically and spiritually those who tithe to Him.

Hence, we see two sides of *Jehovah Sabaoth*. First, He will attack the enemy as an offensive army and lead His people to victory. Second, *Jehovah Sabaoth* will guard, or protect, from enemy attacks, offering the faithful defensive protection from God Himself.

Application

1. Jehovah Sabaoth *brings heavenly power to the aid of His children.* This name, "the LORD of Hosts," indicates the power with which God will help His children. When Israel came to the Promised Land, and their leader Joshua approached Jericho, he wondered how he could take such a city. On an observation trip, he saw a stranger standing before him. Joshua asked, "Art thou for us, or for our adversaries?" (Josh. 5:13). The reply came, "Nay; but as captain of the host of the LORD am I now come" (v. 14). Note that the Lord came to Joshua as Captain of the Hosts in Joshua's hour of need to encourage him. While not actually bearing the name *Jehovah Sabaoth*, this was indeed the One who helped Joshua. Some commentators believe that this was a Christophany—that the One who appeared to Joshua in his time of need was Jesus Christ Himself.

2. *The* LORD *of Hosts rules the armies of heaven so that they will obey His will.* The LORD has hosts who will not only fight for Him but who will obey His command. One of the difficulties in an army is getting the average soldier to obey. Sometimes threats of death, court martial or physical torture are used to get him or her to do so. But the LORD of Hosts has an army that obeys. There is no evidence of His having to punish the armies of heaven, because His angels carry out His will. "Are they not all ministering spirits, sent forth to minister for them who shall be heirs of salvation?" (Heb. 1:14).

How many are in the army of the LORD of Hosts? Jesus said on one occasion, "Thinkest thou that I cannot now pray to my Father, and he shall presently give me more than twelve legions of angels?" (Matt. 26:53). Beyond this number, the writer of Hebrews referred to "an innumerable company of angels" (12:22)—so many that they could not be numbered. The apostle John wrote in Revelation 5:11 that there were in excess of two million angels in heaven. This large group could not function efficiently without organization or a leader. The various groups of angels identified in Scripture all have their duty and their rank—and they obey their Leader.

3. *The Lord will allow His faithless people to be defeated.* There are two wrong ideas that Christians have about problems. First, some have the mistaken idea that being a Christian relieves them from problems and attacks. But a Christian will have pressures in life. "My brethren, count it all joy when you fall into various trials" (Jas. 1:2, *NKJV*). Note that James does not say "*if* trials come" but "*when* they come."

The second mistaken idea is that being a Christian automatically gives one the victory over all attacks. Old Testament Israel apparently had that idea. They felt that no enemy could defeat them because they had the presence of *Jehovah* in the Temple. They treated God like a rabbit's foot—as long as the Temple or the Ark was around, they could not be defeated. However, their sins of legalism, pride and selfish arrogance led to deeper sins of idolatry, adultery and even the sacrifice of their children in fiery holocaust.

The LORD of Hosts who would have defended Israel sat on the sidelines instead and allowed heathen nations to destroy Jerusalem and the Temple and then rape the women, slaughter many of its population, and take a large number of the people into exile (see 2 Kings 25:1-21; 2 Chron. 36:17; Zech. 14:2). God would have been honored by a victory against Israel's enemies, as a judgment of their enemies' sins. But the LORD of Hosts is also honored by the defeat of His people as judgment against their own sins. God does not enjoy the suffering of His people, but at times He allows it. Even then, His holiness is vindicated.

9

The Lord / Master: Adonai

THE HEADSHIP NAME OF GOD

When a sales representative makes a presentation of his product, he calls his client by the proper title and name in order to help earn a contract. If he walked into a small hot-dog stand and asked to talk with the executive vice president, he might be laughed at. Everyone would realize that the salesman doesn't know his customers. If he walked into the executive office suite and asked for an appointment with the foreman, he wouldn't get to see the president or the CEO.

Names and titles are important, because they open doors. Wrong use of names reveals our ignorance and says that we don't know what we are doing or where we are going. Using wrong names and titles shuts doors because it shows that we are not worthy of an opportunity.

We have seen that the Bible uses different names of God to reflect His different roles and functions. When we use the correct name of God in prayer, it shows that we respect Him and know how to approach Him. I don't think God would refuse to hear our prayers because we used an inappropriate title. But our wrong use may reflect our spiritual immaturity, and the fact that we haven't taken time to get to know our Master well. Since His name is *Adonai* (Master), we who are His slaves should learn its meaning as well as how to approach Him properly in that name.

Adonai comes from the Hebrew word *adon*, a word used to describe either a master who owns slaves or a husband in his relationship to his wife (it does not imply that husbands own wives). *Adonai* is a plural form implying the Trinity, just as *Elohim* is also plural, implying the Trinity. Both are a reference in the Old Testament to the Father, Son and Holy Spirit.

The word *Adonai* ("Lord," with only the first letter capitalized) occurs 340 times in the Hebrew Old Testament. However, the rabbis eventually began to use the name *Adonai* as a substitute for the name *Jehovah*. Since *Jehovah* was holy, they could not even speak or write His personal name. On many occasions when copying the Scriptures, they substituted the word *Adonai* for *Jehovah*. Then to make sure that people knew that the terms were substituted, they prepared a parallel manual called the *Sopherim*, which listed the 140 places in the Scriptures where *Adonai* had been substituted for *Jehovah*.

Adonai expresses the personal relationship between a master and his slave. Hence it is a term that symbolizes the relationship of God with His people. The relationship does not emphasize ownership but implies a working relationship.

Just as there is a relationship between a horse and his rider, there has to be a oneness between a person and God if they are to enjoy a trust relationship. Hence, *Adonai* has a twofold meaning.

The relationship between master and servant does not begin with the servant but with the master, who must do two things for his slaves. First, he must provide for the needs of his slaves—give them a place to sleep, food, clothing and the basic necessities. Second, the master must provide direction, training and accountability for the work of the slave.

Hence, the term *Adonai* puts more responsibility on God than on His people. In a sense, the Master serves the slave, for once a person is a slave he or she looks to the master for direction, protection and care.

When Americans try to illustrate the master-slave relationship, it is tempting to think of the book *Uncle Tom's Cabin*. But this would not accurately illustrate God's relationship to us because of the abuse of black slaves portrayed in the book. The relationship of slave and master in the Bible was more often one of love and allegiance. In the Jewish relationship, a slave had more privileges than the hired help. A slave could participate in the Temple sacrifices and was a member of the household. The hired help was excluded from these privileges.

The Master-Slave Relationship

The term *Adonai* ("Master") explains the very heart of Christianity—the relationship between God and the believer. A Christian is different from non-believers because he or she relates to God; the world is the world because in practice it denies that relationship.

What does the name *Adonai* ("Master") assure for us as believers? First, it assures us that our God and Master has the resources and ability to take care of us. Thus as Christian slaves, we trust our Master for these things. Second, it implies that help is available to carry out our Christian duty as a servant. Finally, as servants of the Lord, we have the privilege of calling upon our relationship with the Master to get the help that we need.

The first use of the word *Adonai* ("Master") in Scripture reveals something about its meaning. Abraham had been in the Promised Land for 10 years when this term was first used. When Abraham had first arrived in the land, God had promised him the land and a son—from these his great inheritance would come. But Abraham and Sarah were past the age of bearing children. After 10 years it was only natural that Abraham was growing restless and impatient. He prayed, "Lord GOD [*Adonai Jehovah*], what will You give me, seeing I go childless?" (Gen. 15:2, *NKJV*).

In this reference Abraham had a burden for two things. First, he wanted offspring—a son. Second, he wanted the inheritance that had been promised him. Perhaps Abraham realized that the inheritance was tied to the son. After 10 years Abraham did not have either a son or the Promised Land. Inasmuch as Abraham had a slave-Master relationship to God, it is only natural that he came to God using the names *Adonai* ("Master") and *Jehovah* ("the covenant-keeping God").

Again, Abraham prayed, "Lord GOD [*Adonai Jehovah*], how shall I know that I will inherit it?" (Gen. 15:8, *NKJV*). God had promised him that He would take care of him. Now Abraham wanted some assurance.

Moses, the servant of God, also had a servant-Master relationship with God. He felt inadequate when his Master commissioned him to go to Pharaoh and demand the release of God's people in bondage. Moses only had the rod of God against the power of the Egyptian nation. After offering several excuses to God, he finally prayed, "O my Lord [*Adonai*], I am not eloquent" (Exod. 4:10, *NKJV*). Moses had a speech impediment. Yet he knew he must speak to Pharaoh, king of the strongest nation on Earth. So the servant went to his Master and asked for help. It is only natural that he used the title *Adonai*.

Joshua led Israel across the Jordan River and into battle against Jericho. Because God was with him, Joshua experienced a great victory (see Josh. 6). Shortly thereafter he allowed some of his men to go to battle against Ai. But there was sin in Israel's camp, and God's people were defeated. Joshua approached God in prayer (see 7:1-6). He went as a slave reminding his Master that he needed direction and power to conquer the Promised Land. Therefore, in this context it is only natural that Joshua used the title *Adonai* ("Master"). He prayed, "O Lord [*Adonai*], what shall I say when Israel turns its back before its enemies?" (v. 8, *NKJV*). The prayer of Joshua is based on his servant relationship with God. Obviously, God answered by pointing out the sin, giving them a strategy and finally leading them to victory in battle (see 7:10–8:28).

Gideon was a young man who was fearful of the raiding Midianites, who swept through the Promised Land destroying the Israelites' cattle and crops (see Judg. 6:1-6). The angel of the Lord came to Gideon when he was hiding in the valley in a wine-press, threshing his grain. As background, only those who were fearful and hiding would have attempted to thresh grain in a valley. Usually the threshing floor was on the highest elevated peak, un-obstructed so that the wind could blow away the chaff. The angel of the Lord came to Gideon and said, "The LORD is with thee, thou mighty man of valour" (v. 12). This may have been an attempt to compliment or affirm Gideon, who was apparently an intro-vert with a self-acceptance problem. "And Gideon said unto him, Oh my Lord [*Adonai*], if the LORD be with us, why then is all this befallen us?" (v. 13).

Gideon prayed to God in a servant-Master relationship. He rec-ognized that the Master could give him guidance and power. The angel of the Lord promised that Gideon was going to have a great victory, saying, "Go in this thy might, and thou shalt save

Israel from the hand of the Midianites: have not I sent thee?" (v. 14). But Gideon still wanted answers from his *Adonai* Master. He prayed, "Oh my Lord [*Adonai*], wherewith shall I save Israel?" (v. 15). And based on this prayer, the Lord gave Gideon the direction for his victory.

Others in Scripture have claimed the relationship between slave and Master in their service to God. When Manoah, who was childless, received word of God's promise of a son, he prayed to the Lord (*Adonai*, see 13:8). When Samson prayed to defeat the Philistines, he called upon God in his slave-Master relationship (see 16:28). When David prayed to build a temple, he assumed a slave-Master relationship. Since he knew that God would give his son Solomon the resources and wisdom to build the Temple, David prayed as a slave, knowing that *Adonai* would supply (see 2 Sam. 7:18).

The psalmist joins the names *Jehovah* and *Adonai* in an outburst of praise in Psalm 8:1: "O LORD [*Jehovah*], our Lord [*Adonai*], how excellent is thy name in all the earth!"

When Isaiah was praying in the Temple, he saw the Lord (*Adonai*) high and exalted, sitting on the throne (see Isa. 6:1). Isaiah's hero and friend, King Uzziah, had died of leprosy. Some might assume that Isaiah's personal world had collapsed. What he needed was a vision of his Master *Adonai*. The Lord who was sitting on the throne was also *Jehovah*. For the angels about the throne said, "Holy, holy, holy, is the LORD [*Jehovah*] of hosts" (v. 3).

When Isaiah was called to serve the Lord, he was a proud, young diplomat-bureaucrat who worked for the king. He needed to be broken to enter into a Master-slave relationship. Therefore, God showed Isaiah his sin, and Isaiah cried, "Woe is me!" (v. 5).

The call of Jeremiah had the opposite dynamic. Jeremiah was a weak man, apparently afraid of his own shadow. He is called the weeping prophet. Jeremiah needed the same relationship with God that Isaiah did. He needed a Master, but he did not need to be broken; he needed to be encouraged. Jeremiah prayed, "Ah, Lord [*Adonai*] GOD! behold, I cannot speak: for I am a child" (Jer. 1:6).

God did three things to fulfill His role as Jeremiah's Lord, or Master, and to answer the reluctant prophet's prayer. First,

He encouraged Jeremiah by assuring him that he would not have to rely on his own wisdom: "Whatsoever I command thee thou shalt speak" (v. 7). Second, God promised him His personal presence in the midst of any critics: "Be not afraid of their faces: for I am with thee to deliver thee" (v. 8). And third, God gave his servant Jeremiah a vision of success: "I have made thee this day a defenced city, and an iron pillar, and brasen walls against the whole land. . . . They shall not prevail against thee" (vv. 18-19).

Application

1. *As servants, our first duty is to submit to our Master.* The Old Testament Hebrew *Adonai* ("Master") is the counterpart for the Greek New Testament *kurios* ("Lord"). Jesus Christ is the Christian's Lord and Master. He said, "Ye call me Master and Lord: and ye say well; for so I am" (John 13:13). He also said, "The disciple is not above his master, nor the servant above his lord. It is enough for the disciple that he be as his master, and the servant as his lord" (Matt. 10:24-25).

The Christian should recognize Jesus as Lord and submit to that relationship. Recognizing that relationship, the Christian who submits to his or her Master will hear the words, "Well done, thou good and faithful servant: thou hast been faithful over a few things . . . : enter thou into the joy of thy lord" (25:21).

2. *We can trust the Master's care for His servants.* The title *Adonai* gives the believer the privilege of having Jesus Christ as our Master who will care for us, supply our need and give us direction in life. As Christians, we do not have to be anxious about our "daily bread" (6:11)—supplying that is the Master's responsibility. We do not have to fret over what job we should do or where we should serve— there is a "Master" plan for our lives (see Rom. 12:1-2). We do not have to be concerned about whether we can do the things that God has for us to do—the Master promises the gifts of the Holy Spirit to enable us to serve God (see vv. 3-8).

10

God: Elohim

THE STRONG CREATOR

One time a pastor came up to me at a conference at which I was speaking. I barely remembered him as one of my students. He reminded me of all the things he had done for me while he was in school. He claimed to have carried books for me and washed my car, plus some other things. I was embarrassed because I couldn't remember any of them.

As he left, the former student said, "Tell your wife, Peggy, hello."

I smiled, and I suddenly felt better. I understood that the man had mistaken me for another professor, and that he really hadn't done for me all those things he had claimed.

My wife's name is Ruth.

Names are important to people and their friends. When someone calls a friend by the wrong name, it probably means that he or she is not as close as a real friend would be.

When people say, "God saved me," or, "I know God," although I do not question them outwardly, I sometimes have my inner doubts. For God is an impersonal title for deity. All religions have a god. We who are saved use the personal name of the God who saved us. We say, "The LORD saved me," and we talk about "knowing the LORD."

The difference between God and the LORD may be very subtle to some, but those who know the LORD know the difference. The study of the word *Elohim* ("God") in this chapter will form a basis for the study of the word *Jehovah* ("LORD") in the next chapter.

God is a universal term for deity, used by almost all religions. To review, *Elohim* is one of the three primary terms used in the Bible to describe God. God (*Elohim*) is the strong Creator who is the source of everything. The LORD (*Jehovah*) is the covenant-keeping God who relates to man. *Adonai* ("Master") reflects the servant-Master relationship of man to God.

Elohim comes from *El*, meaning "strong one," and *alah*, meaning "to swear or bind with an oath." The term *Elohim* is used 2,500 times in the Bible to identify the Creator God, the One usually identified with this world, with objects or with the unsaved.

Elohim is the name first used for God in the Scriptures: "In the beginning God [*Elohim*] created the heaven and the earth" (Gen. 1:1). The final reference to God in the Bible is the Greek word *theos*, found in Revelation 22:19. The Bible therefore begins and ends with God, even though it includes many other names, titles or functions to give us other aspects of His nature and work.

Who Is God?

There are many definitions of God. The God of the Bible is the Supreme Being, the divine One whom we worship. Definitions must have a definitive term, such as "the man is a husband." From the Bible we can draw at least seven definitive terms used to describe God.

Who Is God?

---

1. God is life.
2. God is a Person.
3. God is Spirit.
4. God is a Self-existent Being.
5. God is a unity.
6. God is unchangeable.
7. God is unlimited in space and time.

God Is Life

When Joshua told his people, "Ye shall know that the living God is among you" (Josh. 3:10), he was giving one of the definitions for God. Even young David recognized this definition when he spoke of Goliath defying "the living God" (1 Sam. 17:26). To call God "life" is more than describing Him as the One who created life or as the source of life. God is the essence, or nature, of life. The world may say that life is energy, power or force—or even a bowl of cherries. But the Bible says that the life *behind* all these forms of life is the living God who used His energy to create the world. The energy that holds atoms and molecules together is the life of God. The Bible expands this truth when it says, "By him all things consist" (Col. 1:17).

God Is a Person
Whereas most of the religions in the world identify their deities by concepts such as a force or other kinds of impersonal beings, the Bible paints a higher picture of God. He has intellect, emotion and will, which are the elements of personality. In addition to this, God has self-awareness and self-determination. This personality of God is projected into humanity in what Scripture calls the image of God. Mankind mirrors God when we exercise our personality.

The personality of God is seen in His intelligence. God knows (see Gen. 18:19; Exod. 3:7) and has infinite wisdom (see Jer. 51:15).

Next, God has feelings or emotions, sometimes called "sensibility." God feels grief (see Gen. 6:6), kindness (see Ps. 103:8-13), empathy (see Exod. 3:7-8), anger (see Ps. 7:11), and a whole array of other feelings.

Then God has a will, which is the volitional reflection of His personhood. He can make decisions and choose His own actions. God is not bound by any force in the universe, for He is free. Because God has given people an intellect in His own image, we can predict some of His actions. We know, for example, that He will always act in love. But we cannot coerce His actions, since He is perfectly free. No outside stimulus can make Him go against His will, or choice.

God Is Spirit
In the New Testament, Jesus told the Samaritan woman, "God is a Spirit; and they that worship him must worship him in spirit and in truth" (John 4:24). Even though the *King James Version* uses the article "a" with spirit, God is not one spirit among many spirits. It means He is Spirit by nature. As such, God does not have a physical body; He is an incorporeal Being. God is a real Being who has personality and life, but He does not live through a physical body.

Another way of saying this is that God is invisible. Some Bible references imply that people saw God (see Gen. 32:30; Exod. 34:5-8; Num. 12:6-8; Deut. 34:10; Isa. 6:1). Actually, they did not see Him directly but only a reflection of Him. The only ones who have seen God are those who saw Jesus Christ, "the image of the invisible God" (Col. 1:15). To say that God is Spirit is to say that people have not seen Him. One of the reasons the second commandment prohibits making idols or images is because God is not physical or material (see Exod. 20:4). He is Spirit, and He wants man to worship Him in His true nature.

God Is a Self-existent Being

Even though this chapter is defining *Elohim*, God's second name, "LORD" (*Jehovah*), indicates that He is self-existent. The name *Jehovah* comes from the verb "I am." When Moses prayed to God in the burning bush (see 3:1-15), he asked God to identify Himself. God answered by saying, "I AM THAT I AM" (v. 14). This is another name for LORD, or *Jehovah*. The phrase "I AM THAT I AM" actually means "the Self-existent God." In essence, *Jehovah* was saying, "I exist by Myself and for Myself." The existence of God is not dependent upon this world, humanity or anything else.

God Is a Unity

The great *Shema* recited by observant Jews is based on the nature of God: "Hear [Hebrew: *shema*], O Israel: The LORD our God is one LORD" (Deut. 6:4). There can only be one God. To say that there are two supreme Gods or two Creators makes about as much sense as speaking of a square circle. There can only be one Supreme Being; if there were two, these forces would clash. The nature of God excludes all others, for no other one can do what God can do. This truth is taught in Scripture: "Thus saith the LORD the King of Israel, and his redeemer the LORD of hosts; I am the first, and I am the last; and beside me there is no God" (Isa. 44:6).

God Is Unchangeable

Since God is perfect, He cannot become better; therefore He is immutable—He cannot change in His essence. And since He is perfect,

He cannot become corrupt and be less than God. The Bible states, "God is not a man, that he should lie; neither the son of man, that he should repent" (Num. 23:19).

This does not mean that God cannot change His mind. The *King James Version* says that man became so wicked before the Flood that "it repented the LORD that he had made man" (Gen. 6:6). God also "repented" that He had made Saul king (see 1 Sam. 15:11). But a careful study of such passages reveals that man turned from God in sinful rebellion. God did not change in His essence—rather, consistent with His unchanging nature, He judged man's sin. The real change was in humanity; and this called for a change in the way that God responded to people.

This is true even today. God is still unchanging, even though His way of responding to us depends on our response to Him. Obedience will bring reward, and disobedience will bring punishment. God does not change; men and women just move from one side of God's nature to the other. The changing lifestyles of people cause the consistent behavior of God to appear to change, but the essential change is not in God. He is unchangeable.

God Is Unlimited in Space and Time

In the beginning God created everything, including time and space. This means that He is Lord of time and space; He is not bound by His creation. The Bible says that God "inhabiteth eternity" (Isa. 57:15)—a realm beyond time and space. Abraham recognized God as "the everlasting God" (Gen. 21:33). Moses observed that "even from everlasting to everlasting, thou art God" (Ps. 90:2). The psalmist wrote, "But thou art the same, and thy years shall have no end" (102:27).

What is time? Time is the measurement of events that appear in sequence. God existed before the first event—creation. He never had a beginning point, and He will continue without a terminal point. He will always exist.

What is space? Space is all the area in which there is physical reality and being. Space is the distance between objects. But God is greater than space. "God that made the world and all things therein, seeing that He is Lord of heaven and earth, dwelleth not in temples made with hands" (Acts 17:24).

Since time and space are the results of God's creative acts, He is not limited by His creation. He is infinite in relationship to time (the sequence of events) and to space (the distance between objects). God is the only being who exists without limitations.

If there were another God, then *Elohim* would not be the self-existing, all-powerful, unlimited God. Since there cannot be two unlimited beings, there cannot be another God besides *Elohim*. For if there were another God, then neither God could be an unlimited God. The infinity and immensity of God are strong arguments for His sovereignty in the universe and in our lives.

God Is Three in One

If God is One, why is *Elohim* a plural word? Because the New Testament doctrine of the Trinity is latent in this Old Testament name, *Elohim*. God is a unity in plurality. Although the Trinity is not taught in so many words in the Old Testament, the footprints of the Trinity are found throughout its pages.

The compound unity implies the Trinity. The name *Elohim* is a compound unity. This is evidenced in several Scriptures: "Let us make man in our image" (Gen. 1:26); "The man is become as one of us" (3:22); "Let us go down" (11:7); "Who will go for us?" (Isa. 6:8). This does not mean that there are two Gods but that the One God manifests Himself in more than one personality.

Some modern-day Jews call this a "plural majesty" instead of a Trinity. Queen Victoria is credited with the statement, "We are not amused." Although she was speaking only of herself, she used the plural "we," as is common among royalty. But the use of the plural in reference to God reflects more than plural majesty. It is God speaking to Himself within the three Persons of the Trinity.

Old Testament "blessing" formulas imply the Trinity. The formulas for blessing in the Old Testament imply a Trinity. The Aaronic benediction was repeated three times: "The LORD bless thee, and keep thee: the LORD make his face shine upon thee . . . : the LORD lift up his countenance upon thee, and give thee peace" (Num. 6:24-26). The seraphim in Isaiah's vision of the Lord cried, "Holy, holy, holy" (Isa. 6:3), suggesting that each Person in the Godhead is holy. Even the Hebrew *Shema*, which maintains the unity of God, implies a Trinity when it repeats God's name three times: "The LORD our *God* is one LORD" (Deut. 6:4, emphasis added).

Three names imply three Persons. Although some disagree, many Bible scholars believe that Isaiah 54:5 is one of the strongest references to the Trinity in the Old Testament: "For thy Maker is thine husband [Father]; the LORD of hosts [Spirit] is his name; and thy Redeemer [Son] the Holy One of Israel."

The Old Testament distinguishes between God and God. Some Old Testament passages seem to make a distinction between God and God. Zechariah, speaking prophetically, writes, "And I [Father] will pour upon the house of David . . . the spirit [Spirit] of grace and of supplications: and they shall look upon me whom they have pierced, and they shall mourn for him . . . his only son [Son]" (12:10). Psalm 2:7 says, "The LORD hath said unto me, Thou art my Son." And in Genesis 1:1-2, the Spirit who broods upon the face of the water is distinguished from God who creates the world.

Clear statement of the Trinity. Again, some scholars think that Isaiah 48:16 speaks clearly of God as a Trinity: "I have not spoken in secret from the beginning; from the time that it was, there am I: and now the Lord GOD [Father], and his Spirit [Holy Spirit], hath sent me [Son]."

So can we define God in one sentence? No! Even though the Bible has given us such information as that in the above description of God, a neat definition of Him escapes our finite minds. If we could define Him, we would be pouring God into the limitation of our words. God is ultimately greater than any of the definitions we give Him.

Application

1. *Cursing is prohibited.* The Ten Commandments prohibit a person from taking God's name in vain. When a person lightly uses the name of God, he is speaking lightly of God Himself. When a person curses by the use of God's name, he is rejecting God and His control in his life.

2. *We are to seek God by His name.* There is a clear command in the Bible to "be still, and know that [He is] God [*Elohim*]" (Ps. 46:10). We are to seek and come to know God through His name, for His

name reveals to us the nature of His Person and His work. We should remember, however, that as we are searching to know God, He also is searching us and examining us. As David gave his son Solomon the plans for the Temple, he said,

> Know thou the God of thy father, and serve him with a perfect heart and with a willing mind: for the LORD searcheth all hearts, and understandeth all the imagination of the thoughts: if thou seek him, he will be found of thee; but if thou forsake him, he will cut thee off forever (1 Chron. 28:9).

3. *We must know God to know ourselves.* "God created man in his own image, in the image of God created he him; male and female created he them" (Gen. 1:27). Therefore, the more we learn about God, the more we learn about ourselves. Because we are created in God's image, we subconsciously long to become like our Creator. But a part of knowing ourselves is realizing that this longing to be like God can never be realized perfectly. The sin of Lucifer was thinking that he could become like the Most High (see Isa. 14:12-14).

4. *Knowing God leads to eternal life.* When Jesus prayed in the garden the night before His death, He said, "And this is life eternal, that they might know thee the only true God, and Jesus Christ, whom thou hast sent" (John 17:3). Those who know God receive eternal life. But it is impossible to know God without being saved. And the saved have learned of God by faith. "But without faith it is impossible to please him: for he that cometh to God must believe that he is, and that he is a rewarder of them that diligently seek him" (Heb. 11:6). And, "If thou shalt confess with thy mouth the Lord Jesus, and shalt believe in thine heart that God hath raised him from the dead, thou shalt be saved" (Rom. 10:9).

11

Lord: Jehovah

THE SELF-EXISTENT GOD

A little boy sat down at his kindergarten desk and announced, "I'm going to color a picture of God."

"But no one knows what God looks like," responded his teacher.

"They will when I get finished," the boy said, with childlike confidence.

Often we think that we can determine what God is like by what we want or by our need of the moment. But God reveals different names to us in our crises. The name *Jehovah* ("LORD") is one of the earliest of His names that God revealed to His people to give them an indication of what He is like. Whereas the little boy's teacher was right—no one knows what the LORD looks like—we are given a word-picture of Him in this name.

"The LORD" (*Jehovah*) is the second name used for deity in the Old Testament. The name "God" (*Elohim*), the universally recognized name for deity, appears first. But the second name, "LORD," is the name that is used most often in Scripture, occurring 6,823 times in the Old Testament. And to modern Jews, it is the primary name for God.

Recall from chapter 1 that the word *Jehovah* or *Yahweh*—it can be pronounced either way—stands behind the word "LORD" and that it comes from the Hebrew verb *hayah*, which signifies "to be" or "to become." (Remember too that it is spelled with capitals and small capitals in most translations, to distinguish it from "Lord" [*Adonai*], or "Master.") When translated in the first person, it becomes "I Am" said twice. Hence, when Moses anticipated that the Israelites would ask about God's name, God said to tell them,

"I AM THAT I AM" (Exod. 3:14). Then the LORD said, "Thus shalt thou say unto the children of Israel, I AM hath sent me unto you" (v. 14).

The name "LORD," therefore, points to the God who is continuously becoming "the Self-existing One." He that is who He is, therefore, is the eternal One. Some interpret the name "LORD" as containing two truths in one name. The first meaning of LORD is "the One who exists in Himself" and the second is "the One who reveals Himself."

The name "LORD" goes beyond the meaning of the first name: "God" (*Elohim*), "the strong Creator." God (*Elohim*) created the world in Genesis 1:1, but in Genesis 2:4 *Elohim* is identified as *Jehovah* ("LORD God"): "These are the generations of the heavens and of the earth when they were created, in the day that the LORD God made the earth and the heavens."

This second name, "LORD," is perhaps God's favorite name. He told Moses, "I appeared unto Abraham, unto Isaac, and unto Jacob, by the name of God Almighty [*El Shaddai*], but by my name JEHOVAH was I not known to them" (Exod. 6:3). Throughout Scripture God constantly refers to Himself by the name "LORD," seldom by the name "God." Why does He do this? Perhaps because there are so many gods; every false religion has its substitute god. But there is only one LORD who is the Self-existing One.

The uncertainty about how to pronounce the word *Jehovah* comes because there were no vowels in the original Hebrew. There were only the consonants that we transliterate into English as JHVH or YHWH. The vowels were developed later from pronunciation marks. Out of reverence for the name of the LORD, the rabbis in later Judaism would not write it or pronounce it—perhaps because of the verse, "Holy and reverend is his name" (Ps. 111:9). Hence, the way they pronounced YHWH became obscure. (But they would write and pronounce the name "God.")

The name "LORD" (*Jehovah*) is used in relationship to people, while the name "God" is used primarily in references that relate to nature or His creation. After *Elohim* created the world, the name "LORD" was added because the strong Creator wanted to relate to those He created. First, He was identified: "The LORD God had

not caused it to rain upon the earth" (Gen. 2:5). Next we find, "The
LORD God planted a garden eastward in Eden" (v. 8). Man was given
the task of tending the garden. Finally, "The LORD God said, It is
not good that the man should be alone" (v. 18). As a result of seeing
the loneliness of man, "the LORD God caused a deep sleep to fall
upon Adam" (v. 21). He took a rib from Adam, then from "the rib,
which the LORD God had taken from man, made he a woman" (v.
22). Hence, the LORD God is concerned about man's relationship
to woman and about both man and woman's relationships to Him.

Next, the element of evil is introduced into the story because
it broke the relationship between God and His created ones. "Now
the serpent was more cunning than any beast of the field which the
LORD God had made" (3:1, *NKJV*). Because they did not resist the
serpent's temptation, Adam and Eve fell into sin. But a redemptive
LORD came seeking them: "They heard the voice of the LORD God
walking in the garden in the cool of the day" (v. 8). The LORD did
not come to judge them but ultimately to save them. He asked a
question: "The LORD God said unto the woman, What is this that
thou has done?" (v. 13).

The LORD warned the serpent that the seed of woman would
bruise its head (see v. 15). Here is the protoevangelium—the first
hint of the gospel, the good news that Jesus Christ, born of woman,
would conquer evil and be the means of salvation. But the LORD was
not finished. "Unto Adam also and to his wife did the LORD God
make coats of skins, and clothed them" (v. 21). In this act the LORD
obviously had to take the life of an animal, presumably a lamb.
This animal became a foreshadow of all the lambs that would be
sacrificed for the sins of man until the ultimate Lamb, Jesus Christ,
took away the sins of the world (see John 1:29). Hence, early in the
book of Genesis, the name "LORD" reflects a redemptive relationship with man.

What Is the Lord Like?

In the last chapter, God (*Elohim*) was defined under the question
"Who is God?" In this chapter, *Jehovah* is described in answer to the
question "What is the LORD like?" The last chapter gave a definition
of God, while here we focus on a description of the LORD.

God has traditionally been described by His attributes. An attribute reflects that which comes from the nature of God. Just as the rays from the sun give meaning to the sun and reflect its nature, so too the LORD'S attributes reflect His nature. People know what the sun is like because of its rays. In much the same way, we can know something of what the LORD is like from His attributes.

We will discuss six attributes in this chapter. The first three are called absolute, or moral, attributes because they deal with moral qualities that are beyond comparison with human attributes: (1) the LORD is holy, (2) He is love, and (3) He is good. The second three are called comparative, or non-moral, attributes because they deal with natural attributes that to some extent can be compared with human qualities. Hence, the LORD is (1) omniscient, or all-knowing, (2) omnipresent, or present everywhere, and (3) omnipotent, or all-powerful. Some people believe that God has many other attributes that we will not know until we get to heaven. The hymn writer Charles Wesley spoke of God's attributes as "glorious all and numberless." Since the LORD is the Self-existing One who continuously reveals Himself, He has many attributes of which we are not yet aware. Apparently He will continue to reveal Himself throughout all eternity, and we will continue to learn more about Him.

Moral Attributes

The LORD Is Holy

We have noted the description of the LORD as "holy, holy, holy" in Isaiah 6:3 and Revelation 4:8. Note that the word "holy" is repeated three times, perhaps recognizing each member of the Trinity or each of the three primary names of God. The word "holy" means "to cut off" or "to separate." Hence, the person who is holy is cut off or separated from the world yet separated to God.

It is important that we recognize the holiness of God, because so much of our relationship with Him depends upon it. God is synonymous with holiness. "Holy and reverend is his name," said David (Ps. 111:9). Isaiah wrote about "the high and lofty One that inhabiteth eternity, whose name is Holy" (Isa. 57:15). Jesus called the Father "holy Father" (John 17:11) and instructed His disciples to pray, "Hallowed be thy name" (Matt. 6:9).

Positive holiness. Holiness is both positive and negative. Positive holiness means the LORD is the personification of all that is good and pure. When John says, "God is light" (1 John 1:5), he is saying that God is pure, just as light is pure. The positive holiness of God means there is no sin in God's nature or in His presence. His people must be separated to Him and live holy lives.

Negative holiness. But there is a second aspect to God's holiness—negative holiness, which deals with the justice of God. Because the LORD is holy, sin cannot exist in His presence. When God must look on sinful people, He punishes sin. The judgment of the LORD is negative holiness. Hell was created because of this attribute of God: He must punish sin.

When we realize that God is so holy that He must judge all sin, we begin to understand the necessity of coming to God through Jesus Christ. When Jesus hung on the cross and cried out, "My God, my God, why hast thou forsaken me?" (Matt. 27:46), we understand that God was actually unable to look upon His own Son as He died bearing our sins. An understanding of the holiness of God reminds us of the degree to which God loves us: "For God so loved the world, that he gave his only begotten Son" (John 3:16).

The LORD Is Love

To understand God, you must understand love. Most people, in fact, describe God only with the attribute of love. But in God's case, love is more than an attribute, more than a virtue. Love is the nature of God. The Scriptures teach that "God is love" (1 John 4:8,16). When children are asked to describe God, they most often respond by saying, "God is love."

What is love? Love has been described as "a rational and volitional affection having its ground in truth and holiness"—an affection that "is exercised in free choice." Love is the attitude that seeks the highest good in the person who is loved. Love is basically an outgoing attribute, as expressed in an act of God giving to those outside Himself.

It is this outgoing aspect of God's nature that is highlighted when we say that God is love. Love is an attitude of giving oneself to another person. When God loves, He gives Himself to His creation. God created humanity because He wanted to share Himself with people. Because people are made in the image of God, men and women mirror God. Someone described love as "the perfection of divine nature by which God is eternally moved to communicate Himself."

The apostle John describes love in these terms: "Greater love hath no man than this, that a man lay down his life for his friends" (John 15:13). Laying down one's life is the ultimate act of giving. Then John takes the definition of love a step further: "Hereby perceive we the love of God, because he laid down his life for us: and we ought to lay down our lives for the brethren" (1 John 3:16). Finally, John points straight to love: "Herein is love, not that we loved God, but he loved us, and sent his Son to be the propitiation for our sins" (4:10).

The love chapter of the Bible, 1 Corinthians 13, also describes love in terms of giving. The *King James Version* translates the Greek word for love here (*agape*) with the word "charity," which is now an out-of-date word. Charity today means giving time and money to a worthy cause. But originally it meant giving of oneself to a needy cause or to needy people. Today that idea is conveyed by the word "love." Since humanity is in profound need of the deity, it is a profound blessing that God can be described as the essence of love.

The LORD Is Good

When Jesus told the rich young ruler, "There is none good but one, that is, God" (Mark 10:18; see also Matt. 19:16-22), He was relating a truth that the young man already knew. When God told Moses His name, He described Himself as "The LORD, The LORD God, merciful and gracious, longsuffering, and abundant in goodness and truth, keeping mercy for thousands, forgiving iniquity and transgression and sin" (Exod. 34:6-7). Moses later told the nation, "The LORD thy God . . . will do thee good" (Deut. 30:5).

When children pray, "God is great, God is good, let us thank Him for the food," they are focusing on the most positive of all aspects of God: His goodness. The goodness of God is His mercy, kindness, long-suffering and grace that are manifested to those who are in misery and distress. The book of Hosea emphasizes this attribute. It pictures God's people as an unfaithful wife whom God pursues and wins back not because of any merit of her own but because of God's goodness and mercy.

Comparative Attributes

The three remaining attributes discussed here are non-moral and comparative in nature, meaning that they primarily deal with God's power in relationship to creation. The moral attributes deal primarily with His attributes in relationship to people. Each of the following attributes is introduced by the prefix "omni," which means "all."

Therefore, to say that God is omniscient means that He is all-knowing. That He is omnipresent means that He is in all places, or everywhere. And that He is omnipotent means that He is all-powerful. These attributes of God show that human abilities reflect God's divine nature. Every person has a degree of power, but only God possesses omnipotence; everyone has presence, but only God is omnipresent; and everyone has some knowledge, but there is only One who is omniscient.

These three attributes of God may be defined by a comparison of the degree to which God and man share each characteristic. Psalm 139 lays a foundation for understanding the comparative attributes of God. The omniscience of God is seen in verses 1-6; the omnipresence of God is seen in verses 7-11; and the omnipotence of God is seen in verses 12-16.

The LORD Is Omniscient

The word "omniscience" has the word for "knowledge" or "science" added to the prefix "omni," which, as we already saw, means "all." It means that God has perfect knowledge of all things at all times. He knows everything, actual and potential. He "calleth those things which be not as though they were" (Rom. 4:17). The omniscient God has all knowledge in the world. God has never had to learn anything. He has never forgotten anything He has ever known. God knows everything possible. That means He knows and understands the sum total of all the world's knowledge and even those things that mankind has yet to discover.

The Lord knows Himself, and He knows humanity. He knows His creation, because He is the Creator. David wrote, "Great is our Lord, and of great power: his understanding is infinite" (Ps. 147:5). Most Bible commentators agree that wisdom in Proverbs is personified in Christ. As Christians seek guidance in the daily affairs of life, it is good to realize that God guides us, because He knows the answers to questions we have not yet fully comprehended.

The LORD Is Omnipresent

This means that *Jehovah* is everywhere present at the same time. The psalmist asked the question "Whither shall I go from thy spirit?" (Ps. 139:7). From heaven to the grave, early or late, near or far, God is present (see vv. 8-10). Hagar, Abraham's handmaiden, even named the LORD "the-God-Who-Sees" (Gen. 16:13, *NKJV*). The fact of God's omnipresence is a constant source of guidance, comfort and protection for the believer. We can never find ourselves beyond the presence of God.

Yet God's omnipresence is one of the most difficult of His attributes to comprehend. The perfections of God demand that He exist everywhere at the same time. This does not mean that God is spread out so that part of Him exists here and another part of Him is in a room down the hall. Everything of God is here, in the room down the hall and in every other place at the same time.

The LORD Is Omnipotent

When we say that God is omnipotent, we mean that He can do everything He wants to do. He can do anything that is in harmony with His nature. He can do the impossible (raise the dead; see John 11:1-44) and the improbable (walk on water; see 6:19). "With God all things are possible" (Matt. 19:26).

There are some things that God cannot do, but they are things that are either contrary to His nature or the result of His own self-limitation. Hence, they do not limit His omnipotence.

God cannot deny Himself (see 2 Tim. 2:13), lie (see Heb. 6:18), or be tempted into sin (see Jas. 1:13). If God could do any of these things, He would not be God. This limitation represents things contrary to His nature. It is still proper to say God can do anything He wants to accomplish.

How to Know God

The Bible commands that we know and love God for Himself. This creates a dilemma for mankind. Job experienced this dilemma when he cried out, "Oh that I knew where I might find Him! that I might come even to his seat!" (Job 23:3). Thus the question is sometimes asked, "How can a man know God?"

By Faith

It is impossible to know God apart from faith. Faith is accepting what God says about Himself. The Bible says, "Without faith it is impossible to please him: for he that cometh to God must believe that he is, and that he is a rewarder of them that diligently seek him" (Heb. 11:6).

By the Word of God

The Bible gives us a self-revelation of God. We see Him in the pages of Scripture. We can learn about Him through His names, actions, speech, miracles and manifestations.

By Desire

Some people are perfectly content to deny the existence of God without any serious consideration of the subject. These people are prevented from knowing God, because they do not want to know Him. Unless people have a desire to know God, they never will. Why? The Bible says, "Ye shall seek me, and find me, when ye shall search for me with all your heart" (Jer. 29:13).

By Involvement

Our knowledge of God can grow just as our knowledge of a friend grows, but just as in the case of human friendship, this requires interaction and involvement with God. We must apply scriptural content to our lives. Jesus said,

> Not everyone that saith unto me, Lord, Lord, shall enter into the kingdom of heaven.... Many will say to me in that day, Lord, Lord, have we not prophesied in thy name? and in thy name have cast out devils? and in thy name done many wonderful works? And then will I profess unto them, I never knew you: depart from me, ye that work iniquity (Matt. 7:21-23).

By Love

Knowing God is the highest privilege afforded to men and women. Unfortunately, most people fail to recognize the priority that ought to exist in this area. If the greatest commandment is to love God with our total being (see Matt. 22:37-38), then we must know Him to love Him.

12

The Father: Pater

THE INTIMATE NAME FOR GOD

The favorite title for God used by Jesus Christ in the New Testament is "Father" (Greek: *pater*). In the Gospel of John, Jesus called God His Father 156 times. He not only claimed intimacy with the Father, but also He claimed to be one with the Father, which is one reason the Jews hated Him (see John 5:18). Neither the Jews nor their Scriptures regularly called God by the name "Father." To them God was the majestic, powerful Creator, or Master. They did not know Him or approach Him in the intimate relationship of Father.

On a few occasions the Old Testament does identify God as having paternal instincts, as in Jeremiah 31:9, where God says, "I am a father to Israel." But this was a metaphor or a picture, not a name or relationship. To Israel God thundered from Mount Sinai in judgment. He was the Holy One in the midst of the Shekinah glory cloud that rested in the holy of holies. The writer of Hebrews best summarized the Old Testament perspective of God: "For our God is a consuming fire" (12:29).

Jesus revealed a loving relationship with God by calling Him Father. He taught His disciples a new introduction to their prayers: "Our Father which art in heaven" (Matt. 6:9). Because Jesus' revelation of the Father was counter to the view of the religious rulers of His day, they wanted to stone Him (see John 5:18; 10:30-31).

To understand the Father, we must look to the Trinity. The Father, Son and Holy Spirit are all equal persons within the Godhead, yet one God. They are equal in nature, separate in Person and submissive in duty. All that the Father is in holiness, power and wisdom so too are the Son and the Holy Spirit. They are separate in Person, for each has His own personality, that is, intellect, emotion and will. They are submissive in function, for the Father sends the Son, and the Father and the Son both send the Holy Spirit (see 14:26; 15:26).

The first recorded words of the young Jesus revealed new truth about God. At age 12 Jesus said, "Wist ye not that I must be about my Father's business?" (Luke 2:49). Notice that Jesus used the name "Father" in reference to God rather than to Joseph. We learn from this first reference that God is a Father, that the Father must have priority in our lives and that the Father had sent the Son on a mission.

Because of the structure of the family, the world understood the nature and function of a father before Jesus revealed that God is our Father. This does not mean that the doctrine of God the Father gets its meaning from earthly fathers. Actually, the opposite is true—the human family on Earth reflects the eternal family in heaven.

Since God is our Father, all who are saved enter a spiritual family. Believers have a spiritual kinship with each other and with God. Believers in Christ are brother and sister to one another. They are "sons of God" (John 1:12) and "children of God" (see 13:33). As such they call God their Father. They do not come to God in prayer as mere subjects to a king in his court. They crawl into the lap of a heavenly Father as a child who comes for protection or help.

Notice the terms used for God as Father in the New Testament: "O Father, Lord of heaven and earth" (Luke 10:21); "heavenly Father" (11:13); "the Father" (John 4:23); "my Father" (5:17); "God the Father" (6:27); "one Father, even God" (8:41); "holy Father" (17:11); "righteous Father" (17:25); "God our Father" (Rom. 1:7); "Abba, Father" (8:15); "Father of our Lord Jesus Christ" (15:6); "Father of mercies" (2 Cor. 1:3); "God and Father of all" (Eph. 4:6); "Father of spirits" (Heb. 12:9); and "Father of lights" (Jas. 1:17).

Some have interpreted the New Testament emphasis on God's new name, Father, to mean that everyone born in the world is a child of the Father in heaven. This view is called the "Fatherhood of God," which states that all people are the children of God, no one is lost, and all will eventually go to live with the Father in heaven. This works out to the "Brotherhood of Man," which implies universal salvation.

But the Fatherhood of God and the Brotherhood of Man are not biblical truths. Actually, the opposite is taught in Scripture. The Bible teaches that all are sinners (see Rom. 3:23), that the wages of sin is eternal death (see 6:23), that only those who believe in Jesus Christ will be saved (see Acts 4:12; John 14:6), and that eternal life requires regeneration (see 3:3,7).

What Does It Mean for God to Be Our Father?

After a Christian understands the nature and function of the heavenly Father, he or she asks, "What does it mean to me?" The believer under the New Testament has certain benefits that were not available under the Old Covenant. In addition to God being majestic and lofty, the believer now has intimate access to His presence.

Fellowship with the Father

It is possible for us to crawl up into the lap of God as a small child will cuddle in the lap of his father for protection. "Our fellowship is with the Father," said John (1 John 1:3). God will protect His children even more than any father on Earth will care for his child.

Access to the Father

No matter where we are, we can have immediate entrance into the throne of the majesty of God, who is also our Father. Paul notes that because we are adopted into the family, "we cry Abba, Father" (Rom. 8:15). God knows our needs before we cry, and we can go to Him at anytime.

Guidance by Father

First, the Father teaches His children the way they should go (see Ps. 32:8). Second, He actually guides them, through the indwelling Holy Spirit and principles of the Word (see Prov. 3:5-6; John 16:13). Third, the Father speaks through the conscience and will give guidance to His children (see Rom. 2:15).

Security from the Father

The Father wants all His children "to be conformed to the image of his Son" (8:29). Because of that He works all things together for their good (see v. 28). But sometimes the Father must correct His children by allowing trials to come into their lives. Like most children, we do not enjoy laborious teaching sessions. However, the Father does everything for our good. "He that spared not his own Son, but delivered him up for us all, how shall he not with him also freely give us all things?" (v. 32).

Inheritance of the Father

Because we are children of the heavenly Father, we are His heirs. "And if children, then heirs; heirs of God, and joint-heirs with Christ" (v. 17). All the riches of the Father will one day belong to those who are His children. Jesus promised, "In my Father's house are many mansions: if it were not so, I would have told you. I go to prepare a place for you" (John 14:2).

What Does the Father Do?

The God of the Old Testament was Creator (*Elohim*), Master (*Adonai*) and the Self-existent One who gives life to His people (*Jehovah*). What could God as Father do for us that He could not or did not do before? When Jesus revealed God as the Father, a further self-revelation was given of God's nature and function.

A Father Gives Life to His Children

A child inherits his physical and immaterial nature from his parents. A child who is born again into God's family also gets several things. First, he gets a new nature, which is God's nature (see 2 Cor. 5:17). As such, he is known as a child of God. Second, he gets God's life, which is eternal life. He will live forever because he has the life of God in him (see John 3:36). Third, he gets a new standing in heaven. He is adopted into the family of God and is called a son of God (see Rom. 8:14-16). Fourth, he has new desires, indicating his new nature. He will desire to pray, read the Word and show forth the fruit of the Holy Spirit (see Gal. 5:22-23). Finally, he is now a member of the family of God. He calls God his Father, and other Christians are his brothers and sisters in Christ.

A Father Loves His Children

Many people think, when a calamity comes into their lives, that God doesn't love them. This is a wrong view of God. God is a Father who loves His children, not a Father who hates them. As a result of this love, He will do good things for them. "If ye then, being evil, know how to give good gifts unto your children: how much more shall your heavenly Father" (Luke 11:13). Of course, when His children err, there is a place for the heavenly Father to correct them, just as there is for a father on Earth. But the basic premise is that God loves His children.

A Father Protects His Children

The natural desire of every father is to protect his child. So the Father will give eternal life to those who trust in Him. "They shall never perish, neither shall any man pluck them out of my hand. My Father, which gave them me, is greater than all; and no man is able to pluck them out of my Father's hand" (John 10:28-29). The greatest protection of all is that no one can separate us from the love of God the Father.

A Father Provides for His Children

Many fathers work all week because they love to work. But underlying that, the truly loving father desires to provide for his wife and children. The Bible says, "Ye fathers, provoke not your children . . . but bring them up in the nurture and admonition of the Lord" (Eph. 6:4).

When an earthly father nurtures his child, he is providing him with positive training. Likewise, the heavenly Father will care for His children. "Wherefore, if God so clothe the grass of the field, which to day is, and tomorrow is cast into the oven, shall he not much more clothe you, O ye of little faith?" (Matt. 6:30). The promise includes food, drink and other basic necessities, for as it concludes, "Your heavenly Father knoweth that ye have need of all these things" (v. 32).

BOOK TWO

The Names of Jesus

KNOW THE LORD YOU LOVE
MORE INTIMATELY

ELMER L. TOWNS

The chapters in this book were preached as 12 messages at Muskoka Baptist Conference, Canada, during the summer of 1986. Appreciation is extended to Reverend Richard Holiday, director of the conference, for giving me the opportunity to minister the Word of God to over 1,000 delegates each summer. Also, recognition is extended to Reverend Douglas Porter of Oakville, Ontario, who typed the manuscript from the cassette messages. Reverend Porter was my graduate assistant at Liberty Baptist Theological Seminary, Lynchburg, Virginia, where he earned the M.A. degree. His knowledge of resources on the names of Jesus was invaluable. As we examined the various lists of the names of Jesus in Scripture, we felt that many names had been omitted. I want to recognize his diligent search that has produced what I feel is the most complete available list of the names of Jesus in print.

Then they that feared the LORD spake often one to another: and the LORD hearkened, and heard it, and a book of remembrance was written before him for them that feared the LORD, and that thought upon his name.
MALACHI 3:16

Introduction

The Epistle to the Philippians expresses the overwhelming desire of the apostle Paul: "That I may know him" (Phil. 3:10). Thousands of Christians everywhere have since shared the same sentiment. But Paul and Christians were not the first to long for such an intimate knowledge of God. Many years earlier Moses had prayed, "Now therefore, I pray thee, if I have found grace in thy sight, shew me now thy way, that I may know thee" (Exod. 33:13). God answered that prayer of Moses in an interesting manner: "And the LORD descended in the cloud, and stood with him there, and proclaimed the name of the LORD" (34:5).

To really know God, one must get to know Him by name. The names of God in Scripture are really a self-revelation of God in His nature and attributes. The sheer number of such names and titles in Scripture suggests something of the immensity of God. A devout Muslim exhausts his knowledge of his god when he knows the 99 names and attributes of Allah in the Koran. But the Bible identifies more than 800 descriptive names and titles of Jesus Christ. And as Charles Haddon Spurgeon once put it, "God the Father never gave his son a name which he did not deserve." How many of these names do you know and understand?

This book is written to help you get to know Jesus Christ more fully by studying several of His key names and titles. Of course, a volume of this size on the names of Jesus Christ cannot be exhaustive. But it is an introduction to an important subject—important to those who, like Moses and Paul, desire a more intimate knowledge of the One the angels years ago named Jesus.

PART 1

Our Lord Jesus Christ

1

The Names of Jesus

And she shall bring forth a son, and thou shalt call his name JESUS:
for he shall save his people from their sins.
MATTHEW 1:21

Of the more than 800 names and titles of the Lord Jesus Christ
in Scripture, none is perhaps more venerated by Christians than
the name "Jesus" itself. A contemporary songwriter acknowledges
simply, "There's just something about that name." The very sound
of that name is precious in the ears of Christians worldwide. That
name has brought about a sense of overwhelming comfort to many
in their darkest hours. It is that name that is most often verbalized
in prayer and preaching, in testimony and witnessing. Many relate
dramatic, even miraculous experiences of life to the significance
of that name.

The name "Jesus" was, at the time of our Lord's earthly sojourn,
among the most popular of names selected by parents of Hebrew
boys. In the writings of the Jewish historian Josephus, the name
identifies at least 20 different men, 10 of whom were contempo-
raries of Jesus Christ. Its popularity was probably to a large extent
due to its relationship with one of Israel's great leaders, Joshua, the
son of Nun and successor to Moses. In the Egyptian papyri, the
name occurs frequently right through the early part of the second
century. Then, abruptly, both Jews and Christians stopped using
"Jesus" as a name for their boys. The Jews did so because it was
so closely related to Christianity, which many of them rigorously
opposed and hated. The Christians refused to use the name for
opposite reasons. To them, the name was special and held in ven-
eration. It was almost thought sacrilegious that anyone but Jesus
should bear that name.

When one reads the New Testament, he or she must be impressed with how often this name appears. It is by far the most often used name in the Gospels; and even in the book of Acts, where we see the title "Lord" so often, the use of "Jesus" outnumbers "Lord" three to one. In the Epistles, the name of Jesus continues to occur, though not so often. It formed an intrinsic part of the great Pauline formula by which the apostle often referred to the Lord (Jesus' title), to Jesus (His name), and to Christ (His office).

What is perhaps most surprising about the name "Jesus" is not its use but the absence of its use. With the possible exception of the thief on the cross (see Luke 23:42), there is no record of anyone ever addressing Jesus directly by the name "Jesus" during His earthly life and ministry. Further, Jesus Himself apparently used this name to identify Himself only twice, on both occasions to persons after His ascension to and glorification in heaven (see Acts 9:5; Rev. 22:16).

The Meaning of His Identification

In all likelihood, when Mary and Joseph talked to their son, they used their native language and called Him *Yeshua* or Joshua. If they used the Greek trade language, then they called Him Jesus, for as we noted previously, "Jesus" is the Greek form of the Hebrew name "Joshua." The name "Joshua" was a contraction of "Jehoshua," meaning "Jehovah the Savior." It was used to identify several men in the Old Testament, the best known being Joshua the son of Nun, who led Israel into the land of Canaan. Actually, Joshua's given name was "Hoshea," meaning "salvation," and was changed to "Jehoshua" or "Joshua" by Moses, probably when he sent him to spy out the land at Kadesh-barnea (see Num. 13:16).

The name "Jesus," or "Joshua," is built on the Hebrew verb stem *yasha*, meaning "saved." The first use of this verb in Scripture is also the embryonic first mention of the doctrine of salvation (see Exod. 14:30). The salvation of Israel is there defined in terms of the destruction of the army of Egypt in the Red Sea. This miracle, so often referred to in the Old Testament, is also a type of the salvation from sin provided by Jesus on the cross.

As borne by Joshua, the name was an expression of faith in what *Jehovah* could and would do for His people and a testimony to the effect that he, Joshua, was willing to be a part of it. No doubt a major aspect of that salvation was viewed in a military light as the nation went out to destroy the inhabitants of the land and to settle it as their own. Still, the spiritual salvation of the nation and its families, individually or corporately, was not overlooked.

Several Bible commentators have noted the typical significance of Joshua, which goes far beyond a mere similarity of names. Joshua was the shadow of what Jesus is in reality. This is particularly true in the Lord's name. When Jesus was so named by the angel, it was more than simply an expression of the messianic hope of Israel. It was an affirmation of Jesus' real identity and primary concern. "Jesus" means "Jehovah the Savior," but when applied to our Lord, it is a declaration that He is *Jehovah* the Savior. It both enshrines and expresses the mystery of His Person and the marvels of His work.

The Mystery of the Incarnation

In the first mentions of the name of Jesus in Scripture, it is clear that Jesus was more than just another baby boy born to a young Jewish mother. The first to hear His name was Mary, who was informed not only that she would bear a son but that she should "call his name JESUS" and that He would also "be called the Son of the Highest" (Luke 1:31-32). When Joseph first heard the name, he was told, "That which is conceived in her is of the Holy Ghost" (Matt. 1:20). The name "Jesus," when applied to the virgin-born child of Bethlehem, was an affirmation of who He is: *Jehovah* the Savior.

Jehovah was the most venerated name of God in the Old Testament. So careful were the Jews not to violate the fourth commandment that they refused to verbalize this name lest unknowingly they were to use it in vain. When they came to read it in their Scriptures, by habit they substituted the name *Adonai*, another name for God in the Old Testament. Because the Hebrew language lacks vowels, words are pronounced as they are learned audibly. But when the pious Jews refused to pronounce the name *Jehovah*, people soon became unsure as to the actual pronunciation of it. Most evangelicals apply the vowels of *Adonai* to it and pronounce the name *Jehovah*. More critical scholars have chosen to pronounce the name *Yahweh*. Actually, because accents and dialects of a language change as the language is used over the years, it is impossible to be certain how Moses first pronounced this name of God when he introduced it to Israel.

To think that the greatly respected *Jehovah* of the Old Testament was Jesus in the New Testament! *Jehovah* Himself became a man. This mystery concerning the Incarnation has baffled theologians and Bible students for years, yet it remains a part of human history that one day the One who made this world and created all things, including the human race, voluntarily chose to become a man without compromising in any way who He was. No wonder that this name has such special significance for Christians. Certainly if the unsaved Jews were so concerned about using *Jehovah*'s name in vain that they avoided any possibility of doing so, Christians today ought also to reverence and respect the name of *Jehovah* incarnate, Jesus, and never use it in vain as a curse.

When we realize the true nature of Jesus, we have no problem understanding the necessity of the virgin birth. It is not simply an early Christian legend that found its way into the Bible or a novel little miracle to give us yet something else to believe. The virgin birth was the only possible way in which *Jehovah* could become a man and at the same time remain *Jehovah*. Jesus needed a human mother to have a human nature, but if He had had a human father, He also would have received the sin nature of His father. With a pair of sinful human parents, it would have been impossible for Him to be the Son of God.

When God created man, He made man holy—that is, without sin. But man's holiness was conditional, and it ended when Adam fell. Since then, men have been born sinners by nature, because they inherited that nature from their father, Adam. "Wherefore, as by one man sin entered into the world, and death by sin; and so death passed upon all men, for that all have sinned" (Rom. 5:12). That would also have been the fate of Jesus had He been the physical son of Joseph. In contrast, the Scriptures teach that

Christ "knew no sin" (2 Cor. 5:21), was "without sin" (Heb. 4:15), and "did no sin" (1 Pet. 2:22).

The Marvels of His Occupation

When Joseph learned that his legal son would be named Jesus, he was also told the nature of Jesus' work: "He shall save his people from their sins" (Matt. 1:21). Jesus *was* the salvation that would also *provide* salvation for His people. It is not clear whether the full nature or the extent of that salvation was fully understood at first. Initially, it was widely believed that the salvation provided by Jesus was exclusively for the Jews. This view is evident even in the book of Acts, when Peter was reluctant to go to Cornelius's household and later when the Jerusalem conference became a necessity.

Surprisingly, it was the Samaritans who first recognized the broader extent of the salvation that Jesus would effect. Their understanding of Jesus as "the Christ, the Saviour of the world" (John 4:42) was unheard of in Jewish circles and largely ignored in the early days of the Church. One might argue that the extent of the work of Christ was never fully realized in practice even by the Church until the Moravian and later the Methodist movements, with the possible exception of the evangelistic outreach of the Church following the Jerusalem conference (see Acts 15:1-31).

The Majesty of His Reputation

A name is a reputation. Sometimes one gains a reputation from a name, and at other times a person gives his name a reputation. When I was growing up in Savannah, Georgia, my mother would frequently remind me to live up to my name. "Remember, you're a Towns," she would say. Our family history went back several generations in Georgia and included a number of prominent medical doctors, one of whom served for a time as governor of our state. As children, my brother, sister and I were encouraged to live up to the historical reputation of our name.

Just as my mother reminded me to live up to the reputation of my family name, we all need to be reminded to live up to the reputation of the name of Jesus. The apostle Paul told the Jews in Rome that "the name of God [was] blasphemed among the Gentiles" (Rom. 2:24) through them as a result of their inconsistent living. The same could be said of Christians today. When we behave in a manner inconsistent with the name of Jesus, the unsaved world takes note of our hypocrisy and lowers its estimate of Jesus and Christianity. How many Christians have been reminded of hypocrites in the church by their unsaved friends, relatives, associates and neighbors as they have tried to win them to Christ?

Regardless of the nobility of the name or title ascribed to Jesus in Scripture, He always added something to the reputation of the name. Many Christians today conclude their prayers with the phrase "in Jesus' name." Sometimes they will cite John 14:13-14 or 16:23 as biblical authority for that practice. In those texts Jesus encouraged His disciples to "ask in [His] name." Actually, to ask in Jesus' name means to ask in His Person and does not mean that every prayer must end with the words "in Jesus' name." Some who pray this way do so wrongly, viewing the mention of Jesus' name as a kind of magical incantation that will guarantee an answer to their prayers. Others use the expression as a constant reminder that when they pray, they do so on the merits of Jesus and not of themselves.

There is a certain power in Jesus' name, however, that transcends our ability to understand it fully. It is a power over demons themselves. Even the Jewish exorcists of the first century recognized this spiritual power and sought to harness it by addressing and commanding demons in Jesus' name (see Acts 19:13). The failure of the sons of Sceva to overcome the demons on that occasion emphasized the fact that the name that possesses the power is not the mere recital of a formula but the Person of Jesus Himself. The sons of Sceva did not have a personal relationship with Jesus and therefore could not effectively use His name in prayer in order to cast out demons.

Jesus encouraged His disciples to ask for "anything" (John 14:14, *NKJV*), including the salvation of unsaved friends, relatives, associates and neighbors, problems in one's family or finances, difficult responsibilities or relationships. The name of Jesus is the "name which is above every name" (Phil. 2:9). Jesus is powerful to save and powerful to keep those who are saved. He alone is powerful enough both to control demons and to influence God. We should speak, sing, meditate on and glory in the name of Jesus. It is even proper to fall in adoration and worship at the name of Jesus (see v. 10).

CONCLUSION

Have you ever noticed how many of your favorite hymns make specific reference to the name of Jesus? Leaf through the average church hymnal, and you will agree that this name has certainly inspired its share of songs. Many of the most familiar hymns referring to our Lord use the name "Jesus." And this is not only a phenomenon among English-speaking Christians. Though pronounced differently in other parts of the world, the name "Jesus" has found a prominent place in the expression of biblical Christianity, regardless of the linguistic or cultural background of the Christian. Constantly it is sung and preached by those who have come to love the One who first loved them and who demonstrated that love from a cross.

Is it any wonder that the name of Jesus is so deeply loved by Christians around the world? It is the name that brings us salvation and provides all the assistance we need in facing the struggles of life. It bears witness to the fact that *Jehovah* the Savior became a man at a point in history that we might spend eternity with Him in heaven. It challenges us to come with boldness to the throne of grace in prayer, knowing before we pray that He is there to give us the grace we need even before we recognize our need. The songwriter was right: "There is something about that name"!

FOR DISCUSSION

1. What does the name "Jesus" mean? Why was it popular when Joseph and Mary gave it to their Son?
2. Why did parents discontinue naming their sons Jesus? What does this teach us about our attitude toward the name of Jesus?

3. What does it mean to "live up to the name of Jesus"?
4. Should we end our prayers by saying "in Jesus' name"? Why or why not?
5. Name your favorite hymn about Jesus. Why is it your favorite hymn?

2

The Title "Lord"

Unto you is born this day in the city of David a Saviour,
which is Christ the LORD.
LUKE 2:11

Let all the house of Israel know assuredly, that God hath made the
same Jesus, whom ye have crucified, both LORD and Christ.
ACTS 2:36

If thou shalt confess with thy mouth the LORD Jesus, and shalt believe in thine
heart that God hath raised him from the dead, thou shalt be saved.
ROMANS 10:9

People change their names as their role in life and office changes. When I began teaching, my students referred to me as Professor Towns. Later, after receiving my first doctorate, I began to be called Dr. Towns. When I was dean of the B. R. Laken School of Religion, I was sometimes referred to as Dean Towns. The changing titles mark changes in my life. When my children began having children of their own, I thought I was too young to be a grandfather! I told my children not to teach my grandchildren to call me Grandfather or some cute name like Poppa. My daughter, not wanting to offend me, taught her daughter to address me as Dr. Towns. For a while it worked, but the child soon learned that this man was really Poppa. Also, the little girl noticed that her father often called his father-in-law "Doc." Soon she began addressing me as Poppa Doc. Although the title was once that of a Haitian dictator, I am now more than pleased to be called Poppa Doc by my grandchildren.

Similarly, the name of Jesus has changed over the years as His role and office have changed. In the Gospels, He is most often called

"Jesus," although both His title, "Lord," and His office, "Christ," were emphasized at His birth (see Luke 2:11). It was not until the book of Acts that the title "Lord" became more commonly used and began to take on the characteristics of a name. When Luke was writing the early history of the Church, he chose "Lord" as his narrative name. Probably "Jesus" was considered too familiar to be used and "Christ" at that time sounded too formal. Another advantage of this title is that it conveyed the idea of relationship. If Jesus is Lord, then He is Lord of something or someone.

Jesus is the Lord of our lives whether we let Him operate in our lives or not. He is by nature the Lord. Ultimately a lord has dominion over a person, and the Lord will be the Lord. If He is not recognized as Lord now, He will be someday when every tongue will "confess that Jesus Christ is Lord" (Phil. 2:11). We may choose to recognize Him as Lord today or be coerced into recognizing Him as Lord at His return.

The normal posture of prayer traditionally practiced by Christians is a symbolic recognition of the lordship of Jesus. As we pray, it is common for us to bow our heads. That is the usual way of approaching a monarch or supreme ruler of a region. That is the way in which we approach the King of kings and Lord of lords. When we bow, we are symbolically showing that we owe our allegiance to Him.

The Meaning of This Name

In calling Jesus "Lord," a speaker could have been using the term in one of several ways. The Greek word *kurios*, often translated "lord" or "master," is used in the New Testament with reference to an owner (see Luke 19:33), to one who has control of something (see Matt. 12:8) to a master to whom service is due (see 6:24), or to an emperor or king (see Acts 25:26; Rev. 17:14). It is used as a title of respect for a father (see Matt. 21:30), a husband (see 1 Pet. 3:6), a master (see Matt. 13:27), a ruler (see 27:63), an angel (see Acts 10:4), or a stranger (see 16:30). And it is used as a designation of a pagan idol or deity (see 1 Cor. 8:5), and as a translation of the name of God from the Old Testament (*Jehovah*, see Matt. 4:7; *Adonai*, see

1:22; *Elohim*, see 1 Pet. 1:25). There is no indication that Christians used this term for anyone but Jesus, suggesting that it was used as a recognition of His deity.

The translation of the Hebrew titles *Jehovah, Adonai* and *Elohim* by the Greek word *kurios* (Lord) emphasizes that these titles of God in the Old Testament are also to be included among the names of Jesus. The use of the word *kurios* in this way recognizes that several rights belong to Jesus. First, there is the right to respect. This word *kurios* was commonly used as an address of respect not only to those in authority, such as kings and fathers, but even to strangers. Second, there is the right to be served. When one used the title "Lord," it normally expressed a willingness to serve the person or idol so addressed. A third implied right is the right of disposal. As owner, a lord could dispose of his property in any way he saw fit. This is an important concept to remember in the area of our stewardship of the Lord's resources. Finally, the right to rule and hold authority over others is also implied in the name "Lord."

In the cultural context of that day, a lord had absolute authority over his subjects. When Jesus was called "Lord" by Christians, who reserved that word as a title of deity, each of the four above rights were intensified in their experience.

The use of this name is significant in the lives and experience of the disciples, particularly in three instances. When Jesus told Peter to let down his nets, Peter respectfully addressed Jesus as Master and consented to let down a net (Luke 5:5). That he let down only one net suggests that he was doing so merely as a courtesy to Jesus and did not expect to catch anything. Later, when the net broke because of the size of the catch and Peter realized that Jesus was more than just another religious teacher, he addressed Jesus as Lord (see Luke 5:8).

A second significant use of this title in the Gospels occurred at the Last Supper. Again the speech of the disciples betrayed the nature of their faith and their true attitude toward Jesus. When Jesus announced that one of the twelve would betray Him that night, the eleven asked, "Lord, is it I?" (Matt. 26:22). Later Judas also asked but said, "Master, is it I?" (v. 25). The eleven disciples had come to recognize Jesus as Lord, but for Judas, He was only Master.

The third significant use of this title by a disciple in the Gospels is when Thomas answered Jesus' invitation to touch His wounds by crying out, "My LORD and my God" (John 20:28). His affirmation of faith in Jesus as *Jehovah El* of the Old Testament is the apex of the Gospel of John and the highest statement of deity yet attributed to Jesus. John writes his Gospel in such a way as to build to a climax with Thomas's affirmation of the lordship of Christ. This expression of faith is that of Thomas, the disciples and—hopefully—you, the reader.

"Lord" is the most often used name of Jesus in the book of Acts. It was the name that God used of Jesus at the resurrection (see Phil. 2:9-11). The lordship of Christ is a post-resurrection emphasis. It was a constant theme in apostolic preaching: "For we preach not ourselves, but Christ Jesus the Lord; and ourselves your servants for Jesus' sake" (2 Cor. 4:5).

The Message of This Name

As is true with each name of Jesus in Scripture, the name "Lord" has a special significance in the life of every Christian. It closely relates to what it means to be a Christian: "That if thou shalt confess with thy mouth the Lord Jesus, and shalt believe in thine heart that God hath raised him from the dead, thou shalt be saved" (Rom. 10:9). Some evangelists erroneously argue that this means that a person is not saved if his or her conversion is not accompanied by a dramatic evidence of repentance. Although repentance is as important as faith in conversion, the *evidence* of repentance differs in every experience.

If the Lord has convicted an unsaved person about a particular sin, and that person refuses to repent of that sin, the individual cannot be saved until he or she is willing to recognize the Lord Jesus in that area. Often, however, it is not until after a person is saved that he or she is convicted by the Holy Spirit of sin in his life. This presence of sin does not mean that Jesus is not the person's Savior, only that Jesus is not recognized as the person's Lord.

Recognizing the lordship of Christ is a work of the Holy Spirit in our life. "No man can say that Jesus is the Lord, but by the Holy Ghost" (1 Cor. 12:3). All Christians at some point in their walk with God need to put Jesus Christ on the throne of their life as Lord. "But sanctify the Lord God in your hearts" (1 Pet. 3:15), the apostle Peter exhorted. Paul urged essentially the same things of the Romans when he said, "I beseech you therefore, brethren, by the mercies of God, that ye present your bodies a living sacrifice, holy, acceptable unto God, which is your reasonable service" (Rom. 12:1). This is the foundation of practicing biblical stewardship. Stewardship is not just fundraising; it is also managing our life. It is placing our all on the altar for God. Stewardship is recognizing not just the tithe as the Lord's—that is, 10 percent—but realizing that all things are His. "The earth is the LORD's, and the fullness thereof; the world, and they who dwell therein" (Ps. 24:1). He is Lord both by creation and by redemption.

Lordship is an experience of the believer rather than of the unsaved. What is today referred to as lordship salvation is almost a statement of salvation by works, but the Scriptures teach that we are saved solely by grace. Lordship is for the Christian; grace is for the unsaved. Failure to recognize Jesus as Lord in your life will result in frustration in your Christian experience. If you never yield control of your life to Jesus, you will constantly have doubts concerning the certainty of your salvation.

Lordship marks the progress or growth of our Christian life as we confess and forsake known sin in the process of becoming more Christlike. George Mueller grew in grace as a Christian. On several occasions God revealed areas in his life to be corrected. As Mueller confessed his sin and surrendered these areas of his life to Christ's lordship, he continued to grow in Christ.

Lordship means surrender. In a meeting of several well-known Christian workers in the last century, the question was asked, "What is the greatest need in Christian circles at this time?" Without hesitation a Scottish missionary leader summed up that need in two words: absolute surrender. He went on to explain that most of the problems he dealt with in his ministry would resolve themselves if Christians would surrender themselves totally and absolutely to the lordship of Christ.

Many Christian leaders today would agree that this is still the greatest need of the Church. Jesus said, "If any man will come after me, let him deny himself, and take up his cross daily, and follow me" (Luke 9:23). The key to the victorious Christian life is found in this surrender, or yielding, of oneself wholeheartedly to God. "Neither yield ye your members as instruments of unrighteousness unto sin: but yield yourselves unto God, as those that are alive from the dead, and your members as instruments of righteousness unto God" (Rom. 6:13).

Paul uses four key verbs in Romans 6 that describe various aspects of what it means to call Jesus Lord. These are keys to the victorious Christian life. The first verb is "know" (vv. 3,9). We must first know the doctrinal basis of victory in the Christian life—that is, that we are united to and identified with Christ in His death and resurrection. The next verb is "reckon" (v. 11), which means to count or rely upon these facts to be true concerning ourselves. The verb "yield" (vv. 13,16,19) means to present ourselves once and for all to God as His possession and for His use. The fourth verb, "obey" (vv. 16-17), urges us to be continuously obedient to the revealed and known will of God.

Lordship is more than just yielding; lordship means control. An overemphasis on yielding sometimes results in passive Christians. But God wants more than yielded Christians; He wants control of our life. When He has control, we will take up our cross. When He has control, we will deny self and the flesh. When He has control, we will find ourselves saying no to the old man and yes to the new man.

When Jesus taught the parable of the talents, He emphasized several principles of lordship, or biblical stewardship. One of the most significant is that God expects production from what He has given us to use. To take the resources of God, which He has entrusted to our keeping, and hoard them or bury them in the ground is the greatest wrong we can do toward the Lord. When God entrusts us with His resources, He expects us to use them and multiply them. It is impossible to invest what God has given us without seeing a return on it.

CONCLUSION

Recognizing the lordship of Christ should be the norm in the Christian's life. Jesus taught a parable concerning the duty of the servant constantly to obey his master, and He concluded with the words, "So likewise ye, when ye shall have done all those things which are commanded you, say, We are unprofitable servants: we have done that which was our duty to do" (Luke 17:10). The concept of a Christian who does not recognize the lordship of Christ in his life is foreign to the New Testament ideal.

Yet such Christians are all too common today. The greatest need of the Church is still absolute surrender. Someday, of course, "at the name of Jesus every knee should bow, of things in heaven, and things in earth, and things under the earth; and that every tongue should confess that Jesus Christ is Lord, to the glory of God the Father" (Phil. 2:10-11). When it comes to recognizing the lordship of Christ, we have a choice. It can be our decision now or His coercive act later.

FOR DISCUSSION

1. What did the word "Lord" mean in the culture of our Savior's day?
2. Explain the term "lordship of Christ."
3. Can you recall a time when you surrendered your life to the Lord? Write your experience, or share it with a friend.
4. Explain the statement, "Jesus is the Lord of our life whether we let Him operate in our life or not."
5. Where will you be on that day when everyone recognizes the lordship of Christ?

3

The Office of Christ

*Come, see a man, which told me all things that ever I did:
is not this the Christ?*

JOHN 4:29

At least 49 times in his epistles, Paul uses the expression "the Lord Jesus Christ" or "our Lord Jesus Christ," bringing together the three primary names of Jesus. As noted already in our study, "Lord" is His title, "Jesus" is His name, and "Christ" is His office. Actually, "Christ" is a favorite name of the apostle Paul, and he uses it independently of other titles some 211 times in his writings. In addition, he often uses this title with other names and titles of Christ. For this apostle, the title "Christ" had a very special significance.

The Greek word *Christos*, translated "Christ," literally means "anointed one" and was used in the Septuagint to translate the word "Messiah" (see Dan. 9:25-26). The Messiah in the Old Testament and the Christ in the New Testament, therefore, refer to the same Person, although their contextual use affects their perspective somewhat. In the Old Testament, "Messiah" is always used in the context of a messianic hope, whereas the predominant use of "Christ" in the New Testament is as an official name of Jesus in the context of a work completed.

Theologians speak of the three anointed offices of Christ, meaning Christ as prophet, priest and king. This expression seems to have been first used by Eusebius in the third century to explain the biblical teaching concerning the office of Christ. Even though the writers of Scripture did not express it in so many words, the fact that Christ was viewed by them in the context of the Old Testament-anointed offices is evident, particularly in the book of Revelation. The title of the book implies the nature of the prophetic office in revealing or making known what was otherwise hidden from man (see Rev. 1:1). In John's first vision of Christ, the Lord is viewed wearing a *talar*, a technical word referring to the robe of the priest (see v. 13). The office of king is seen in Revelation 11:15, where the theme of the book may be summarized: "And the seventh angel sounded; and there were great voices in heaven, saying, The kingdoms of this world are become the kingdoms of our Lord, and of his Christ, and he shall reign for ever and ever." This theme is developed throughout the book until the Lord is pictured as returning and having "on his vesture and on his thigh a name written, KING OF KINGS, AND LORD OF LORDS" (19:16).

Although the Old Testament context is important in understanding the implications of the name "Christ," we must again remember that Jesus not only took the reputation of a name upon Himself but also added something of His reputation to the name. This is certainly evident as we see how the apostle Paul gave the title "Christ" greater clarity in his writings. Paul ministered mostly among Gentiles, to whom the title "Christ" would have been meaningless without the Old Testament background. In his various epistles he gave the title a fuller meaning for such readers, particularly in the context of the union and communion of Christ and the believer. In many respects, therefore, the apostle must be credited with transforming the office of Christ into a personal name for the One who was the Messiah and much more.

When a young man graduates from medical school and moves to a small town to begin private practice, the members of the community might use the title "Doctor" with great respect as a prefix to his name. But as the years pass and the doctor becomes more and more a part of the community, the title "Doctor" often becomes the nickname "Doc." Similarly, Paul took the title "Messiah" and made it the personal name of Christ, by which many Christians today refer to Jesus Christ.

The Messiah in the Old Testament

Throughout the pages of Old Testament revelation, the prophets of Israel and Judah displayed a pervasive messianic hope. In their messages, which were often characterized by judgment or doom, often there was also a distant hope that ultimate deliverance would come from God. This deliverance was more than a supernatural phenomenon; it was the work of an anointed servant of God designated "the Messiah" (see Dan. 9:25).

This title, which became a name of Jesus, was a title of the preincarnate Christ in that eternal day before the beginning of time. From the very beginning, opposition to God was the same as opposition to "his anointed" (Ps. 2:2). In the consummation of this age, the kingdom of *Jehovah* is identical to the kingdom "of his Christ" (Rev. 11:15).

In the context of the Old Testament, the term "Messiah" or "Anointed One" had specific relevance to the three offices into which the candidate was normally initiated by an act of anointing: the offices of prophet, priest and king. Because of this I have called it the "threefold anointed office." Prophetically, the coming Messiah (the Anointed One) was portrayed as holding each of the offices. Typically the New Testament identifies Christ in the context of the past principal holders of these offices, namely, the prophet Moses (see Deut. 18:15-19), the priest Melchizedek (see Ps. 110:4), and the king David (see 2 Sam. 7:12-13). The candidate for each of these offices was anointed with oil (see Exod. 29:6-7; 1 Kings 19:16; 1 Sam. 16:13). In fulfillment of the type, Jesus was anointed by the Holy Spirit as He began His public ministry (see Matt. 3:16; Mark 1:10-11; Luke 3:21-22; John 1:32-33).

We must assume that the early disciples understood the title "Christ" in the Old Testament context of the Messiah. John the Baptist confessed that he himself was not the Christ (see John 1:20), yet those who left John to follow Jesus announced boldly, "We have found the Messias" (John 1:41). The divine anointing of Jesus for specific service was important in both the teaching of Jesus and in the Jerusalem church (see Luke 4:18; Acts 10:38). From the very beginning the Early Church understood Jesus in terms of His threefold anointed office of prophet, priest and king.

The Anointed Prophet

Few people would deny the prophetic ministry of Jesus even if they might reject the content of His teaching. It is a common practice among those who deny His deity and the unique redemptive nature of His work at least to acknowledge Him to be a moral teacher and a religious prophet. Of course, the prophetic office of Christ as revealed in Scripture was far more specific than the vague description of Jesus as a prophet by a liberal teacher.

There are no fewer than five designations that identify the prophet in the Old Testament. First, a prophet was called the "man of God" (see Deut. 33:1; 1 Sam. 2:27; 9:6; 1 Kings 13:1; the title of Ps. 90). This expression related particularly to his unique relationship to God and the uniqueness of his message. Most probably it also assumed that the prophet had a godly character.

The second title of the prophet was the "servant of God" (see 2 Kings 17:13,23; 21:10; 24:2; Ezra 9:11; Jer. 7:25). Although no prophet ever called himself the servant of God, God often referred to His prophets as His servants. Some commentators think that this might be part of the reason that the writers of the New Testament so often began their epistles with such expressions as "servant of God" or "the servant of the Lord Jesus Christ." Also, inasmuch as it was customary for a Jew to begin his prayer to God by identifying himself as the servant of God, we may assume that this title, when applied to the prophets, referred to them as men of prayer. The predominant feature of this designation is that of the Master-slave relationship that existed between God and His servants the prophets.

A third and by far most common designation of the prophet in the Old Testament was the Hebrew word *nabi'*. Although there is some debate as to the origin of this word, scholars generally agree that it derives from an Akkadian root meaning "to call." The word could be identifying the prophet as one who is called by God, one who calls to men in the name of God, or one who calls to God on behalf of men. In the Old Testament, each of the above descriptions was characteristic of the prophet, and it might be best to think of the term as implying all three aspects.

The final two terms applied to Old Testament prophets derive from Hebrew roots for "sight." *Ro'eh* is an active participle of the verb "to see" and is always translated "seer" in Scripture. The second term, *hozeh*, is an active participle of another verb for "seeing" that has no English equivalent. It is sometimes translated "seer" (1 Chron. 29:29) and sometimes "prophet" (Isa. 30:10). It is, with one exception, always mentioned in the context of a king, leading some to conclude that this kind of prophet was a resident court historian with prophetic ability (see 2 Chron. 29:30).

First Chronicles 29:29 seems to prove that these three Hebrew terms distinguish three varieties within the prophetic office, for the verse uses each term of different persons who were prophets. That there are similarities in these three kinds of prophets is evidenced in passages such as Amos 7:12, in which Amaziah addresses Amos as a *hozel*, asking him to prophesy (*nabi'*) in Judah. Amos on that occasion refused, claiming he was not a *nabi'*.

In the New Testament two Greek verbs identify prophesying. The word *prophaino* means "to reveal" and includes the idea of predicting the future and revealing the message of God. The other term, *prothemi*, conveys the meaning "to tell forth," to speak to others on behalf of God though not necessarily with a predictive message. The noun *prophetes* was used by the Greeks as early as the fourth century B.C. to identify those who could interpret the oracles of the gods. The word literally refers to one who speaks forth or speaks openly and was loosely applied to anyone who proclaimed a divine message. The word *prophetes* was used in the Old Testament Greek version (the Septuagint, or LXX) to translate both *nabi'* and *ro'eh*. It therefore came to be understood by the Jews to refer to one anointed of the Holy Spirit who received revelation from and communicated a message for God.

One of the early messianic prophecies of the Old Testament was that God would raise up a Prophet like unto Moses (see Deut. 18:15). Although the character of this Prophet came to be the standard by which other prophets were evaluated, the Jews clearly understood the prophecy as messianic. Many Old Testament prophets engaged in prophecy, but only Jesus possessed the credentials and practiced the ministry of the Prophet in perfection. His ministry gave evidence of all three of the following aspects of prophetic preaching.

1. *A spokesman for God—"for-teller."* Jesus was a spokesman for God and so fulfilled the office of the Prophet. Everything Jesus said was the Word of God. Also, "His name is called The Word of God"

(Rev. 19:13). Jesus consciously said and did the will of the Father while here on Earth. He told the religious leaders of His day, "The Son can do nothing of himself, but what he seeth the Father do: for what things soever he doeth, these also doeth the Son likewise" (John 5:19). Later in the same conversation, Jesus said, "I can of mine own self do nothing: as I hear, I judge: and my judgment is just; because I seek not mine own will, but the will of the Father which hath sent me" (John 5:30).

2. *Predicting the future—"foreteller."* Normally when people think of prophecy, their first idea is that of predicting future events. In His role as foreteller, Jesus made several prophecies. He told His disciples about the coming of the Holy Spirit (see John 14:26), which was fulfilled at Pentecost (see Acts 2:1-4). Further, He described the ministry of the Holy Spirit in this age (see John 16:13-14) and the details of His own death, burial and resurrection (see Matt. 16:21). Additional predictive teachings of Christ dealt with His return (see John 14:2-3), the existence of the Church (Matt. 16:18), and the course of the Church age (see Matt. 13).

3. *A preacher to people—"forth-teller."* Jesus taught the people truth concerning God. Nicodemus, a Pharisee and ruler of the Jews, acknowledged, "Rabbi, we know that thou art a teacher come from God: for no man can do these miracles that thou doest, except God be with him" (John 3:2). When Jesus taught, "the people were astonished at his doctrine: for he taught them as one having authority" (Matt. 7:28-29). Jesus spoke with authority for God. Several extended discourses of Jesus are recorded in Scripture, including the Sermon on the Mount (see Matt. 5-7), the mystery parables (see Matt. 13), the Olivet discourse (see Matt. 24-25) and the Upper Room discourse (see John 13-16).

Jesus was certainly consistent with the prophetic tradition of Israel; and, as such, those who heard Him understood Him to be a prophet (see Matt. 21:11). But Jesus was more than just another prophet; He was *the* Prophet. Although there were many similarities between Jesus and the other prophets, there were also differences. The most notable of these was His authority in preaching. The prophet of God almost always prefaced his remarks with the expression "Thus saith the Lord"; but Jesus characteristically began by saying, "I say unto you."

The Anointed Priest

A second anointed office in the Old Testament is that of the priest. Primarily, the priest acted as man's representative before God. The priest offered the sacrifice upon the altar. Because God is by nature both just and forgiving, the priest could always tell the people that God would forgive them if they met His conditions. The priest was a channel of forgiveness, whereas the prophet was usually the channel of judgment. Priests were by far more popular than prophets.

The office of the priest was an anointed office, because the candidate could not practice this office until he was first dipped in water and anointed with oil. This normally occurred at age 30, and for 20 years the candidate then served as a functioning priest. It is significant that Luke notes that Jesus was 30 years of age when He was baptized by John and anointed with the Holy Spirit (see Luke 3:23).

The fullest development of New Testament teaching on the priesthood of Christ is understandably in the book of Hebrews. There it is demonstrated that He is both a priest and a high priest. His priesthood is considered superior, because it succeeds in the order of Melchizedek rather than of Aaron. Some commentators have interpreted this claim to mean that Melchizedek was a Christophany, but it is more likely that we should view him as a type of Christ. Actually, "Melchizedek" was not a name but a dynastic title, which may also be applied to Jesus. This explains why the Scriptures appear to call Melchizedek Jesus. In reality, they are calling Jesus Melchizedek.

The office of the priest was unique in nature. First, if one was a priest, the implication is that he had been called of God to that task. Also, as a priest, he could represent another before God. If Jesus is a priest, then He serves two major functions: that of offering sacrifices and that of intercession for others.

Jesus was not only a priest but also the high priest. In addition to his other responsibilities as a priest, the high priest was particularly involved in the activities of the Day of Atonement (see Lev. 16) and in the use of the Urim and Thummin (see Num. 27:21). He was Israel's mediator on the Day of Atonement, for he took the blood of the slaughtered goat into the holy of holies, where he offered propitiation for the nation's sins and effected the atonement, or covering, of its sin for another year. He wore the Urim and Thummin on his breastplate, which contained the names of the twelve tribes and, as such, represented the nation. By using this means, he alone could discern the will of God for the nation. In contrast with the limited national ministry of Israel's high priest, Jesus "is the propitiation for our sins: and not for ours only, but also for the sins of the whole world" (1 John 2:2).

The names "priest" and "high priest" primarily relate to the redemptive work of Christ, for they help explain this work within the context of the legal system of Moses. Yet these names also relate to Christ's Person, as He fulfilled the ideal qualifications for these offices. Jesus is both in person and in ministry our priest, high priest, propitiation, mediator and guide. Many of the secondary names of Jesus, to some extent, belong to the function and office of the priest.

The Anointed King

In the Old Testament one of the designations of the coming Messiah was that of Israel's king (see Ps. 2:6; Zech. 9:9). It is interesting to note Nathanael's recognition of Jesus as "the Son of God . . . the King of Israel" (John 1:49). In the Gospel of Mark, the title "king" occurs six times but always as a term of contempt or derision. It is the Gospel of Matthew that really develops this theme. Matthew begins with the legal genealogy of Jesus, noting Him to be the legal heir to the throne of David. The number 14 is particularly emphasized in this genealogy (see Matt. 1:17). This is significant for two reasons. First, the numerical value of the name "David" is 14. Second, 14 is the product of two times seven, seven being the number of perfection or completeness. Most Jews considered David their most nearly perfect king, and Matthew is introducing the "second David." Although several kings are listed in the genealogy, only David is called king.

In the second chapter of Matthew, the magi looking for Jesus ask, "Where is he that is born King of the Jews?" (v. 2) and Herod responds by inquiring of the chief priests and scribes "where Christ should be born" (v. 4). Matthew develops this theme further until he records Jesus Himself acknowledging, "All power is given unto me in heaven and in earth" (28:18). Jesus is the King with ultimate authority. When the Early Church practiced the implications of this aspect of who Christ is, it was not without negative consequences. They called Jesus their King (see Acts 17:7), recognizing Him alone as the supreme ruler in their lives; but this was offensive to Rome, who viewed Caesar as both god and king. Much of the later persecution of the Church was related to Rome's view that recognition of Jesus as king was seditious. It is therefore significant that the theme of the final book written to the persecuted Church is the regal status of Jesus (see Rev. 11:15; 19:16).

Jesus Is King

The kingship of Christ follows from His deity. Because He is God, He is also King. Paul gave praise to King Jesus: "Unto the King eternal, immortal, invisible, the only wise God, be honour and glory for ever and ever" (1 Tim. 1:17). In heaven "they sing the song of Moses the servant of God, and the song of the Lamb, saying, Great and marvellous are thy works, Lord God Almighty; just and true are thy ways, thou King of saints" (Rev. 15:3). The Romans considered their Caesar to be a god. Christians, on the other hand, recognized Jesus alone to be their King. Calling Jesus King implied that they believed in His deity.

Jesus Has a Kingdom

Every king has a domain over which he rules, and Jesus is no exception. He acknowledged, "My kingdom is not of this world" (John 18:36), but He never denied that He had a kingdom. It was the custom of the Romans to identify the crime of a condemned man by writing it on a shingle and nailing it on the cross upon which he died. Jesus was executed as "THE KING OF THE JEWS" (19:19). When He returns to this earth, He will do so to establish His kingdom for a thousand years (see Rev. 20:1-6).

Jesus Has Subjects

Christ is now a ruler to those who submit their wills to Him. Someday, "at the name of Jesus every knee should bow, of things in heaven, and things in earth, and things under the earth; and ... every tongue should confess that Jesus Christ is Lord" (Phil. 2:10-11). Today those who receive Christ as Lord and Savior recognize the kingship of Christ in their lives. Jesus taught a parable that equated His disciples with servants (see Luke 17:10), and that was the attitude of the Early Church. They were eager to serve their King.

The Christ in the New Testament

Many of the New Testament references to Christ must be understood in the context of the Old Testament Messiah. This was the probable meaning when Peter confessed that Jesus was "the Christ, the Son of the living God" (Matt. 16:16) and when Caiaphas asked Jesus whether He was the Christ (see 26:63). On the day of Pentecost, Peter concluded his sermon by declaring Jesus to be "both Lord and Christ" (Acts 2:36), again to be understood in the context of the Old Testament Messiah. But "Christ" was also the favorite title of Paul, who ministered primarily among Gentiles who lacked the understanding of the Jews concerning the Messiah. In Paul's letters the title "Christ" took on a special significance—a new dimension.

Jesus did not use the title directly of Himself, although He answered "I am" (Mark 14:62) when people asked Him whether He was the Christ, and He approved of others calling Him by that title (see Matt. 16:16-17; John 4:25-26). On occasion He also mentioned that His disciples belonged to Christ, although we cannot be conclusive from the context that He was necessarily referring to Himself (Matt. 23:10; Mark 9:41).

In his epistles Paul often used the title "Christ" with the name "Jesus," and when he did so, the order of the names was significant. The name "Christ Jesus" referred to the exalted One who emptied Himself (see Phil. 2:5-9), emphasizing His preexistence and having reference to His grace. The reverse order of "Jesus Christ," however, referred to the despised and rejected One who was afterward glorified (see v. 11).

One of the great themes in Paul's epistles is that of the union and communion of the believer with Christ. In this connection, he uses the expression "in Christ" 172 times and speaks also of

Christ's indwelling the believer. Interestingly enough, it is always "Christ," never "Jesus," that he uses to teach indwelling. Paul's use of this title of Jesus is foundational to our understanding of the Christian life.

Union with Christ—Our Position in Heaven

The expression "in Christ" refers to our union with Christ, an aspect of the Christian's experience of salvation. Being in Christ is a non-experiential state—that is, it occurs at the moment of salvation in the life of every believer, whether he or she realizes it or not. This is our position, or standing, in heaven. In Paul's writings "Christ" becomes the positional name of Jesus after His resurrection.

The nature of the union between Christ and the believer is difficult to define and may be best understood if we describe several aspects of this relationship. Although in itself each aspect falls short of what this union is, together these aspects give us a more complete portrait of the nature of this union.

This union is a mystical union, for in a sense, there is a blending of the life of God into the life of the believer so that although believers remain distinct persons, there is the development of oneness with God in our will and purpose. This union transcends the limits even of the marriage union. By this union we also become Jesus' friend (see John 15:14-15).

Second, there is a legal or federal aspect of this union. In this sense our union with Christ becomes the basis of our justification and adoption. It is legal, or federal, in the sense that we are "in" our lawyer or senator while he or she represents us before the court or in government. Again, although this is one aspect of our union, this union also goes much deeper.

Our union is of an organic nature in which not only does the believer become a member of the body of Christ, but Christ also becomes a part of the believer. Furthermore, the Christian life is the result of a vital union with Christ. It is Christ living in us, not merely influencing us from without. Because the Holy Spirit is the author of this union, we call it a spiritual union.

Moreover, this union is both indissoluble and inscrutable. The believer is so bonded to Christ that he or she has entered into an indissoluble relationship with Him. The omnipresence of Christ makes this union possible. Also, because this union involves the nature of God, there is a sense in which we can never fully understand it.

Finally, the union of the believer and Christ must be regarded as both complete and completed. The idea of a believer being partially united with Christ is as impossible as that of a woman being only partially pregnant. Although we may grow in the realization of this truth, we are never more deeply united with Christ by any means than we are at conversion.

Communion with Christ—Our Experience on Earth

Not only are we in Christ, but Christ is also in us. This is the basis of our communion with Christ, which is an experience of our sanctification. The writings of Paul sometimes use the title "Christ" without the article. Paul does this consistently in order to signify the One who by the Holy Spirit and also His own Person indwells the believer and molds the believer's character into a closer conformity to Christ (see Rom. 8:10; Gal. 2:20; 4:19; Eph. 3:17). The practical application of this truth results in our abiding in Christ.

Many writers distinguish two aspects of abiding in Christ. First, it means to have no known sin unjudged and unconfessed that would hinder our communion or fellowship with Christ. Second, it assumes that we give all burdens and concerns to Him and rely upon Him for the strength, wisdom, faith and character that we need to meet the particular challenges of life. Not only is His position our position (union), but His life is also our life (communion).

CONCLUSION

When the prophets of Israel and Judah spoke of the coming Messiah, their highest thoughts of Him were those of prophet, priest and king. Jesus functions today in each of those offices in the life of the believer. But He is also far more. He is no longer merely "the Christ" but also "Christ," the One in whom we dwell and depend upon for the very essence of spiritual life and the One who lives within, providing all that is necessary for effective Christian living.

FOR DISCUSSION

1. What is the literal meaning of the name "Christ"? Why was it Paul's favorite name for the Savior?
2. How did Christ fulfill His office as prophet?
3. As an anointed priest, how does Christ minister to us today?
4. Describe the kingdom and rule of Jesus Christ the King.
5. God's Word teaches that believers are "in Christ" and that Christ abides in believers. What effect does this have on your everyday life?

PART 2

Groupings of the Names of Jesus Christ

4

The Old Testament Prophetic Names of Jesus

Philip findeth Nathanael, and saith unto him,
We have found him, of whom Moses in the law, and the prophets,
did write, Jesus of Nazareth, the son of Joseph.
JOHN 1:45

Beginning at Moses and all the prophets, he expounded unto them
in all the scriptures the things concerning himself.
LUKE 24:27

It has often been said that the Old Testament is Christ concealed and the New Testament is Christ revealed, and yet the Old Testament was the Bible by which the Early Church preached the gospel of Christ to a lost world. Hidden in the pages of law, history, poetry and prophecy is a wealth of revelation concerning the Lord Jesus Christ. He is revealed in every book through types, metaphors, analogies and indisputable titles. Although it would be impossible for us to consider every title in a single chapter, we shall discuss in this chapter several of the principal titles of Jesus Christ in the Old Testament. Some important Old Testament names are omitted here because they are covered in later chapters.

Shiloh

One of the earliest of the titles the book of Genesis applies to the coming Messiah in the Old Testament is "Shiloh." As Jacob was blessing his sons and prophesying concerning the twelve tribes of Israel, he said, "The sceptre shall not depart from Judah, nor a lawgiver from between his feet, until Shiloh come; and unto him shall the gathering of the people be" (Gen. 49:10).

The name "Shiloh" means "peace maker" and closely relates to one of Isaiah's birth names for Jesus, the "Prince of Peace" (Isa. 9:6). This prophecy affirms that Shiloh would come from the royal tribe of Judah, wield a temporal scepter and possess a sovereignty of a different character.

Prophet

The great prophet in the history of Israel was Moses, although before he died he prophesied of a future Prophet that the Jews came to understand to be the coming Messiah. "The LORD thy God will raise up unto thee a Prophet from the midst of thee, of thy brethren, like unto me; unto him ye shall hearken" (Deut. 18:15). This prophet would speak as a "forth-teller," preaching a message; as a "for-teller," preaching for God; and as a "foreteller," predicting things to come. The preaching of Jesus conformed to each aspect of this prophetic preaching.

The Branch

Our English Bible translates three Hebrew words for "branch" as a name or title of Jesus. The first word, *tsemach*, literally refers to a green shoot or sprout growing out of an old stump. A similar word, *netzer*, was used of a small, fresh, green twig. A third word, translated "rod" in Isaiah 11:1, was *choter*; this refers to a shoot growing out of a cut-down stump. These three words describe Jesus as the Branch.

This title of Christ had both positive and negative connotations. A puzzling verse in Matthew refers to an Old Testament prophecy to the effect, "He shall be called a Nazarene" (Matt. 2:23). To be called a Nazarene by those living outside Nazareth was insulting, for the town had a reputation as the city of garbage. Even one of Jesus' first disciples asked, "Can there any good thing come out of Nazareth?" (John 1:46). But the puzzling thing about this verse is that no verse in the Old Testament identifies Nazareth as the home of the Messiah. Most commentators argue that Matthew was here alluding to one of the Branch prophecies, having noted the similarity of sound between *netzer* and Nazareth.

Isaiah did use the word *netzer* in a negative sense when he said of the king of Babylon, "But thou art cast out of thy grave like an abominable branch." (Isa. 14:19). Here the word describes a useless shoot cut off a tree and left to rot. Although Isaiah's use of the word in this context does not specifically refer to Christ, it does demonstrate how Matthew could have understood a Branch prophecy to imply that Jesus would have to live with the reputation of being a Nazarene.

Positively, these words for "Branch" are used in four ways corresponding to the four Gospels in the New Testament. First, Christ is the King Branch. This corresponds to the Gospel of Matthew, which emphasizes the life of Christ as the King of the Jews. Jeremiah noted, "Behold, the days come, saith the Lord, that I will raise unto David a righteous Branch, and a King shall reign and prosper, and shall execute judgment and justice in the earth" (Jer. 23:5). This title specifically applies to the coming kingdom of God during the millennial reign of Christ.

Jesus is also spoken of as a Servant Branch. This corresponds to the Gospel of Mark, which portrays Jesus as the Servant of the Lord. The prophet Zechariah announced, "Hear now, O Joshua the high priest, thou, and thy fellows that sit before thee: for they are men wondered at: for, behold, I will bring forth my servant, the BRANCH" (Zech. 3:8). Jesus was not only a king but also a servant. Several passages in Isaiah more fully describe this One who is the Servant of *Jehovah*.

This Branch is described as a man. This corresponds to the unique emphasis of the Gospel of Luke, which 80 times refers to Jesus as the Son of man. Again, it was the prophet Zechariah who announced this aspect of the Branch: "And speak unto him, saying, Thus speaketh the LORD of hosts, saying, Behold the man whose name is The BRANCH; and he shall grow up out of his place, and he shall build the temple of the LORD" (Zech. 6:12).

The final aspect of this name is that the Lord Himself is the Branch. This corresponds to the emphasis of the Gospel of John, which begins with a statement as to the deity of Jesus the Word. "In that day shall the branch of the LORD be beautiful and glorious, and the fruit of the earth shall be excellent and comely for them that are escaped of Israel" (Isa. 4:2). Again, this name specifically applies to the millennial reign of Christ still to come.

The Desire of All Nations

Perhaps no preacher in history left behind such a brief record of ministry with as great accomplishment as the prophet Haggai. The book that records his name consists of five sermons that range in length from a single line to several verses. Yet it was primarily the preaching of this prophet that led to the resumption of work and the completion of the second temple in Jerusalem. Because some Jews had seen the previous temple in all its physical splendor, they became discouraged as they saw the builders erecting a smaller wood frame structure. Haggai knew that the people were failing to realize that it was not the architecture of a building but rather God's presence that made a building a holy place. To encourage the people, Haggai prophesied of the days when "the desire of all nations shall come" (2:7).

Commentators debate among themselves about the meaning of this phrase "desire of all nations." Some argue that Haggai meant that the wealth of other nations—that is, the desirable things of those nations—would someday be brought to this second temple. A more probable interpretation is that the phrase is a title of Christ, who would come to the temple that seemed so insignificant in the eyes of some of the workers.

Jewish writers have noted that the second temple lacked five objects that were present in the first temple: (1) the Ark of the Covenant with its mercy seat, or place of propitiation, (2) the tables of the Law, (3) the holy fire, (4) the sacred oracle in the breastplate of the high priest, and (5) the Shekinah glory of God. Although God did not give these things to the remnant that returned and built the temple, He did promise to send the "desire of all nations," who was all these things and more.

Jesus is the reality of which the Ark was only the type. He is not only the place of propitiation but also "the propitiation for our sins" (1 John 2:2). The early Christians applied the title "lawgiver" to the Lord (Jas. 4:12). He is a "wall of fire" (Zech. 2:5), the Urim and Thummin and our high priest. But above all these things, He is the incarnate Shekinah glory of God. As the apostle John noted, "And the Word was made flesh, and dwelt among us (and we beheld his glory, the glory as of the only begotten of the Father), full of grace and truth" (John 1:14). The Shekinah glory was indeed absent at the dedication of the second temple, but eventually it was present in Christ in a greater sense than ever was true of the first temple. The "desire of all nations" came; He was the fullness of the Godhead, and He dwelt, or tabernacled, among us.

Although this prophecy had partial fulfillment in the first advent of Christ, many commentators point out that the context of this prophecy applies to the second coming of Christ. In the Millennium Christ will be King and Lord of the nations. In that sense the "desire of all nations" is still yet to come. However, in a sense He is the "desirable one of all nations" today, since Christians around the world echo the final prayer of the Scriptures: "Even so, come, Lord Jesus" (Rev. 22:20).

The Ensign of the People

One of the many titles for Christ in the book of Isaiah is "an ensign of the people" (11:10). Of the seven times the word "ensign" appears in Scripture, six are singular and found in the prophecy of Isaiah. The word itself refers to a national flag to which people rally. It is the symbol of the nation, and loyalty to that flag is the most common form of patriotism.

While I served as president of Winnipeg Bible College, the Canadian government designed a new national flag. At the time a great debate arose over the proposed action. Many Canadians remembered fighting for liberty in World War II and the Korean War under the old Red Ensign. To change that flag seemed unpatriotic and an attack on the national heritage of Canadians. Today, almost two decades later, most Canadians feel a sense of deep-seated patriotism when they see their new maple-leaf flag blowing in the wind.

Just as the old Red Ensign was an untouchable symbol of the nation in the early sixties, so too many Canadians would respond the same way if the government tried to change the maple-leaf flag today.

In the same way in which a nation rallies around its flag, Christians rally around Jesus. The history of the Church is a record of various conflicts and debates over different interpretations of doctrine, but true Christianity has always been grounded upon an agreement concerning Christ. There have been times when good people thought it wrong to baptize, to send out missionaries or to be involved in political action, but believers have always found a rallying point around the Person and work of Jesus Christ. He has been the ensign to which they have been drawn.

As an ensign for the peoples, Jesus is not just the flag that brings a group of Christians from one country together but rather the flag that brings believers from all places together. Commenting on this title of "Christ," Charles J. Rolls exclaimed,

> What a distinction! To be high above all principality and power.
> What a recognition! To be revered by myriad hosts of men and angels.
> What a coronation! To be crowned Lord of lords and King of kings.
> What a commemoration! To be admired in all them that believe.

El Shaddai—The Almighty

When the LORD appeared to Abraham to confirm His covenant with him, He revealed Himself to the 99-year-old man of faith as *El Shaddai* (see Gen. 17:1). Linguists do not agree about the etymology of this title and usually suggest one of three possibilities. Some link the word to the Hebrew *shadad*, meaning "to devastate," and argue that the title lays emphasis on the irresistible power of God. Others believe that the word relates the Akkadian word *shadu*, meaning "mountain," and argue that the title means something like "God of the Mountains." The third and most probable meaning of this word is based on its relationship to the Hebrew word *shad*, meaning "breast."

El Shaddai is naturally a tender title for God. Scripture uses it exclusively of God in relation to His children. When trying to explain more fully the implications of this name, some writers have spoken of the mother love of God. To the child held to its mother's breast, the mother is the all-sufficient one who provides both the physical necessities and the emotional support that the child needs. Similarly, *El Shaddai* is the all-sufficient One in the believer's experience. He has been accurately described as "the God who is enough."

El Shaddai was Job's favorite name for God. Thirty-one of its 48 occurrences in Scripture appear in the book of Job. For Job in the midst of his suffering and despair, *El Shaddai* was enough. This title suggests supplying the need and comforting the hurting. Over the years many Christians have discovered the true nature of *El Shaddai* only in their darkest hours. When we understand this name of Jesus, we can grow in our Christian experience, knowing the tenderness that characterizes Christ, until we can confess with Job, "Though he slay me, yet will I trust in him" (Job 13:15).

CONCLUSION

Throughout the Old Testament the prophets of God looked forward to the day when their coming Messiah would arrive. As God continued to reveal more and more about Him, they chose names to describe Him more accurately. Hundreds of such names appear in the pages of the Old Testament, but they describe only part of the character and nature of Jesus. Although these names were given to nourish a sense of anticipation and expectation, we can enjoy them even more, for now, at least in part, the fulfillment of them has come. Jesus has proved to be far more than what the prophets could have imagined.

FOR DISCUSSION

1. What is probably the earliest name of Christ in the Old Testament? What do we know about our Savior from this title?

2. One of the favorite titles for Christ in the prophets was "Branch." How is Christ our Branch?
3. Haggai called Christ the desire of all nations. How does Christ fulfill this title?
4. Isaiah called Christ the ensign of the people. What should be our reaction to this name?
5. Share an experience when you realized that Christ is your *El Shaddai*.

5

The Salvational Names of Jesus

I know that my redeemer liveth,
and that he shall stand at the latter day upon the earth.
JOB 19:25

Let the words of my mouth, and the meditation of my heart,
be acceptable in thy sight, O LORD, my strength, and my redeemer.
PSALM 19:14

Theologians refer to certain names and titles of Jesus Christ as the soteriological titles because they have particular reference to the work of Christ in salvation. I call these names the salvational names of Jesus because they are the names that reveal or clarify our salvation more fully. Although the Bible speaks of salvation in three tenses (past, present and future), the names I'll discuss in this chapter refer primarily to salvation past, that is, to our conversion rather than to our sanctification and eventual glorification with Christ. We might designate these names as evangelistic names, for they tend to preach or explain the *evangel*, or gospel, of salvation.

Redeemer

When we think of the doctrine of salvation, sooner or later we must consider the concept of redemption. It is a little surprising, however, that the title "Redeemer" is never used of Jesus in the New Testament, although its verbal form occurs both in the Gospels and Epistles in connection with His work of redemption (see Luke 1:68; 24:21; Gal. 3:13; 4:5; Titus 2:14; 1 Pet. 1:18; Rev. 5:9; 14:3-4). This name was, nevertheless, a popular title in the Old Testament, particularly in the psalms (see Job 19:25; Ps. 19:14).

Although the New Testament does not call Jesus Redeemer, it certainly emphasizes His work of redemption throughout. The term "redemption" comes from a word that means "to buy back." Christ gave His blood as a ransom for sin; by it He redeems the lost (see 1 Pet. 1:18-20). In the context of soteriology, the price of redemption is blood, which is paid to procure the remission of sins (see Heb. 9:12,22). The Greek words for "redeemed" denote the purchase of servants in the ancient slave market. The Bible applies the terms to the redemption of all men.

First, the Bible teaches that Christ purchased the sinner in the marketplace. The verb *agorazo* means "to go to the marketplace [*agora*] and pay the price for a slave." The verb was common in deeds of sale and generally meant the paying of a price for a group of slaves. Those who were "sold under sin" (Rom 7:14; see also Gal. 3:10) are redeemed. Each of the following Scriptures uses the term *agorazo*: Revelation 14:3-4 speaks of the 144,000 as those redeemed from the earth; Revelation 5:9 notes that Christ's blood was the price paid for redemption; and 2 Peter 2:1 shows that Christ redeemed (paid the price for) not only the saved but also the false teachers. *Agorazo* is simply the payment, the purchase price—the price of redemption, which is blood.

A second word in the Bible for "redemption" is *ekagorazo*, meaning "to buy out from the marketplace." The prefix *ek* means "out." Therefore, this term refers to the fact that Christ paid the price with His blood and bought the slave "out of the marketplace" of sin. The slave was never again exposed to sale (see Gal. 3:13). When Christ took mankind out from under the law, He placed us in a different relationship with God by providing for us the opportunity to become adopted children of God (see 4:5). *Ekagorazo* emphasizes the removal of the curse of the law (see 3:13; 4:5).

The third word that refers to redemption is *lutrao*. This word means "to pay the price for the slave and then release him" (see 4:5). It emphasizes the freedom that Christ brings to those whom He has redeemed. This verb suggests that Christ works to separate us completely from all sin (see Titus 2:14).

A consideration of each of these terms and the contexts in which they appear in the New Testament indicates that Christ has provided redemption for all people by the shedding of His own blood (see Heb. 9:12). That redemption includes the price of redemption (*agorazo*), removal from the marketplace of sin (*ekagorazo*), and the provision of liberty to the redeemed (*lutrao*). This is the work of the Redeemer. But the sinner is not prepared to go to heaven until he responds by faith to the Redeemer.

Savior

It is interesting that Scripture rarely uses the name "Savior" of Jesus, especially in view of the fact that saving is fundamental to all Jesus is and did. At His birth the angel announced, "Unto you is born this day in the city of David a Saviour, which is Christ the Lord" (Luke 2:11). Early in His ministry, a group of Samaritans concluded the same truth and told the woman who met Jesus at Sychar's well, "Now we believe, not because of thy saying: for we have heard him ourselves, and know that this is indeed the Christ, the Saviour of the world" (John 4:42). But these are the only two instances in the Gospels of this title being applied to Jesus. He is seldom called Savior in the Epistles, although both Peter (see Acts 5:31) and Paul (see 13:23) used this title of Christ in their preaching.

Men have wondered why this name that embodies the very essence of the work of Christ should be almost neglected by the apostles. Two reasons suggest themselves. First, the apostles may have been trying to avoid a major confrontation with Roman authorities. One of the titles of Caesar was "savior of the world." A second reason for its infrequent use may have been that all Christ is and does in His saving work led the New Testament writers to take the title for granted. Both Peter and Paul used this title in an evangelistic appeal in which they were trying to explain the fundamentals of the gospel. If this were characteristic of the evangelical preaching of the Early Church, we would not expect a special emphasis in the Epistles, which were written largely to correct problems in the Church. The emphasis on Jesus as Savior may be absent because early believers widely understood and accepted it.

The Greek word *soter* means "savior," "deliverer" or "preserver." It is a title used of the Father as well as of the Son. It shares a common root with the verb *sozo*, which is the most commonly used expression of conversion in the Scriptures. This verb is used in three tenses in the New Testament to describe complete and full salvation. First, the believer has been saved from the guilt and penalty of sin. Second, he is being saved from the habit and dominion of sin. Third, he will be saved at the return of Christ from all the bodily infirmities and the curse that results from sin.

The Lamb of God

In the first 26 books of the New Testament, only John the Baptist used the title "Lamb of God." The expression occurs 26 times in the final book of the New Testament. When we think of the book of Revelation, we usually think of the Lord as the Lion of the tribe of Judah—that is, the coming King—but the most frequent title of Christ in that book is "the Lamb." The reason is that His coming as King is possible only because of His sacrifice as a Lamb.

Being the son of a priest, John the Baptist was no doubt familiar with the importance of the lamb offered every morning and evening in a whole burnt offering. He was acquainted as well with the other sacrifices, including that of Passover. This title of Christ probably derived from Isaiah's description of the suffering servant of the Lord (see Isa. 53:11) and the Levitical system of sacrifice in Israel. Just as a lamb was offered on the altar for sin, so too the Lamb of God would be offered for the sin of the world.

John predicted that the Lamb of God would take away sin. The verb *airon*, translated "takes away," conveys the idea of taking something up and carrying it away and in that sense destroying it. Jesus took away sin by bearing it in His own body (see 1 Pet. 2:24) and so He removed our transgressions from us as far as the east is from the west (see Ps. 103:12). Even before the Cross, John spoke of Jesus as the Lamb already taking away sin.

At least 10 times in Scripture we read about the taking away of sin:

1. Before the foundation of the world (see Rev. 13:8)
2. At the fall of man (see Gen. 3:15)
3. With the offering of a sacrifice (see 4:7)

4. On the Day of Atonement (see Lev. 16:34)
5. At a time of national repentance (see 2 Chron. 7:14)
6. During the public ministry of Jesus (see John 1:29)
7. On the cross (see 1 Pet. 2:24)
8. At conversion (see Rom. 6:6)
9. At the Second Coming (see 8:18-23)
10. At the end of the Millennium (see Rev. 20:15; 21:8)

Propitiation

A title of Christ that relates to the Lamb of God is "The Propitiation." The Greek word *hilaskomai* occurred in pagan literature to describe the sacrifices offered to idols in order to appease their wrath. The translators of the Septuagint used this word in a technical sense to identify the mercy seat, the place of reconciliation between God and man. The term conveys the idea of a full satisfaction to appease the wrath of God. Jesus bore the full brunt of God's wrath, and so He is the Propitiation for sin (see 1 John 2:2).

In an effort to escape the connotation that the wrath of God must be appeased, some translators prefer to translate this term "expiation." They consider that "propitiation" applies in Scripture only to pagan deities. But this view fails to recognize the offensiveness of sin in the eyes of God and the reality of the wrath of God against sin.

That Jesus is our Propitiation has deep meaning for every believer. First, it is the basis of our salvation. The so-called sinner's prayer, "God be merciful to me a sinner" (Luke 18:13), is literally, "God be propitious to me the sinner." Also, it is the incentive for our love for other Christians. "Herein is love, not that we loved God, but that he loved us, and sent his Son to be the propitiation for our sins. Beloved, if God so loved us, we ought also to love one another" (1 John 4:10-11).

The Last Adam

The apostle Paul taught that the human race consisted of two groups: those who were "in Adam" and those who were "in Christ." In presenting this contrast he used several comparative names of

Christ, including "the last Adam" (1 Cor. 15:45) and "the second man" (v. 47). These two related titles are fundamental to the doctrine of imputation, the means by which God reckons our sin to Christ and His righteousness to us.

When we speak of the headship of the race, we do so in two senses. First, Adam was the Federal Head of the race, and when he sinned, we sinned in the same sense as when our representative government takes a course of action and we who elected certain candidates as our leaders are involved in the decisions they make. Second, Adam was the Seminal Head of the race in that he was the physical father of the human race. When Adam sinned, he became a sinner by nature, a nature that we as Adam's descendants also received, much as the child of a mother who is a drug addict may be born with an addiction to that drug.

Christ as the Last Adam and the Second Man is the head of a new race in the same way Adam was the head of the old race. When Jesus died for us, He paid the price for our sin on our behalf much as a government might pay off its national debt, which is the debt also of those who elected that government. When Christ rose from the dead, He did so as a quickening, or life-giving, spirit, able and willing to impart new life to all who come to Him.

History and society are the result of two men and their respective acts. Adam, by disobedience, plunged this world into the slavery of sin. Jesus, by obedience, brought this world back to Himself. Because of what the first Adam did, we need to be saved. Because of what the Last Adam did, we may be saved. In order to be saved, we must be "in" the Last Adam.

Author of Eternal Salvation

Describing Jesus, the writer to the Hebrews notes, "He became the author of eternal salvation unto all them that obey him" (Heb. 5:9). The Greek word used here for salvation is *aitios*, denoting that which causes something else. Jesus is the "Author of Salvation" as one might be an author of a novel. The author knows all that is to be written before the book is published. He or she develops the plan of the book, its underlying thesis, the characters and the plot, or story line. And when the book is completed, it contains a part of the author, an investment of a part of his or her life.

When we speak of Jesus as "the Author of Eternal Salvation," this illustration is accurate only in part. Jesus is not merely the formal cause of salvation; He is the efficacious and active cause of it. Not only is salvation caused or effected by Christ, but also Christ is Salvation itself (see Luke 2:30; 3:6). Although an author may invest a part of himself or herself in a book, we cannot say that the book is the author. But Jesus is that of which He is the author. When the Scriptures reveal Him as the "Author of Eternal Salvation," they emphasize not only His ability to save but also His power to keep.

Closely related to this title of Christ are several titles that make use of the Greek word *archegos*, translated in Scripture as "prince," "author" and "captain." This is the key word in the titles "the Prince of life" (Acts 3:15), "a Prince and a Saviour" (5:31), "the captain of their salvation" (Heb. 2:10), and "the author and finisher of our faith" (12:2). The term signifies one who takes the lead in something or provides the first occasion of anything. In his English translation of the Scriptures, Moffat consistently translates this word "pioneer." Although translated "author" once in the New Testament, the word really stresses the quality of leadership; it does not necessarily mean that the cause originated with the leader. This is, of course, true of Christ as noted in the above title but not implied in the use of this related Greek word. The emphasis here is that of Christ's primacy. As the *aitios*, Jesus originates and provides eternal salvation for all who will come to Him. As the *archegos*, He leads us into that eternal salvation. In this way He is the Captain of Salvation, the Prince of Life, and the Pioneer (Author) of our Faith.

Mediator

Jesus is also called "the mediator" by the apostle Paul (1 Tim. 2:5; see also Heb. 8:6; 9:15; 12:24). In the first century this was both a legal and a commercial term. It differs from Christ's title as our "Advocate" in that the "Mediator" is impartial; He represents both parties equally. Only Jesus could be the mediator between God and man because only He is both God and man. The Greek word *mesites* literally means "a go-between" and is used in two ways in the New Testament. First, Jesus is the Mediator in that He mediates between God and people to effect a reconciliation (see 1 Tim. 2:5). Second, He is "the mediator of a better covenant" (Heb. 8:6), "of the new testament" (9:15), and "of the new covenant" (12:24) in the sense that He acts as a guarantor so as to secure that which . would otherwise be unobtainable.

CONCLUSION

No wonder the hymn writer exclaimed, "I will sing of my Redeemer"! The more we understand what the Bible describes as "so great salvation" (Heb. 2:3), the more we appreciate the salvational names of Jesus. Some of these names speak of Christ's work in saving us: He is "the Redeemer," "Savior" and "Mediator." Others speak of His Person in saving us: He is "the Lamb of God" and "the Propitiation for Our Sins." Still others mysteriously reveal the One who both produces and is our salvation: He is "the Last Adam," "the Second Man" and "the Author of Eternal Salvation." All our questions concerning our salvation are answered in Jesus' names.

But the meaning of His salvational names ought to be applied to our lives. He is the Propitiation for the sins of the whole world, but we may call Him "our own Propitiation" only when we have received by faith that payment for sin. He is our "Mediator" in the deepest sense when we believe on Him as Savior. Knowing the salvational names of Jesus carries with it a grave responsibility—that of being certain that we have obtained so great a salvation. And if we have, then knowing the salvational names of Jesus provides for us a tremendous privilege, for we can introduce others to the One who loves us and gave Himself for us.

FOR DISCUSSION

1. From what has Christ redeemed us? What was the payment or ransom?

2. Why was the name "Savior" neglected by the apostles? How can we avoid taking this title and work of Christ for granted?

3. How should we feel and act in response to Jesus' work as the Lamb of God?

4. When Christ is called the Propitiation, what does that mean He has accomplished? What influence should this have on our lives?

5. Why is Christ called the last Adam? Are you under the headship of the first or last Adam?

6. Give as many titles of Christ as possible that relate to our salvation. Discuss briefly what each title suggests about salvation.

6

The Birth Names of Christ

The LORD *himself shall give you a sign: Behold, a virgin shall conceive,*
and bear a son, and shall call his name Immanuel.
ISAIAH 7:14

Unto us a child is born, unto us a son is given: and the government shall
be upon his shoulder: and his name shall be called Wonderful, Counsellor,
The mighty God, The everlasting Father, The Prince of Peace.
ISAIAH 9:6

The virgin conception of Christ was prophesied many years before Jesus' birth in Bethlehem and, correctly understood and interpreted, is one of the foundational doctrines of Scripture. Genesis 3:15 is the first reference in Scripture to the coming of Christ; embryonically it anticipated the virgin birth by calling Jesus "the seed of the woman." The miracle of the virgin birth was not so much in the birth but rather in the supernatural conception of Jesus. There are five persons in Scripture with supernatural origins. Adam was created with neither male nor female parents. Eve's origin involved a man but no female. Isaac was born to parents both of whom were beyond the age at which they could physically produce children. John the Baptist was born to parents who were well into old age. But the greatest of the supernatural origins was that of Jesus, whose birth involved a virgin but no man.

As miraculous as the virgin birth of Jesus Christ was, the real significance of the event is that it marked the incarnation of Christ. In the words of John, "the Word was made flesh" (John 1:14). Even Isaiah, the prophet of the virgin birth, alluded to the Incarnation when he differentiated between a human child born and the divine Son given (see Isa. 9:6). The birth of Christ, celebrated each year at

Christmas, marks the time when Jesus emptied Himself to become a man. Though He always remained God, while on Earth the glory of Jesus was veiled, and He chose voluntarily to limit Himself in the independent use of His non-moral attributes.

One of the tasks of the parents of a newborn baby is to give that child a name. Usually the parents will spend several months discussing possible names that they may or may not choose. Often friends and relatives will suggest names that they think are suitable. I have often suggested that expectant parents consider naming a son Elmer, so far without success! The concern of many parents is to choose a name that expresses their aspirations for their child or that suggests by association a positive role model for the child. When that name is chosen, it has a special significance to the proud parents of the newborn baby.

Several of the names and titles of Jesus were given in the context of His birth. It is almost as though the prophets of God sought for the ideal name for the baby Jesus as they anticipated His coming to this world. In this chapter we propose to look at several of what may be called the "Birth Names of Jesus."

The Dayspring from on High

When Zacharias prophesied at the birth of his son John, he called his son "the prophet of the Highest" (Luke 1:76). But the emphasis of his prophecy focused upon the One whom he called "the dayspring from on high" (v. 78). It was to be characteristic of the life and ministry of John that he, "a burning and a shining light" (John 5:35), should seem dim in comparison to his cousin, who was the "light of the world" (8:6).

The word "Dayspring" is a translation of the Greek word *anatole*, literally meaning "a rising of light" or "sunrise." The place of the dayspring was the point along the eastern horizon at which the sun rose, a place that constantly changed with the passing seasons (see Job 38:12). By implication the term came to mean "the east"—that is, the direction of the sunrise (see Matt. 2:1). Zacharias used it metaphorically of Christ, the One through whom the true Light shone not only to Israel but to all the world.

But there is something unique about this particular sunrise. This dayspring originated "from on high" (*ex hupsos*). *Hupsos* refers not only to height but also to the idea of being raised to a high or exalted state (see Jas. 1:9). It closely relates to the adjective *hupsistos*, the word that describes John as the prophet "of the Highest" (Luke 1:76). The use of this particular term in this context implies that this was uniquely a divinely appointed or exalted sunrise. Perhaps the sun shone just a little brighter on the morning following the birth of the Dayspring from on High.

The appearance of the Dayspring from on High on the horizon of human history produced significant effects. Its shining exposes our sin. Its warmth revitalizes our hope in sorrow. And its light redirects our steps.

The Revelation of Our Sin

In speaking of the visitation of the Dayspring from on High, Zacharias suggested His purpose: "to give light to them that sit in darkness" (Luke 1:79). One of the effects of a natural sunrise is the illumination of an otherwise dark world. Someone has observed that the darkest hour of night comes just before the dawn. There is certainly a spiritual reality in the application of this truth. The Greek word *skotia* is used in the New Testament not only of physical darkness but also of the spiritual darkness of sin. Of the various Greek words that describe darkness, this word indicates the darkest. So the effect of sin in the life results in not a mere gloominess but in a blinding darkness in which any measure of illuminating light is absent. So dark is the darkness of sin that even sin itself is hidden by the darkness.

The cresting of the sun over the mountains along the eastern horizon first makes visible the shadows in the night and then that which the shadows hid in the night; so the appearance of the Dayspring from on High first produces the light of conviction in a soul darkened by sin and then floods the soul with gospel light so that we can understand spiritual truth (see 2 Cor. 4:4-6). When Jesus was challenged to pass sentence upon the woman caught in the act of adultery, He merely spoke the word that brought conviction to the conscience of each accuser (see John 8:9). In that passage John uses the verb *eleochomenoi*, translated "convicted" but literally meaning "to bring to light and expose." Just as one might hold a letter up to the light to expose its contents, so too Jesus exposed the sin of self-righteous people by His penetrating light.

Our Revitalization in Sorrow

There is yet another effect of the natural sunrise that finds a spiritual counterpart in the Dayspring from on High. The light and warmth of the early morning sun is that which revitalizes life on Earth. As the light of the sun rises on the eastern horizon, the flowers of the field once again turn and open to absorb the benefits it offers. The animals that hid from the darkness and dangers of the night begin to come out of the caves and hollow logs to enjoy the day. The people of primitive lands begin to remove the coverings that kept them warm in the night as the sunlight of a new day announces yet another opportunity to work while it is still light. It is therefore not without significance that Zacharias should note the shining of light to those who walked in "the shadow of death" (Luke 1:79).

Light was one of the great symbols of messianic prophecy. According to Isaiah, the messianic light was to shine brightest in Galilee of the Gentiles, upon people who walked in darkness (see Isa. 9:1-2). Often those who find themselves hiding in the shadows are the ones who benefit most from the light. Darkness aids the criminal in the successful accomplishment of a crime. For that reason people all over the world fear the night and eagerly await morning. The pilgrims of Israel understood the significance of the coming morning and the greater significance of their coming Lord. As they sang their hymns of worship, they testified, "My soul waiteth for the Lord more than they that watch for the morning: I say, more than they that watch for the morning" (Ps. 130:6).

In our sorrow, pain and hurt, the Dayspring from on High shines His revitalizing light and warmth. How often has the discouraged Christian, groping in the shadows of even death itself, found in that heavenly sunrise the source of strength he or she needs to continue? How encouraging the thought that in our constant struggle with the darkness of this world, the Dayspring from on High shines a light that the darkness cannot hide. French theologian Frederic Godet used to think of the Dayspring in the context of an eastern caravan that had lost its way in the night but, while sitting down and expecting death, soon noticed a star begin to rise over the horizon, providing the light that would lead them to the place of safety. Unquestionably, there are and will be many times in life when, like those discouraged traders, the believer would resign to defeat but for the appearance of the morning light from heaven.

The Redirection of Our Steps

A third benefit of the appearance of the Dayspring from on High is the redirection of our steps, "to guide our feet into the way of peace" (Luke 1:79). The implication is that the light of the sunrise enables us to see how to walk a straight path that leads to "the way of peace." "A man's heart deviseth his way: but the LORD directeth his steps" (Prov. 16:9). That our steps often need redirection is self-evident to any and all who have attempted to live the Christian life. The Word of God is the instrument that God uses to give direction in our lives (see Ps. 119:105). As we continue to walk by faith in the Christian life, we come to know experientially not only "the peace of God, which passes all understanding" (Phil. 4:7) but also "the God of peace" (v. 9) Himself.

The Redemption of Our Souls

The priority in the life of John the Baptist was "to give knowledge of salvation unto his people by the remission of their sins" (Luke 1:77). But that was possible only because of the visitation of the Dayspring "through the tender mercy of our God" (Luke 1:78). "The tender mercy of our God" is literally "the mercy of the bowels or heart of God," meaning that mercy that springs from the innermost seat of His self-existence. In that mercy the benefits of our individual and corporate redemption are found. Zacharias is concerned both with the national deliverance of Israel (see Luke 1:68-75) and the personal salvation of those who come to Christ by faith (see 1:76-79). Both of these aspects of salvation will materialize by a visitation from the Dayspring.

The Scriptures view a visitation of God either positively or negatively. When God visits a people in His wrath, it is a time of great and severe judgment. When God visits a people in His mercy, it is a time of salvation. Like the psalmist's, our prayer must be, "O visit me with thy salvation" (Ps. 106:4).

How penetrating is the light of that brilliant heavenly sunrise! It reaches into the darkest areas of our life, revealing our sin. When convicted of sin by that light, we begin to understand its horror and the inevitable penalty of it—death itself. But that is also the light that revitalizes us in our sorrow. If we were to respond to that light while we remain in our darkness, we would no doubt stumble and fall or miss the narrow way altogether, and so it is the same sunrise that provides the light to redirect our steps. The ultimate effect of that light is the redemption of our souls. Understanding and experiencing these few benefits of the Dayspring from on High will cause our hearts to praise and worship the God who granted to us this merciful visitation.

Immanuel (Emmanuel)

When God gave the faithless Ahaz an opportunity to ask Him for a sign to encourage his faith, he was so apathetic to the things of God as to refuse to accept the gracious offer. But the purpose of God would not be defeated. Ahaz was given a sign that he would not behold because he chose not to ask for a sign that God had offered to him. "Behold, a virgin shall conceive, and bear a son, and shall call his name Immanuel" (Isa. 7:14). That unusual name for a son captured the highest of ideals in the religious life of the pious Jew. It was an affirmation of the highest of blessings: "God with us."

Whenever God called a person or group to a seemingly impossible challenge, He reminded them of His all-sufficient promise, "Certainly I will be with thee." Moses was to deliver Israel from Egypt, but God was with him (see Exod. 3:12). Joshua was to conquer the Promised Land, but God was with him (see Josh. 1:5). Throughout Israel's history, every effective judge and king owed his success to the fact that "the LORD was with him" (1 Sam. 3:19;

18:12; 2 Kings 18:7; 1 Chron. 9:20). When Nebuchadnezzar looked into the fire, expecting to see the flames consuming the physical remains of three faithful Hebrews, he saw them surviving the flames, and the Lord was with them. When the remnant returned to rebuild the temple, they were motivated to action by the prophet's reminder, "I am with you, saith the LORD" (Hag. 1:13).

In contrast to the Old Testament promise of the presence of God, the absence or withdrawal of this presence, when noted, is a foreboding warning of disasters to come. Cain went out from the presence of the Lord to found a society so degenerate that God eventually had to destroy it with a flood. Samson woke in the lap of Delilah, not knowing that the Spirit of the Lord had departed from him, and he was captured by the Philistines. Because of his constant disobedience to the revealed will of God, Saul lost his unique relationship with the Holy Spirit, and God replaced His Spirit that had come on Saul with an evil spirit.

But in the New Testament, that relationship between God and humanity changed and intensified. The Christian now has an unprecedented relationship with God in Christ. In this regard the name "Immanuel" ("Emmanuel") signifies something special in the Christian's life.

First, it is an incarnational name. "The Word was made flesh, and dwelt among us" (John. 1:14); in a unique way in human history, the name was "God with us." Second, it is a dispensational name. The "in Christ" and "Christ in you" relationship is unique to this present dispensation of grace.

The Effect of Immanuel

In every art and industry of mankind, Christians have found a place in which their relationship with Christ can be both enjoyed and expressed. The presence of God is effective, first, in producing a deeper communion with Christ. The Christian life may be summarized theologically in two areas of experience—the point of salvation and the process of sanctification. Before salvation Christ is present knocking at the door of our lives (see Rev. 3:20) and waiting to be received (see John 1:12). In sanctification

Christ is present dwelling within (see John 14:23) and continuously completing the work He began at our conversion (see Phil. 1:6).

The "God with us" relationship is effective secondly in securing a definite conquest over evil with Christ. The Christian is engaged in a spiritual warfare that cannot be waged, much less won, without Immanuel, the presence of God with us. As Joshua prepared to conquer the Promised Land, a type of Christian experience, he was first assured of the presence of God with him (see Josh. 1:5). In describing Joseph being tempted unsuccessfully by Potiphar's wife, the Scripture is both prefaced and concluded with the remark, "The LORD was with Joseph" (Gen. 39:2,21). We are victorious in Christ because Christ is in us working (see Phil. 2:13) and we are in Christ winning (see Rom. 8:37).

Third, a deep consolation in Christ flows from the Immanuel promise. Scripture gives the promise of the presence of God as an assurance to the perplexed (see Gen. 28:15), an encouragement for the servant (see Exod. 3:12), a fortification for the timid (see Jer. 1:8), a confidence for the teacher (see Matt. 28:20), a rest for the pilgrim (see Exod. 33:14), and a strength for the fearful (see Heb. 13:5-6).

The Experience of Immanuel

There is an important distinction between the believer's union with Christ (which exists as a result of the baptism of the Holy Spirit and Christ's work on the cross, both applied at salvation) and the believer's communion with Christ, by which he or she experiences and enjoys the results of that union. We enjoy the benefits of the name "Immanuel"—"God with us"—as we respond in obedience to the multifaceted call of Christ in our lives. The first aspect of the call is the call to salvation. Throughout the New Testament this call has a universal appeal; for God "will have all men to be saved, and to come unto the knowledge of the truth" (1 Tim. 2:4) and therefore "now commandeth all men every where to repent" (Acts 17:30; see also 2 Pet. 3:9).

Second, there is a call to sanctification. By sanctification God sets us apart to holiness. It involves all three aspects of biblical separation (see 1 Thess. 1:9): First, we are separated to God. Further, we are separated from sin. Finally, we are separated to service. Christ is present with us both in our personal sanctification (see John 17:16-23) and in our corporate sanctification as a body of believers (see Matt. 18:20).

We are also workmen together with Christ (see 1 Cor. 3:9). God has a specific call to service for every believer. Not every believer has the same calling, but each has the same responsibility to serve in the place of his or her calling. Scripture describes three aspects of the call. Concerning its source it is a "heavenly calling" (Heb. 3:1). Concerning its character it is a "holy calling" (2 Tim. 1:9). Concerning its challenge it is a call to excellence, or a "high calling" (Phil. 3:14).

A final aspect of the call of God is one that most believers prefer to minimize—the call to suffering. Suffering is a very real part of the experience of the Christian life (see 1 Pet. 2:19-21). There are two extreme positions to be avoided in this area of the Christian life. First, some run from any and all opposition and hardship and, in doing so, often hinder the testimony of Christ and fail to learn what God is trying to teach them in their suffering. A second group seems committed to multiplying their sorrows to the same effect of hindering the testimony of Christ and at times even resisting the will of God when God wants to bless them. Note the five areas of suffering in the Christian life in which Immanuel becomes particularly meaningful: infirmities, reproaches, necessities, persecutions and distresses (see 2 Cor. 12:10).

Wonderful

Another of the birth names of Christ is "Wonderful." This title was first used in an appearance of the angel of the Lord to the mother of Samson (see Judg. 13:8-22) and later was one of the five titles Isaiah ascribed to the child born and the son given (see Isa. 9:6). Although many contemporary writers tend to view this Isaiah list as four compound names, the first being "Wonderful Counselor," the Hebrew word used by the prophet is a noun and not an adjective. Also, the names "Wonderful" and "Counselor" both appear independently elsewhere in Scripture as names of Christ.

A Definition of His Wonder

This word "wonderful" is used in three different senses in the Old Testament. First, a wonder is something marvelous or spectacular. The expression "signs and wonders" is a common Old Testament designation of the miraculous. The New Testament reserves this designation for miracles of the most incredible variety. They were the kinds of miracles that left the witness with a feeling of wonder (see Matt. 15:31; Mark. 6:51; Luke 4:22).

A second aspect of this word "wonder" is something mysterious or secret. F. C. Jennings has commented on this name of Christ: "It both expresses and hides the incomprehensible." In this way the name is closely related to the "name written, that no man knew, but he himself" (Rev. 19:12). Even when this name has been thoroughly studied, an element of mystery will still remain about all that it represents in Jesus.

Third, that which is wonderful is separated from the common and belongs to the majestic. It falls in a class all by itself far above the common or ordinary. Charles Haddon Spurgeon suggested, "His name shall be called the separated One, the distinguished One, the noble One, set apart from the common race of mankind."

A Recognition of His Wonder

Jesus is called Wonderful because He is wonderful. He is wonderful, first, in His identity. Theologians today can analyze the nature of the *kenosis*, the Incarnation, and the hypostatic union of two natures, but after all is said and done, a deep mystery about Christ's Person remains.

He is wonderful, further, in His industry. Whether in His work of creation or His work of redemption, all that Jesus did to accomplish His work was wonderful in the sense that the observer of the act or the finished work feels overwhelmed with a sense of wonder. Christ was wonderful in His ministry to the extent that the multitudes marveled at the content of His message and the authority of His delivery.

Finally, He was wonderful in His destiny. Born in a barn on the backside of Bethlehem, the legal son of a humble carpenter, His closest associates a group of former fishermen, patriots and traitors to their country's ideals, His humiliating death between two thieves and His hometown reputed to be "the city of garbage," this Jesus of Nazareth is destined someday to be declared the King of kings and Lord of lords.

A Response to His Wonder

Charles Haddon Spurgeon once announced to the great crowds who came to hear him preach, "Beloved, there are a thousand things in this world that are called by names that do not belong to them; but in entering upon my text, I must announce at the very opening, that Christ is called Wonderful, because He is so." How do we respond to that wonder?

First, we respond to Christ's wonder with adoration. Jesus ought to be the object of our grateful adoration and worship. Leafing through the pages of an average hymnbook will suggest dozens of suitable expressions of our adoration for Christ.

Second, Jesus ought to be the object of our wholehearted devotion. He alone ought to be the object of our deepest and warmest affections. The great commandment of the Law was to love the LORD supremely with one's total being. That also is a valid responsibility of the Christian today.

Finally, we should respond to Jesus' wonder by entering into a deeper communion with the One who is called Wonderful. The shallow experience of many Christians today is a sad commentary on their interest in the One who loves them and gave Himself for them. If Jesus is Wonderful, and He is, we should long to spend time with Him in Bible study and prayer and to enjoy sweet fellowship with Christ in all that we do.

Counselor

Another of the birth names of Jesus is "Counselor." The world was brought to ruin by the counsel of the serpent in the Garden of Eden. That ruined race can be restored only by another Counselor who advises men in the counsel of God. If Satan is the counselor of ruin, Jesus is the Counselor of restoration.

The significance of this name of Christ is clear in Scripture by the fact that Christ Himself needs no counsel (see Rom. 11:33-34);

He is described as the fount of all wisdom and understanding (see Prov. 8:14) and is presented as imparting counsel to those who seek it (see Ps. 16:7; 73:24; Isa. 25:1; 28:29). As we study the Scriptures, the qualifications of this Counselor and the quality of His counsel become increasingly obvious. But only when we discern and apply His counsel to our life does He become our Counselor.

The Qualification of the Counselor

Most contemporary Christian counselors today affirm that there are three basic qualifications of a biblical and effective counselor. Based upon passages such as Romans 15:14 and Colossians 3:16, they argue that the Christian counselor must be characterized by a knowledge of the meaning of Scripture as it applies to their personal life, by a goodness or empathetic concern for others and by enthusiasm for life and wisdom—that is, the skillful use of Scripture in ministry to others for the glory of God.

If this is what Scripture requires of a counselor, then obviously Christ excels in each and every prerequisite. One of His relative divine attributes is omniscience, the fullness of all knowledge. As God, He alone is truly good. He is also the personification of the wisdom of God. He is the Counselor *par excellence*, for He is the only One who fully meets the qualifications of a counselor.

The Character of His Counsel

Isaiah described the nature or character of Christ's counsel with the words "wonderful in counsel" (Isa. 28:29). A survey of the biblical references to the counsel of the LORD indicates five aspects of its character.

First, the counsel of Christ sets controls. It controls in the sense that it guides the steps of the believer (see Ps. 73:24) and establishes him or her in that which continues (see Prov. 11:14; 15:22; 19:21; 20:18).

Second, the counsel of Christ is creative. It is interesting to note how often the concept of creation stands in close proximity to a reference to the Counselor (see Isa. 40:12-14,26; Rom. 11:34,36). This is an important principle for us to remember. Just because the will of God for someone else in similar circumstances requires a certain course of action does not mean that it is God's will for everyone in that same situation. We must learn to let God be God and allow Him to be creative in His counsel.

Also, the counsel of the LORD comforts: "Ointment and perfume rejoice the heart: so doth the sweetness of a man's friend by hearty counsel" (Prov. 27:9). Jesus in His role as Counselor is one of the implications of the name *Paraclete*, which the New Testament applies to Him as well as to the Holy Spirit ("Advocate," see 1 John 2:1). In both cases one of the functions of this One called alongside to help is to encourage the discouraged and comfort the sorrowing.

Fourth, the counsel of Christ is confidential. This is implied by the Greek word *sumboulos*, used by the Septuagint translators and New Testament writers (see Prov. 24:6; Isa. 9:6; Rom. 11:34). The term literally means "a confidential advisor." When we seek counsel from the LORD concerning an opportunity or a problem, the resulting counsel is confidential, and we do not have to worry about later hearing the subject by the grapevine.

Finally, the counsel of the LORD is corporate. In counseling the Laodicean church to anoint their eyes and improve their vision, Jesus used the Greek verb *sumbouleuo*, meaning "to give advice jointly." The Father as the God of all comfort and the Holy Spirit as the Comforter are the other advisors of the believer. David also called the Scripture his counselor, for it is the instrument that this Trinity of counselors uses to communicate to us the counsel of God.

The Discerning of His Counsel

How can we discern the counsel of Christ in our lives? Among the many principles of Scripture for discerning the will of God, five stand out predominantly. First, the counsel of God is revealed in the Scriptures (see 2 Tim. 3:16-17). Second, this counsel often comes through prayer (see Judg. 20:18,23; 1 Sam. 14:37). Third, we discern it from the help of wise counselors (see Prov. 11:14; 12:15; 24:6). Fourth, we recognize it through circumstances. Eliezer was aware of the Lord's leading in his life, and circumstances confirmed that God was indeed guiding him (see Gen. 15:2; 24:27). Finally, the Holy Spirit reaffirms it. Paul sought to go several places to preach the gospel that were not places God wanted him to go. Because he was sensitive to the leading of the Spirit, he could discern closed doors and had a deep assurance that he was doing what God wanted him to do when the doors finally opened (see Acts 16:6-10).

The Mighty God

Isaiah also called Jesus *El Gibbor*, "The Mighty God" (Isa. 9:6). Although Jesus "emptied himself" (*NASB*), or "made Himself of no reputation" (Phil. 2:7), to become a man, Jesus never abandoned His divine attributes. Is it not paradoxical that the Mighty God should clothe Himself as a newborn child? If there is any question about Isaiah's view of this coming child, clearly here he indicates that He is God incarnate.

Scripture used the Hebrew word *gibbor*, translated "mighty," not only of God but also of the "mighty men" who were soldiers of Israel distinguished in battle. It conveys the idea of exceptional physical strength and prowess. When used of God in the Old Testament, it expressed the assurance that God would defend Israel from her enemies (see Pss. 24:8; 45:3). It emphasizes the relative attribute of omnipotence and suggests that God will use that power on behalf of His people.

The Everlasting Father

Jesus is also called "the Everlasting Father," or, more literally, "Father of Eternity." This is the most emphatic assertion of His deity offered by the prophet Isaiah. This title of Christ has caused some confusion among Christians in trying to understand the mystery of the Trinity. Jesus is not here called the Father in the way that God the Father is the Father. He is a distinct Person of the Trinity. The Persons of the Trinity are equal in nature but distinguishable in Person and distinct in duties.

The title "Father" is used here of Christ in the sense of a "founding father." People will talk about the founding fathers of a country or movement, meaning those persons who were the pioneers of an idea and who gave birth to the movement or nation. In this sense Jesus is the founding father of eternity, existing before it began and giving birth to time and history.

The Prince of Peace

Isaiah also calls Jesus "the Prince of Peace." He is a Prince now and will ultimately be recognized not only as a king but as the King of kings (see Rev. 19:16). As the Prince of Peace, Jesus can meet the deepest need in the human heart—that of peace with God, with ourselves and with others round about us. Peace with God is a result of our justification and based on Christ's shed blood at the Cross (see Rom. 5:1; Eph. 2:13; Col. 1:20). Jesus is both "the God of peace" (Phil. 4:9) and *Jehovah Shalom* (see Judg. 6:24).

Notice how these five names suggested by Isaiah relate to the ministry of Christ. He was Wonderful in life as He performed various signs and wonders to demonstrate who He was. He was our Counselor by example and teaching, and He perpetuated His counsel by giving us the New Testament. In His resurrection He demonstrated Himself to be the Mighty God. He ascended into glory as our Everlasting Father, and when He returns, He will do so as the Prince of Peace.

CONCLUSION

When parents choose a name for their child, they often strive to select one that expresses their hopes for what the child will be someday. Parents name children after people they admire and respect. When God inspired His prophets to select names for the Christ Child, He had the advantage of omniscience. His names not only expressed desire but also affirmed the very nature and character of the Child. Jesus is the Dayspring from on High, Immanuel, Wonderful, Counselor, the Mighty God, the Everlasting Father and the Prince of Peace. Have you acknowledged Him to be each of these in your life?

FOR DISCUSSION

1. Of all the individuals in Scripture with supernatural births, why is the birth of Christ the greatest?
2. How is Christ our Dayspring?

3. How should the name and work of Christ as Immanuel affect our daily lives?
4. Name several ways in which Christians may express their worship of our Wonderful Christ.
5. How and when does Christ counsel the believer?
6. Is Jesus the Prince of Peace today, or is this a future event?

7

The Service Names of Christ

*The Son of man came not to be ministered unto, but to minister,
and to give his life a ransom for many.*
MATTHEW 20:28; MARK 10:45

Jesus described His ministry here on Earth in terms of ministry to others. Although there were times when He was entertained by friends and when others provided for His physical necessities, His primary concern was what He could do for others. Wherever He was, He found needs and met them. The crowds followed Him not so much for His dynamic charisma as for what He did for them. They came for healing, to have demons cast out, or to be fed with loaves and fish. Their motives were often less than noble. Jesus met needs in lives, and some people chose to follow Him. Jesus was primarily a minister to others.

When He ascended to heaven, Jesus continued to be a minister to others. Even today He is primarily interested in meeting the needs of others. Every name of Jesus represents His ability to meet a particular need in someone's life. Sometimes I have asked, "What is the greatest name of Jesus in the Scripture?" Actually, there is no standard answer to that question. The greatest name is the name that meets the greatest need we feel. For some that name is "Jesus," the name that relates so closely to salvation. To others it is "Christ," the name that relates so closely to victorious Christian living. Someone who is often discouraged might think of the name "Comforter" or "Consolation" as the greatest of His names.

Although every name of Jesus ministers to human needs, some names more characteristically describe Jesus in His role as minister. These names I call the service names of Jesus. There are many such names in Scripture because His range of ministry is so wide. Our objective in this chapter is to examine only a few of the more prominent service names of Jesus.

When we think of the service names of Jesus, the subject of where Jesus is necessarily arises. Obviously Jesus can serve only in the place where He is. There are actually five aspects to the presence of Christ in Scripture. First, He is omnipresent. This means that as God, He is at all times in every place wholly present. Then there is a localized presence of Jesus, such as when Stephen saw Jesus standing to greet him as he was being condemned and stoned (see Acts 7:55). We also speak of the indwelling presence of Jesus; Christ lives within the believer (see Col. 1:27). A fourth presence of Jesus is the institutionalized presence of Christ. There is a sense in which Christ dwells in the midst of the Church (see Eph. 1:22-23). Finally, Christ the incarnate Word dwells in the Scriptures, the inspired Word; and the Scriptures are therefore identified as the Word of Christ (see Col. 3:16).

The Creative Names of Jesus

When we think of the service names of Jesus, we must begin with those titles that relate to His creation and sustenance of this world. In this regard Jesus is both the Creator and Sustainer of the world and of all life therein. The prominent references to Christ in two key Christological passages particularly emphasize this fact.

The first of these is John 1, in which Jesus is introduced as the *Logos*. John affirmed, "All things were made by him; and without him was not any thing made that was made" (John. 1:3). In discussing the creative work of Jesus, John uses the verb *egento*, meaning "generated" or "energized." Jesus created by producing life and energy from nothing. The verse following argues, "In him was life; and the life was the light of men" (v. 4). Jesus is life.

The second key passage is Colossians 1:15-22. Perhaps no other statement concerning Jesus Christ is as magnificent as this one. Although Jesus is never mentioned by name in this passage, no fewer than 15 pronouns are used with reference to Christ. Note several of them:

For by *him* were all things created, that are in heaven, and that are in earth, visible and invisible, whether they be thrones, or dominions, or principalities, or powers: all things were created by *him*, and for *him*: and he is before all things, and by *him* all things consist (Col. 1:16-17, emphasis added).

These verses identify Christ as both the Creator and the Sustainer of life. The terms "thrones," "dominions," "principalities" and "powers" are generally considered to refer to various rankings of angels. Christ created them all and came before them all. Here Paul is portraying Christ as more than a super-angel, probably in an effort to correct a false teaching in the Early Church.

The word "consist" (v. 17) literally means "to hold together." This is similar to John's portrayal of Jesus as life. Energy is the glue that holds this universe and all its component parts together. God is the source of energy because life begets energy. Scientists have discovered an incredible amount of energy in every atom, but God is the source of that energy. When viewing this aspect of the nature of God, we must be careful not to go to the extreme of Spinoza, who defined energy as his god. Although God is the source of energy, we must not think of Him as energy itself.

The Instructive Names of Jesus

Several names of Jesus in the New Testament emphasize His role as a teacher. It is interesting that the Scriptures never call Jesus a preacher (although that may be implied by the title "Prophet"), but at least four terms are used to distinguish Him as a teacher. Each of these terms differs slightly in meaning, and together they give a more complete picture of both the nature and emphasis of Jesus' teaching ministry.

Rabbi

The word *rabbi* is an Aramaic word that the writers of the New Testament transliterated into the Greek. In many cases translators have done the same, bringing the word over into the English language letter for letter. This term was a common one with which to address a religious teacher in the first century and was first used to address Jesus by two of His first disciples (see John 1:38). In that passage John explains to his Greek readers that the title was equivalent in meaning to "master" (*kurios*), a common Greek reference to a philosopher or teacher.

The Aramaic word literally means "my great one" and represented the great respect the Jews had for their rabbis. The title included not only the idea of teaching but also a certain content in their teaching. It was used much in the way that we today speak of a charismatic teacher or a deeper-life teacher. When people addressed Jesus as "Rabbi," they were normally discerning the nature or content of His teaching.

Rabboni

The title *Rabboni* is used only on two occasions to refer to Jesus. It was first used by blind Bartimaeus in his request for sight (see Mark 10:51, *NKJV*). Later Mary Magdalene used it upon her recognition of the resurrected Christ. On both occasions it was used by people who had a deep sense of loyalty to or affection for Christ because of a major miracle that He had performed in their behalf. It is an intensified form of the title "Rabbi" and might be translated "My Rabbi." When Mary used it on that resurrection morning, she no doubt spoke it with deepest love for and commitment to the One who was not just another teacher but the One she would claim to be her own (see John 20:16).

Didaskalos

A third instructive name for Jesus is the Greek word *didaskalos*, usually translated "teacher" or "master." This is the title that Nicodemus used when he addressed Jesus as "a teacher come from God" (John 3:2). It was characteristic of Jesus' ministry that the crowds who heard Him teach were astonished at His doctrine or teaching (see Matt. 7:28-29; Mark 1:22,27).

Although it is popular today to speak of the sermons of Jesus, it would probably be more correct to consider His talks as His adult Bible-class lessons, because they refer to Jesus' teaching rather than preaching. Six major blocks of Jesus' teaching are recorded in Matthew, including the Sermon on the Mount (see Matt. 5-7), His instructions to His apostles before sending them out (see Matt. 10), His parables on the kingdom of heaven (see Matt. 13), His teaching on greatness in the church (see Matt. 18), His sermon in the Temple on the day of testing (see Matt. 21-23), and the Olivet discourse concerning things to come (see Matt. 24-25). John includes an additional account of a teaching session of Jesus, the Upper Room discourse (see John 13-16), and several detailed accounts of other lessons. Luke also emphasizes the teaching ministry of Jesus, particularly in recording the various parables that He taught.

The teaching of Jesus was unique in both content and style. He taught not the tradition of men, as was common in His day, but the Word of God. Like the prophets of old, He spoke on behalf of God; but unlike those who prefaced their most authoritative appeals with the remark "Thus saith the Lord," Jesus was unique for His comment "I say unto you." He differed from the scribes, the usual teachers of the Law, not only in content but also in His style of teaching. When a scribe taught the Law, he announced his text and proceeded to recite all the various opinions of other respected teachers of the Law. Only then did he conclude by announcing the consensus of scholarship on the subject. But Jesus spoke authoritatively with little or no appeal to the usual authorities.

Kathegetes

A final name of Jesus that alludes to His teaching ministry is the term *kathegetes*, meaning "guide." It is used only on one occasion in the New Testament, where Jesus urged His disciples, "Neither be ye called masters: for one is your Master, even Christ" (Matt. 23:10). Here this term is twice translated "master" in the *King James Version*, but other translators have used words such as "leader," "teacher" or "instructor" to convey the meaning of this word. It differs from the other words for "teacher" in Scripture in that it conveys the image of a teacher who influences or guides a student not only intellectually but also morally. Jesus is unique among teachers in that He alone can teach the truth and lead us most fully in the way of truth.

The Sovereign Names of Jesus

Several different names of Jesus are translated with the English word "master," including most of the instructive names of Jesus cited above. But at least three titles of Christ include in their meaning the idea of mastery over someone or something. These too are service names of Christ, for they demonstrate Jesus' power and authority over others, and therefore they evince His ability to serve.

Epistates

Luke alone uses the Greek word *epistates*; he uses it six times of Christ (see Luke 5:5; 8:24,45; 9:33,49; 17:13). It is a strong term, meaning "chief," "commander," "leader" or "overseer." It relates closely to the word translated "bishop" in the *King James Version*, which is a title of the pastor in a church (see 1 Tim. 3:1). It designates the absolute authority of the one so addressed and would ordinarily be considered an honorable title. It was apparently never used except by a disciple and in every case occurs within a context in which the speaker's view of Jesus is somewhat defective. It is always followed by the user being rebuked for his action or conclusion or the user experiencing something that causes him to grow in his understanding of who Jesus is.

Oikodespotes

Jesus used the term *oikodespotes* to refer to Himself in several of His parables. It is translated "master of the house" (Matt. 10:25; Luke 13:25; 14:21), "goodman of the house" (Matt. 20:11; 24:43; Mark 14:14; Luke 12:39), and "householder" (Matt. 13:27,52; 20:1; 21:33). This was the usual title for the master over the household stewards. It emphasizes the absolute control of that master over those stewards. Jesus used this title in two contexts. First, He was Master over His disciples, who are stewards of the mysteries of God. Second, in those eschatological parables in which Jesus used this term in the context of His return, He is Master over all mankind.

By this title, Jesus claimed absolute authority over men and women both in this life and in that to come.

Despotes

Only once is Jesus referred to by the term *despotes* and that by Peter in his second epistle (see 2 Pet. 2:1), where the *King James Version* reads "Lord." Vine suggests that this word refers to "one who has absolute ownership and uncontrolled power." It is perhaps the strongest title of Christ that argues for His Lordship. It was commonly used in Greek to refer to a master who exercised a rigid authority over his slaves and is the root of its English derivative, "despot," referring to any ruler having absolute control, particularly a tyrant or oppressive leader. The negative connotation—abuse of power—is not necessarily implied when this term is used of Christ but rather only the absolute nature of His authority.

The Assistance Names of Jesus

Some of the service names of Jesus can best be described as assistance names, for their primary emphasis points out how Jesus assists the believer in living the Christian life. The Christian life has been explained as Christ living in and through the Christian (see Gal. 2:20). Because this is true, every one of the more than 800 names and titles of Jesus, in a sense, is an assistance name. But the names considered in this section more properly belong here because of the more direct role the LORD plays in our Christian life as implied in these names.

The Intercessor

Jesus is our Intercessor; one of His primary works on behalf of the Christian today is that of intercession. The writer to the Hebrews noted, "Wherefore he is able also to save them to the uttermost that come unto God by him, seeing he ever liveth to make intercession for them" (Heb. 7:25). This is one of the two primary functions of Christ as our High Priest.

The need for an intercessor has long been felt by man. In the midst of his despair, Job cried out, "O that one might plead for a

man with God, as a man pleadeth for his neighbour!" (Job 16:21).
He realized man's greatest need was someone who could stand
before a holy God on behalf of a sinful human race and pray effectively for that race. That is why he earlier lamented, "Neither
is there any daysman betwixt us, that might lay his hand upon us
both" (Job 9:33). That missing Daysman was the One whom Paul
in the New Testament called the "mediator" (1 Tim. 2:5).

The twofold purpose of our Intercessor's prayer on our behalf
is to keep us from sinning and, in so doing, to save us to the uttermost. Of the two primary ministries of Christ as our High Priest,
this is concerned most with preventing problems in the Christian
life. Our Intercessor is known for what He does; He pleads that
we might not sin.

The Advocate

The second of Jesus' ministries as a High Priest is advocacy. Jesus
is called "an advocate with the Father" (1 John 2:1), meaning that
He stands before God on our behalf. As Intercessor, Jesus pleads
that we might not sin. As Advocate, He stands by us after we have
willfully sinned. John uses the Greek word *paraclete*, meaning "one
called alongside to help." This is also a name of the Holy Spirit,
translated in another place "Comforter" (John 16:7). The duty of
an advocate is to stand by the person and/or the principles that
he or she supports.

One legal phrase used today to describe an advocate is "a
friend of the court." Years ago when I had to go to court over a
traffic accident, my insurance company supplied a lawyer who
acted on my behalf. Throughout the course of the case, the lawyer spoke on my behalf to ensure that the court heard my side of
the traffic accident. Although I did not speak in the courtroom
myself, my case was heard and won because of the efforts of my
advocate, the lawyer.

Similarly, Jesus acts as our Advocate before the Father in heav-
en when the devil accuses us of sin. Jesus is "the Man in the glory,"
a priest after the order of Melchizedek, who is both qualified and
capable to represent our cause in the court of heaven. He does not
actually have to plead our case every time we sin. His constant

presence before the Father is the sufficient plea for our failings. His defense rests upon His work that He accomplished at Calvary on our behalf.

Because both Intercessor and Advocate are aspects of Christ's work as High Priest, the qualifications for both tasks are the qualifications for the priesthood. To be a priest one needed the right birth, right calling and right qualifications. Jesus qualifies to be our High Priest and therefore both our Intercessor and Advocate, because, after the order of Melchizedek, He was called of God to be our High Priest and was anointed of the Holy Spirit just as priests were anointed with oil to begin their priestly ministry. The Man in the glory (see Heb. 6:19-20; 7:24) is not only our High Priest but also our Intercessor and Advocate.

The Propitiation for Our Sins

A third of the assistance names of Jesus is "the propitiation for our sins" (1 John 2:2). The Greek word *hilaskomai* means "a satisfaction." It was used by pagan Greeks to describe sacrifices to their gods that were offered as an appeasement to their wrath. In the Scriptures this word is never used in connection with any act of humanity that might appease the wrath of God; rather, God is propitiated by the vicarious and expiatory sacrifice of Christ. In the sacrifice of Christ on the cross, the holy and righteous character of God was vindicated, making it possible for God to be a just God and at the same time to forgive sin. Jesus not only accomplished the task of propitiating the Father but also was Himself the propitiation, or satisfaction, by which God was propitiated.

John describes Jesus as the propitiation for our sins (plural). Earlier in this epistle he used the singular form of the noun "sin" (see 1 John 1:7-8). When the word "sin" appears as a singular noun in this epistle, the apostle is speaking of the sinful nature of people. When the noun is plural, John is speaking of the practice of sin. Jesus not only "cleanseth us from all sin" (v. 7) but also forgives us our sins (see v. 9). He is the sufficient payment, or propitiation, for the sins we commit—past, present and future—and not only for our sins "but also for the sins of the whole world"

(2:2). The death of Christ was sufficient to save anyone, regardless of his or her history of sin.

The Indweller

Although the title "Indweller" is not found in Scripture, this name for Jesus is biblical in spirit. The names of Jesus reflect the actions of Jesus, and these acts include indwelling the believer. Many Christians realize that the Holy Spirit indwells them but do not know that Jesus Himself also lives within. Jesus promised to manifest Himself to His disciples and later explained, "If a man love me, he will keep my words: and my Father will love him, and we will come unto him, and make our abode with him" (John 14:23).

The conscious recognition of Christ's indwelling the believer is sometimes called communion with Christ or the deeper Christian life. The condition that the believer must keep in order to enjoy this communion is a deep love for Christ that evidences itself in a willing obedience to do the commands of Christ. We cannot claim to have this kind of love for Christ while we rebelliously resist the lordship of Christ. Our obedience to the Scriptures is born not out of a legalistic spirit or a fear of the consequences of not obeying but rather out of an inner desire to please the One we love.

John uses an interesting word to describe the Father and Son making Their abode within the believer. The word *monai*, translated "abode" in John 14:23, occurs only one other time in Scripture, and there it is translated "mansions" (John 14:2). Obviously, John's use of the word here is significant. While Jesus is in heaven preparing our mansion, we here on Earth are providing Him a mansion. If the LORD were to prepare us a mansion similar to the mansion we are preparing for Him, what would our mansion in heaven be like? When we understand that Jesus is not only in heaven but also living within us, that in itself should be an incentive to holy living.

CONCLUSION

Jesus came not to be served but to serve. In many ways He is still serving us today. When we learn the service names of Jesus, our appreciation of and love for Him increase. But an understanding of the service names of Jesus does more for us than merely increase our love for the Lord. Jesus said, "It is enough for the disciple that he be as his master" (Matt. 10:25). Since Jesus is by name and nature a minister to the needs of others, so we too, as His disciples, minister to others in His name.

FOR DISCUSSION

1. The service names of Christ that relate to His act of creation are "Creator" and "Sustainer." Discuss each of these roles.
2. What are Christ's instructive names? What can we learn about Christ from each?
3. The sovereign names of Christ describe His role in giving direction to the believer. What can we learn about Christ from each of these names?
4. The assistance names of Christ reveal how Christ supports and helps the believer. Discuss the meaning and work involved in these names.
5. Share your reaction to reviewing these service names of Christ. Which is most meaningful to you? Why?

8

The Sonship Names of Christ

I will declare the decree: the LORD hath said unto me,
Thou art my Son; this day have I begotten thee.
PSALM 2:7

The Father's favorite name for Jesus Christ is "Son." It is an Old Testament name (see Ps. 2:7), and it has eternal implications. Christians around the world call Christ "the only begotten Son." On all but one occasion Jesus referred to God as "Father." The exception to this rule occurred when on the cross Jesus asked, "My God, my God, why hast thou forsaken me?" (Matt. 27:46).

In John 5:19-27 Jesus referred to Himself as the Son 10 times in His comments to the Jews. He affirmed that the Son did only what He had seen the Father do (see v. 19), that the Son was the constant object of the Father's love (see v. 20), that the Father had and would continue to reveal all things and greater works to the Son (see v. 20), that the Son had power to give life (see v. 21), that the Father had delegated His authority to judge to the Son (see v. 22), that men should honor the Son as they honor the Father (see v. 23), that those who do not honor the Son offend the Father (see v. 23), that the Father sent the Son (see v. 23), that the dead will rise to life when they hear the Son's voice (see v. 25), that the Son has life in Himself (see v. 26), and that the Father has given to the Son authority to execute judgment (see v. 27). Obviously "Son" is an important title of Jesus.

Of all the many names and titles of Jesus, perhaps more belong to this family or category of names than to all the others. At least 19 names in Scripture relate to the Son. These include "the Son of the Highest" (Luke 1:32), "the carpenter's son" (Matt. 13:55), "the son of Mary" (Mark 6:3), "son of David" (Mark 10:47), "the son of Joseph" (John 1:45), "the Son" (Matt. 11:27), "his Son from heaven" (1 Thess. 1:10), "My beloved Son" (Matt. 3:17, *NKJV*), "the Son of God" (John 1:49), "the son of Abraham" (Matt. 1:1), "the Son of man" (John 1:51), "the Son of the Blessed" (Mark 14:61), "the Son of the Father" (2 John 3), "the son of the freewoman" (Gal. 4:30), "the Son of the living God" (Matt. 16:16), "Son of the most high God" (Mark 5:7), "a son over his own house" (Heb. 3:6), "the Son, who is consecrated for evermore" (Heb. 7:28), and "only begotten Son" (John 3:16).

Although each of these 19 sonship names of Jesus possesses a special and important significance, this chapter will examine only three of the more prominent names closely. Each of these three names is used in John 3 in connection with Jesus' meeting with Nicodemus. Note the phrases "Son of man" (John 3:14), referring to Jesus' messianic office and humanity, "only begotten Son" (3:16), referring to His unique relation to God, and "Son of God" (3:18), having special reference to the divine nature and character of Jesus.

Son of Man

The term "Son of man" is particularly noteworthy because in the Gospels it appears to be the favorite title of Christ for Himself. The Lord never identified Himself as "Jesus" until He appeared to Paul on the Damascus Road and then only one other time to the apostle John 50 years later (see Rev. 22:16). Only once did He call Himself Lord, and that was in quoting from the Old Testament (see Matt. 22:43). Over 80 times during His three-and-a-half-year ministry, Jesus called Himself the Son of man. It is also interesting to note that only Jesus used this term—no one else ever addressed Him as "the Son of man."

Why was this term Jesus' favorite title for Himself? The answer to this question lies in its biblical background. The only occurrence of the term in the Old Testament with any significance appears in Daniel 7:13. There it is a title of messianic expectation. Daniel describes the Son of man in the context of His return and His kingdom. This is the only use of the expression in the Old Testament that refs to Christ. Other occurrences of the term in the Old Testament have a different sense (see, for example, Ezek. 2:1,3,8; 3:1; 4:1).

Daniel's vision contrasts the kingdom of the Son of man with the succession of world empires symbolically represented as the lion (Babylon), the bear (Medo-Persia), the leopard (Greece), and the fourth beast, described only as "dreadful and terrible" (Rome, Dan. 7:7). When these great powers and kingdoms pass, One "like the Son of man" remains (7:13-14). Closely associated with this One are a dominion, a glory and a kingdom that are greater than all that had come before. The Jews expected their Messiah to conquer an existing kingdom (that is, Rome). They refused His messianic claims when He did not fulfill their preconceived notions about what Messiah must be like and must do. But someday Jesus will receive the kingdoms of the world from God. He will claim them as King of kings and Lord of lords. This aspect of the prophecy still awaits fulfillment.

The context of John 3 suggests a second reason that Jesus may have favored this name over others: "No man hath ascended up to heaven, but he that came down from heaven, even the Son of man which is in heaven" (3:13). When Jesus was born in Bethlehem, He acquired something He had never possessed before—a human nature. Although He remained God, He became also a man; He possessed a complete human nature. Because He wanted to identify with those He came to save, He chose to call Himself "the Son of man." The key verse of the Gospel of Luke affirms, "The Son of man is come to seek and to save that which was lost" (19:10). Jesus referred to Himself as Son of man in three contexts: He was, first, the Son of man in the context of His earthly ministry (see Matt. 8:20; 9:6; 11:19; 16:13; Luke 19:10; 22:48). Second, He used this title also when describing His approaching death on the cross (see Matt. 12:40; 17:9,22; 20:18; Mark 10:33; Luke 9:22; John 3:14; 8:28; 12:23; 13:31). Finally, Jesus used this title in an eschatological context with reference to His second coming (see Matt. 13:41; 24:27,30; 25:31; Luke 18:8; 21:36).

The Only Begotten Son

When someone asked a little boy what he had learned in Sunday School, he replied that the lesson was on "God's only forgotten Son."

He went on to explain how people forgot about God, and He had to be born in a stable, and later His parents forgot about Him and left Him in the temple. Although the little boy had misheard the title "Only Begotten Son," he was also right about "God's only forgotten Son." People today still forget Jesus, as was also common during the Lord's life on Earth (see John 1:10-12).

The name "only begotten Son" (John 3:16) did not originate in the Gospels but rather in heaven before time began. In the first of the messianic psalms, David noted, "I will declare the decree: the LORD hath said unto me, Thou art my Son; this day have I begotten thee" (Ps. 2:7). Over the years several suggestions have been offered as to the "day" on which Jesus was begotten. In order to resolve a doctrinal controversy in the Early Church, the Church fathers coined the expression "eternal generation." When we speak of the eternal generation of the Son, we mean that Jesus was eternally the Son and did not become the Son at His birth, baptism, death, resurrection, ascension or at any other historical point in His incarnate life. If Jesus became the Son at a point in time, He would not be the eternal Son and therefore would not be related to the Father as the Son from eternity.

We should understand the difference between being begotten and being identified or named as a son. Traditionally, Jews name their sons eight days after birth, at the time of the child's circumcision. It is not therefore unusual that a period of time should exist between the eternal generation of the Son and the various times when He was named or called the Son.

I have only one begotten son. When my son was born on May 8, 1956, we named him Stephen Richard Towns. About 10 years later, I heard another man calling his son by several terms of endearment that sounded too effeminate for a boy. Turning to Stephen, I said, "If I ever give you a nickname, it is not going to be something effeminate like that. I'll call you something strong, like Sam, a real man's name." For some reason, the name stuck, and to this day my son is known as Sam Towns. He was begotten Stephen Richard Towns in 1956 but called Sam in 1966. Similarly, Jesus is called the Son at His birth, baptism, death, resurrection and ascension, but He was begotten as Son in eternity past.

Two different Hebrew words for "Son" are used in Psalm 2: *ben* and *bar*. Each has its own distinctive meaning, although both are used throughout the Scriptures to identify the male descendant of a father. The first word, *ben* (see v. 7), refers to that which Christ achieves—that is, His lordship. As the firstborn, Jesus is the builder of God's spiritual house. The second word, *bar* (see v. 12), refers to that which Christ receives as heir of all things—that is, His legacy. The first refers to His honor; the latter to His heritage.

The word "begotten" emphasizes Christ's uniqueness. All who receive Christ by faith are "sons of God" (John 1:12) but not in the same sense that Jesus is the only begotten Son. God had only one Son, and He sent Him to be a missionary. To that Son He gave the promise, "Ask of me, and I shall give thee the heathen for thine inheritance, and the uttermost parts of the earth for thy possession" (Ps. 2:8).

This phrase "only begotten Son" occurs on three other occasions in the Gospel of John. John beheld "the glory as of the only begotten of the Father" (John 1:14), noted "the only begotten Son, which is in the bosom of the Father" (v. 18), and later identified Jesus as "the only begotten Son of God" (3:18). This uniqueness of the Son is alluded to prophetically in a birth name given to Him by Isaiah when the prophet distinguished between "a child is born" and "a son is given" (Isa. 9:6). Jesus had both a human nature ("a child is born") and a divine nature ("a son is given"). Neither nature in any way hindered or altered the other. He was the God-man—one Person with two natures. "Generation" and "only begotten" are the terms that best express the eternal relationship that existed between the divine Person of Christ and the divine Person of the Father.

The Son of God

The Gospel of John primarily purposes to produce faith in the reader, more specifically, "that ye might believe that Jesus is the Christ, the Son of God; and that believing ye might have life through his name" (John 20:31). When I first began to study and teach theology, it used to bother me that Jesus did not more often call Himself the Son of God and emphasize His deity. This was especially frustrating when I heard or read the arguments of liberals who noted Jesus' use of the name "Son of man" and insisted that Jesus never claimed to be God, only man. It was not until much later that I began to understand why Jesus did what He did. It is only when we fully understand the humanity of Christ that we see His deity. Likewise, only when we fully see His deity can we then see His humanity.

Although some people like to distinguish between the expressions "God the Son" and "Son of God," the difference is more imagined than real. The phrase "son of" was a common Hebraism to denote a relationship in which the son possessed the very same nature as that of his father. Even today the highest honor a Jew can receive is to be recognized as "a son of Israel" by the Israeli government, meaning that he is by nature the personification of the true spirit of the nation. The expression "Son of God," therefore, means that Jesus is by nature the personification of God Himself: He is of the same essence as the Father.

When we refer to Jesus as the Son of God, we do not mean that He is in any way inferior to or less than God the Father. In every respect the name "Son of God" implies that the Son is both co-equal and co-eternal with the Father. This is also true of other forms of this name, such as "Son of the Blessed" (Mark 14:61), "the Son of the Father" (2 John 3), "the Son of the Highest" (Luke 1:32), "the Son of the living God" (Matt. 16:16), and "Son of the most high" (Mark 5:7).

This relationship of Jesus to the Father was not something that Jesus discovered later in life. As a twelve-year-old boy, He understood He was the Son of God and that He needed to be about His Father's business (see Luke 2:49). This was also reaffirmed at His baptism. When He was dipped into the water by John the Baptist, God "thundered" from heaven, "Thou art my beloved Son, in whom I am well pleased" (Mark 1:11).

When Jesus was tempted by Satan, He did not dispute that He was indeed the Son of God (Luke 4:3,9), and Satan knew full well that Jesus was the Son of God. Jesus later encountered a demon-possessed person who called Him "Son of the most high God" (Mark 5:7). "God Most High" (*El Elyon*) is the name of God that demons most often used. Satan fell from his exalted position when he attempted to be like *El Elyon* (see Isa. 14:14). Melchizedek used this name to identify the Possessor of heaven and Earth (see Gen. 14:19). The constant attack of Satan against *El Elyon* often takes the form of destroying or taking possession of that which rightfully belongs to God.

At His trial Jesus was accused and charged with both insurrection (at the Roman trials) and blasphemy (at the Jewish trials). He was asked by the high priest, "I adjure thee by the living God, that thou tell us whether thou be the Christ, the Son of God" (Matt. 26:63). While He hung on the cross, enemies of Jesus mocked Him with statements such as, "If thou be the Son of God, come down from the cross" (27:40), and, "He trusted in God; let him deliver him now, if he will have him: for he said, I am the Son of God" (27:43).

CONCLUSION

Jesus was not only the Son of man but also the only begotten Son of God. That is what He claimed and taught. That being the case, we must respond to Jesus in one of three ways: If He lied about His identity and knew it, then His attempt at deception was such that He got exactly what He deserved. If He believed that He was the Son of God but was deceived Himself, then, as C. S. Lewis so aptly put it, He should be regarded not as a liar but rather as a lunatic, on the level of a man who thinks He is a poached egg. If, however, Jesus was telling the truth—that is, if He really was the Son of God as He claimed to be—then we must recognize and worship Him as none other than the LORD of life and as very God of very God. Jesus' claim to be the Son of God gives us these three alternatives today. We must all answer the haunting question of Pilate, "What shall I do then with Jesus which is called Christ?" (Matt. 27:22).

FOR DISCUSSION

1. Giving Jesus the title "Son" implies that the first Person of the Trinity is the Father. What do the sonship names reveal about the Trinity?

2. There are 19 sonship titles of Christ. Which three are predominant? Why?
3. Of all His names, which one did Christ use most frequently in reference to Himself? Why do you think He preferred this name?
4. Why was Jesus called the only begotten Son?
5. The title "Son of God" reminds us of the deity of Christ. Can a person be saved apart from belief in Christ's deity? Why or why not?

9

The Godhead Names of Christ

Simon Peter answered and said, Thou art the Christ,
the Son of the living God.
MATTHEW 16:16

Several names of Jesus are commentaries on the character of
Christ, His nature and His attributes. For a complete understanding of who Christ is, we should consider all His names, but certain
names are foundational to Christological considerations. Usually
these names appear in the context of an important Christological
passage of Scripture or stress some unique aspect or attribute of
Christ and/or His relationship to the Godhead. These names describe Jesus as God incarnate—"The Christ of God" (Luke 9:20).

The Word

The apostle John was the exclusive user of the title "Word." Using
the Greek word *logos*, John wrote, "In the beginning was the Word,
and the Word was with God, and the Word was God" (John 1:1).
He also began his first epistle with a variation of this title. There he
noted, "That which was from the beginning, which we have heard,
which we have seen with our eyes, which we have looked upon,
and our hands have handled, of the Word of life" (1 John 1:1).
The apostle also used a form of the title in describing the return
of Christ to this earth: "And he was clothed with a vesture dipped
in blood; and his name is called The Word of God" (Rev. 19:13).

Words are indispensable to language. We use them to communicate a message. Without them we could not explain precise-
ly what we mean. A word defines or describes the idea that we

intend to pass on to others. When the Jews used the word *logos*, they thought in terms of the wisdom literature of the Old Testament.

Scholars debate whether John borrowed the term *logos* from the Greeks or from the Jews. If the term is Greek, there may be numerous philosophical implications in it. If the term is Hebrew, John may be making reference to the wisdom of God personified (see Proverbs, especially chapters 5–8). Probably John calls Jesus "the Word of God" because this phrase is used over 1,200 times in the Old Testament to refer to the revelation or message of God, as in the phrase, "the Word of God came to . . ." Jesus Christ was the message, meaning or communication from God to men. Jesus was everything the written and spoken Word of the LORD was in the Old Testament. Jesus is, therefore, the expression, revelation and communication of the Lord. He is both the incarnate and inspired Word.

Ten Conclusions about the Word

In John 1:1-18

The following listing summarizes the primary ideas of John's introduction concerning the Word:

1. The phrase "in the beginning" is not a reference to a point in time but a reference to eternity past (see v. 1).
2. The personality of the Word is evident in that it is capable of individualization (see v. 1).
3. The Word has active and personal communication with God (see vv. 1-2).
4. There are two centers of consciousness, for the Word was God yet also was face to face, or "with," God (see v. 1).
5. The Word has the essence of deity (see v. 1).
6. The Father and the Word are one (see v. 1).
7. The Word was the Agent by which God expressed, or revealed, Himself (see v. 18).
8. The incarnate Word has a definite continuity with the pre-incarnate Word (see vv. 1,14).

9. As God lived in a tent, spoke in a tent and revealed Himself in the Old Testament Tabernacle, so the Word tabernacled among us (see v. 14).

10. The incarnation of the Word is the unique revelation of God (see v. 4).

The Beloved

The title "Beloved" occurs only once in Scripture (see Eph. 1:6), although many passages affirm the Father's love for the Son. God called Jesus "my beloved Son" at His baptism (Matt. 3:17), and Jesus repeatedly acknowledged that "the Father loveth the Son" (John 3:35; 5:20; see also 17:23). Paul notes that we are "accepted in the beloved" (Eph. 1:6). The particularly comforting aspect of this title is the context in which it is revealed. Jesus is the object of the Father's love, and because we are in Christ, we too are the objects of the Father's love.

The Image of God

The Greek word *eikon*, meaning "image," is twice used in titles of Christ to express His unique relation to God. The word itself denotes an image and involves the two ideas of representation and manifestation. When Paul affirmed that Jesus is "the image of God" (2 Cor. 4:4), he meant that Jesus was essentially and absolutely the perfect representation and manifestation, or expression, of the Father. In another place Paul altered the title slightly by calling Christ "the image of the invisible God" (Col. 1:15). It emphasizes that Christ is the visible representation and manifestation of God to created beings. Both contexts convey the idea of perfection in that image.

A second closely related title is "the express image of His person" (Heb. 1:3, *NKJV*). This is one of seven such statements in the early verses of Hebrews—all designed to demonstrate the superiority of Christ. Various versions translate it in different ways: "the very image of his substance," "an exact representation of his very being" (*ERB*), "flawless expression of the nature of God" (*Phillips*), "stamped with God's own character" (*Moffat*), "the copy of his being" (*Beck*), "the exact representation of God's nature" (Swindoll), "the exact expression of God's nature" (Stibbs), "the impress of the Divine Nature" (F. B. Meyer), and "the exact expression of God's very essence" (Barclay). This wide assortment of translations derives from two key Greek words in this title.

The first of these is the word "character," which is closely related to the verb *charasso*, meaning "to cut," "to scratch" or "to mark." Originally this word referred to a marking agent, such as a die, and then later to the impression made by the marking agent. It is similar to the English word "stamp," which first referred to the instrument that printed the impression and later to the impression itself. It suggests the idea of an exact representation of the person or the person himself—that is, the distinguishing features or traits by which a person or thing is known (as in the English word "characteristics"). What the writer of the Hebrews seems to argue by using this title is that as the wax bears the impression of the seal pressed upon it, revealing all the dominant character traits of that seal, even so Jesus Christ bears the impression of God's essential being, revealing all the attributes of God.

The second word in this title is *hypostasis*, which is more of a philosophical than a theological term. Etymologically, it refers to the sediment or foundation under a building but came to be used by Greek philosophers to refer to the essence or real being of a person thought to rest under the surface appearance of the person. It refers to the substance of what we are. Used here of Christ in this context, it is an argument for the deity of Christ, for He is substantially God.

Attributive Names

Several character names of Jesus may be classed as attributive names, for in their meaning they focus upon the various attributes of God. These names underscore two of the more prominent attributes: holiness and righteousness.

In several passages Jesus is called the Holy One. The child to be born to Mary was "that holy thing" (Luke 1:35); later the apostles called Him "thy holy child Jesus" (Acts 4:30). On several occasions the apostles referred to the LORD as the "Holy One" (Acts 2:27; 13:35; see also Ps. 89:18). The primary thought in these designations is that of consecration or of being set apart uniquely unto God. The holiness of Christ was a fundamental requirement of the worthy sacrifice for sin. Because of Christ's holiness, we become holy. One of the biblical titles for the Christian is "saint," which is connected in thought to the idea of holiness.

Righteousness also is a feature in several of the names and titles of Jesus. Christ is called "the righteous" (1 John 2:1), "a righteous Branch" (Jer. 23:5), "the righteous LORD" (Ps. 11:7), "my righteous servant" (Isa. 53:11), "the righteous judge" (2 Tim. 4:8), "a righteous man" (Luke 23:47), "righteousness" (1 Cor. 1:30), and "the righteousness of God" (Rom. 10:3). Just as holiness refers primarily to the character of Christ, so too righteousness refers primarily to the conduct of Christ. These two titles are closely related, because it is impossible to be righteous without being holy. The righteousness of Christ is an expression of His holiness just as righteousness is the spontaneous expression of the saint.

The holiness and righteousness of Christ are best expressed in His sinlessness. I refer to Christ's sinlessness as a four-legged chair, because there are four Scriptures that affirm that our LORD "knew no sin" (2 Cor. 5:21), "did no sin" (1 Pet. 2:22), was "without sin" (Heb. 4:15), and could not be convicted of sin (see John 8:46). Just as a four-legged chair is the most secure in which to sit, these four statements serve to affirm the sinless perfection of Christ.

Priority Names

Several names and titles of Christ may be called "priority names," for they emphasize the priority of Christ either in His Person or accomplishment. The apostle Paul emphasized this concept when he noted "that in all things he might have the preeminence" (Col. 1:18). Each of the following names refers to the LORD in this sense.

Jesus is called "mine elect" (Isa. 42:1), or "the chosen of God" (Luke 23:35). This title emphasizes the priority of Christ as the uniquely appointed Servant of the Lord. When we have a job that needs to be done, often we will spend time looking for the one most qualified to accomplish the task. The greater the job, the more diligently we seek out the most capable and qualified person available. We want to be sure that the chosen one is the best available. When God sought to redeem a lost world, only One qualified to complete successfully that task, and God chose Him to do it. When the mockers at the foot of the cross called out to Him as "the chosen of God" (v. 35), they no doubt intended insults in order to add to His suffering. Actually, it was a reminder to the One who at any moment could have called on legions of angels to release Him and destroy His enemies that He was God's Elect, chosen to complete the specific task in which He was then engaged.

Several titles of the LORD include the term "the firstborn" (Heb. 12:23). He is "the firstborn among many brethren" (Rom. 8:29), "the firstborn from the dead" (Rev. 1:5, *NKJV*; "first begotten" in *KJV*), "the firstborn of every creature" (Col. 1:15), and the "firstborn son" (Luke 2:7). The emphasis of the Greek *wordprototokos*, translated "firstborn" or "first-begotten" in Scripture, is that of a priority in relationships. When used of Christ, it affirms His priority with the Father and His preeminence over all creation. It does not imply the idea that He first came into existence at some point in time so as not to be eternal in nature; rather, it is used in the sense that He held a certain superiority of position (see Exod. 4:22; Deut. 21:16-17).

Another priority name of Jesus relates to the concept of first fruits (see Rom. 11:16; 1 Cor. 15:20). The Greek word *aparche* closely relates to the verb *aparchomai*, meaning "to make a beginning," and was normally used in Scripture in the context of the offering of the first part of the harvest. As a title of Christ, it is a guarantee of our resurrection after the pattern of His resurrection. Just as the first fruits of the harvest assure the farmer that more produce will follow, so too the resurrection of Christ assures us of our future resurrection.

Christ Our Passover

The apostle Paul urged the church at Corinth to deal with sin in their personal and corporate lives, stating, "Purge out therefore the old leaven, that ye may be a new lump, as ye are unleavened. For even Christ our passover is sacrificed for us" (1 Cor. 5:7). Although Jesus is the fulfillment of all Israel's typical feasts and sacrifices, the need for personal holiness in Corinth caused the apostle to single out the Passover and to apply this word to Christ.

The Passover feast was so named because of the promise of God that accompanied its first observance: "And the blood shall be to you for a token upon the houses where ye are: and when I see the blood, I will pass over you, and the plague shall not be upon you to destroy you, when I smite the land of Egypt" (Exod. 12:13). The final of the 10 plagues in the land of Egypt involved the death of the firstborn son in every home. Israel was instructed to kill a lamb as a substitutionary sacrifice and apply its blood to the doorpost of the home. By midnight "there was not a house where there was not one dead" (v. 30). In the homes stained with blood, the lamb was dead. In the homes lacking the bloodstain, the firstborn son of the family was dead.

Sin is destructive and deserving of the death sentence, but Christ our Passover has died in our place. Because of this, we are spared the inevitable consequences of sin. But when we understand this title of Christ and the work of Christ that it emphasizes, our natural response is to look inward and begin the process of purging ourselves of sinful attitudes and habits that are a part of our being. To effect this response in us, Christ has given us the Holy Spirit. The fact that some things that are wrong in our life still bother us is an evidence of the work of the Holy Spirit reminding us of the real nature of sin and what it cost Christ, our Passover.

Alpha and Omega

It is impossible for finite language to describe exhaustively the meaning of Christ in His Person and work in a single title or name, but if one comes close, it is the title "Alpha and Omega" (Rev. 1:8). Two other related titles are "the first and the last" (v. 17) and "the beginning and the ending" (v. 8). These names are significant not so much for what they say as for what they imply. Alpha is the first, or beginning, letter of the Greek alphabet. Omega is the last, or ending, letter of the same. The expression should not, however, be limited only to the literal first and last letters of the alphabet, for the expressions were used much in the way that we today speak of "everything from A to Z."

Jesus is everything from the first to the last, the beginning to the ending, the alpha to the omega, A to Z. He is, as the apostle put it, "all, and in all" (Col. 3:11). These related titles of Christ serve to emphasize His inexhaustibility. What does Jesus mean to you? Perhaps you have passed through a particular experience in which He met an unusual need in your life. Even if you cannot find the specific name or title of Jesus in Scripture to express adequately that meaning, it is covered under these expressions. Remember, there are more than 800 names of Christ in Scripture. Jesus is all these and more. One name cannot express all that He is, and over 800 names cannot exhaust what He is.

CONCLUSION

On the day when Peter affirmed that Jesus was the Christ of God, he probably did not comprehend all that was involved in the character of Christ. Jesus was uniquely related to His Father as the Beloved and as the eternal Word who had been face to face with God in eternity past. He was the One whose names suggest the very attributes of God. He was the One who holds preeminence in all things and priority before all. He was God Himself, the express image of His Person, and the visible image of the invisible God.

But in the experience of the believer, Jesus is even more than that. He is Christ our Passover, the One who died in our place in order to redeem us from the infection of sin. In fact, Jesus is everything to the child of God. He is Alpha and Omega, the First and the Last, the Beginning and the Ending and everything in between.

FOR DISCUSSION

1. Why is Jesus called the Word? What does this indicate about His character and work?
2. What does "accepted in the beloved" (Eph. 1:6) mean?
3. As the Image of God, what does Christ reflect? How does this term relate to believers?
4. There are several names of Christ that come from the attributes of God. Discuss how each of these names reflects a different aspect of God's nature.
5. Does the title "Firstborn" imply that Christ came into existence at some point in time? Why or why not?
6. As the Passover, what does Christ do for the believer?
7. Christ is Alpha and Omega. He is the beginning and ending of what? In light of this truth, how should we view our trials and struggles?

10

The Jehovistic Titles of Christ

Jesus said unto them, Verily, verily, I say unto you,
Before Abraham was, I am.

JOHN 8:58

The Bible records many statements concerning the deity of Christ, but perhaps none were so impressive to the Early Church as those that identified Him with *Jehovah* in the Old Testament. Although the name *Jehovah* was used before the time of Moses, it was not until He commissioned Moses that God revealed the uniqueness of its meaning (see Exod. 6:3). It was the covenant name of God in the Old Testament and a form of the verb "to be" repeated twice. When Moses maintained that he did not know the name of God, God revealed His name as "I AM THAT I AM" (3:14). *Jehovah* is the I AM. This name is printed in the English Bible as the title "LORD," in which all four letters are capitalized.

Jehovah was the most respected name of God in the Old Testament. When scribes were copying the Scriptures and came to this name, they would change their clothes and find a new pen and fresh ink to write the name. They refused even to pronounce the name as they read the Scriptures; they substituted for it the name *Adonai*. As a result of this misguided expression of reverence, considerable debate has arisen over the actual pronunciation of the name.

Although most conservative theologians argue that it should be pronounced as *Jehovah*, many liberal teachers argue that it should be pronounced as *Yahweh*. It is impossible to resolve this debate now at a time when the name has remained unpronounced for generations. Even if the Hebrew language included vowels, our task of deciding how to pronounce this name would be difficult. Dialects change within languages over years of use so that a word pronounced one way today may sound totally different 200 years from now. If we did not know the history of the region, it would be hard for us to believe that the original settlers of the Southeastern United States spoke English with a thick British accent. Over the years and generations since they first settled, they have developed their own unique dialect of English. The same thing no doubt happened to the Hebrew language over a long period.

Jesus used the expression "I am" in eight contexts within the Gospel of John in each of which He revealed something about His character as *Jehovah*. The Greek words that John used on those occasions, *ego eimi*, emphatically draw attention to their significance. The following listing identifies the eight contexts in which Jesus called Himself "I am" and is the group of names that this chapter discusses.

The Jehovistic Names of Jesus in the Gospel of John

1. "I am the bread of life" (John 6:35).
2. "I am the light of the world" (8:12).
3. "I am the door" (10:9).
4. "I am the good shepherd" (10:11).
5. "I am the resurrection, and the life" (11:25).
6. "I am the way, the truth, and the life" (14:6).
7. "I am the true vine" (15:1,5).
8. "I am . . . I am" (4:26; 8:58; 18:5-6,8).

The Bread of Life

The Jews widely believed that they would recognize the Messiah, because He would find the lost Ark of the Covenant hidden by Jeremiah and produce the jar of manna hidden therein. Hence, Messiah would be identified with manna, or bread. Also, the Jews thought that being a Prophet like unto Moses (see Deut. 18:15) meant that

Messiah would produce the bread from heaven. One rabbinical saying declared, "As was the first redeemer, so was the final redeemer; as the first redeemer caused the manna to fall from heaven, even so shall the second redeemer cause the manna to fall." Further, the Jews thought that manna would be the food in the kingdom of God. In the Jewish mind manna excited messianic expectations.

In light of this cultural context, it is not surprising that those who were one day ready to declare Jesus to be the Messiah should the next day raise the subject of manna. Twice in a meeting with Jesus, they requested that Jesus produce this manna (see John 6:30-31,34). In response Jesus identified *Himself* as the manna when He declared, "I am the bread of life" (v. 35). In the discourse in which He revealed this Jehovistic title, Jesus explained that He was the bread of everlasting life (see vv. 32-34), the bread of satisfying life (see vv. 35-36), the bread of resurrection life (see vv. 37-47), and the bread of indwelling life (see vv. 48-59).

Just as a person eats bread in order to sustain his or her physical life, so too the Christian must "eat" the Bread of Life in order to sustain his spiritual life. In His address on the Bread of Life, Jesus used two different verbs for "eating," showing two responses to the Bread. First, He used the verb *phagein*, always in an aorist tense and with reference to eternal life (see vv. 50-53). When a person receives Christ as Savior, he or she is, in this context, "eating His flesh" (see vv. 51-56). This is a reference to once-and-for-all salvation. The second verb, *trogon*, is a present active participle, which emphasizes a continual or habitual eating. It was used of munching on fruit, vegetables or cereals. The change in tense that accompanies the change in verb emphasizes the continual satisfying of a spiritual appetite through constantly or habitually munching on the Bread of Life (see vv. 54,56-58). If the first act of once-and-for-all eating speaks of our salvation, this constant munching speaks of our uninterrupted communion with Christ.

The Light of the World

On several occasions the religious leaders in Jerusalem tried to destroy Jesus. One attempt involved bringing to Him a woman caught in the act of adultery and calling on Him to pass judgment. It created for the LORD what the leaders thought was an impossible situation. If Jesus condemned the woman as required by the Law, the people would be disappointed and would stop following Him. If He failed to uphold the Law, He would be guilty of teaching contrary to Moses and could be thrown out of the synagogue and stoned for blasphemy. Jesus upheld the Law in its true spirit by bringing conviction to the woman's accusers and salvation to the guilty woman. At the same time He increased His already growing popularity with the common people.

Immediately following that incident, Jesus announced, "I am the light of the world" (John 8:12). That simple statement was rich in meaning in the context in which it occurs in this Gospel. Jesus uttered it in the court of the women, where He had been teaching. In that place were located the four golden candelabra, each with four golden bowls. As part of the previous week's celebration of the Feast of Tabernacles, these bowls had been filled with oil and lighted. Contemporary observers affirmed that the light was so brilliant as to illuminate the entire city of Jerusalem. Those who gathered around Jesus that morning would no doubt still remember the spectacle of the night before.

By calling Himself the "Light of the World," Jesus may have been alluding to the cloud and pillar of fire that led Israel through the wilderness. The ceremonial illumination of the Temple was a reminder to the people of that cloud and pillar. Most Jews would have considered that phenomenon a theophany, a manifestation of God Himself. If Jesus was thinking of this background, then His claim to be the Light of the World is a clear title to deity.

Jesus may also have been referring to the rising of the sun. He had begun teaching very early in the morning—that is, just before sunrise (see John 8:2). By the time Jesus made this claim, the sun would have been bursting over the horizon. Because of the mountainous terrain, the sunrise in Palestine is sudden and spectacular. Within an hour, the degree of light changes from the darkest hour of the night to the brilliance of the day. It was this unique sunrise that caused David to compare the sun to "a bridegroom coming out of his chamber" (Ps. 19:5).

Another possible context for better understanding Jesus' statement about the light of the world is that of the Old Testament prophecies that associate the coming of the Messiah with light. On the preceding day, Nicodemus's colleagues in the Sanhedrin had mildly rebuked him with the statement, "Search, and look: for out of Galilee ariseth no prophet" (John 7:52). It may be that Jesus called Himself the Light of the World in order to remind these Jewish leaders of important prophecies that they seemed to have forgotten (see Isa. 9:1; 42:6; 49:6; 60:1-3; Mal. 4:2). These prophecies concerning the light specifically named Galilee as the place in which the light would particularly shine.

One other context clarifies the sense in which Jesus is uniquely the Light of the World. Jesus is the light that repels the sinner who will not repent of his sin but that attracts those sinners who will. In the confrontation prior to His claiming to be the Light of the World, Jesus spoke so as to bring conviction to the self-righteous Jewish leaders who had sought to exploit the woman caught in the act of adultery. The word John uses in this context for "convicted" (John 8:9) is *elegchomenoi*, literally meaning "to bring to the light and expose." It describes the act of holding a letter to a lamp so as to see what is inside. Jesus was the Light of the World in the sense that He could hold up people's lives to the light to expose the sin hidden deep within. When He convicts of sin and people are not willing to repent, they cannot remain in His presence. Many people today are trying to run from God because they are convicted of some sin for which they will not repent.

Jesus is the Light of the World, and one of the primary functions of light is to shine so as to reveal what would be otherwise hidden. Christ shines to reveal Himself (see John 8:12-20), the Father (see vv. 21-27), and the Cross (see vv. 28-30). He not only exposes the hidden sin in humanity but also shows us how the sin problem can be ultimately resolved. He is the light in a world of moral darkness.

The Door

When Jesus identified Himself as the door, He was comparing Himself to the purpose or function of a door (see 10:9). A door was the means by which the sheep entered into the fold. By way of application, Jesus is the door to the fold of salvation. In this context He emphasized the exclusiveness of Himself as Savior by using the definite article *he* ("the") and by identifying salvation exclusively with entering into the fold through that door. The Greek expression *di'emou* ("by me") stands in an emphatic position so as to identify clearly the door by which men and women may find salvation.

There are at least three specific applications of this particular title of the LORD in the Christian life. "I am the door: by me if any man enter in, he shall be saved, and shall go in and out, and find pasture" (v. 9). First, Jesus the Door provides salvation when we enter. Second, we have liberty to go in and out—in for salvation and out for service. Third, we shall find spiritual food in Christ.

The Good Shepherd

Jesus twice identified Himself as "the good shepherd" (see John 10:11,14). In doing so He used the Greek word *kalos*, which carried with it certain moral overtones. In classical Greek this word was used to describe that which was beautiful, useful, auspicious, noble, wholesome, competent and morally good. It would be correct to use any or all of these adjectives to describe the Good Shepherd. This word emphasizes the essential goodness of our Shepherd that, because it is evident to the observer, results in His being admired, respected and loved by others.

Many commentators believe that this title is a reference to *Jehovah Roi* of the 23rd Psalm. The primary emphasis of the title, however, is the Shepherd's giving His life for His sheep and therefore is probably better understood within the context of Psalm 22, the first of the trilogy of shepherd psalms (Pss. 22–24). The title "Shepherd" was a Church name of Jesus, for Scripture occasionally identifies the Church as the flock of God (see 1 Pet. 5:2).

The Resurrection and the Life

When Jesus met with Martha just prior to the raising of her brother Lazarus from the dead, He introduced another of His Jehovistic names: "Jesus said unto her, I am the resurrection, and the life: he that believeth in me, though he were dead, yet shall he live: And whosoever liveth and believeth in me shall never die" (John 11:25-26). Martha had expressed her faith in the resurrection as a principle, but Jesus revealed to her the resurrection as a Person, that Person being Himself. One of the titles of Christ is "Life," and Jesus is the resurrection because He is life in its fullest sense.

This title carries with it a twofold promise for the believer: First, those who have experienced physical death shall rise to immortality. Second, none who believe shall be hurt in the second death. Although we commonly hear this title of Christ at funerals, where these promises are repeated, they are conditional promises, and this name for Christ has meaning and benefit only to those who believe.

The Way, the Truth, the Life

Alone with His disciples on the last night of His life here on Earth, Jesus revealed two additional Jehovistic titles. The first of these is "the way, the truth, and the life" (14:6). The Greek word *hados* literally means "road" or "highway." In the context of the language of a journey, Jesus is the highway to heaven. Further, He is the only highway to heaven. The New Testament consistently teaches an exclusiveness with respect to Christ as the only Savior. Christ claimed to be the only Savior (see v. 6), and the disciples acknowledged this also (see Acts 4:12). This description of Christ was so characteristic of the nature of New Testament Christianity that followers of Jesus were described as being "of the way" or "this way" (see Acts 9:2; 19:23; 22:4; 24:14,22).

Christ was not only the way but also the truth in its most absolute nature. He is the fountain and standard of truth. This was important to the Jews. One Jewish legend reports that a group of rabbis were praying in order to determine the essential nature of God when God sent a scroll down from heaven with the first, middle and last letters of the Hebrew alphabet on it. These three letters spell the Hebrew word for "truth." Although the story is no doubt apocryphal, it does serve to illustrate the importance of truth to the Jews, especially as an attribute of God.

And Jesus is the life. He is unique among men in that He has life in Himself. He is described in the context of His resurrection as a "quickening," or life-giving, spirit (see 1 Cor. 15:45). Life is fundamental to His being and is described early in the fourth Gospel as the life that was the light of all men (see John 1:4).

The True Vine

The second Jehovistic title Jesus revealed that night in the Upper Room was "I am the true vine" (John 15:1; see also 15:5). Vineyards were so plenteous in Israel that the vine had become a national symbol. A golden vine had been engraved over the Temple gate area, and it had been used on coins minted during the Maccabean revolt. Throughout the Old Testament, God had used the image of a vine or a vineyard to describe the nation (see Ps. 80:8; Isa. 5:1-7; Jer. 2:21; Ezek. 15; 19:10; Hos. 10:1). When Jesus called Himself the true vine, He was obviously drawing a parallel between Israel and Himself.

The Greek word *alethine*, meaning "true," is repeatedly used in the Gospel of John to distinguish the reality and genuineness of Jesus in contrast to that which is false and unreal. Although in the Old Testament God often talked of Israel as a vine, the image always appears in a negative sense. In contrast, Jesus is the real or genuine vine, a vine that is cared for and carefully pruned by the husbandman and that is characterized by consistent fruit-bearing. Israel was never a vine like this; the nation was a spurious vine that produced sour grapes.

I Am . . . I Am

The Greek expression *ego eimi* is used in the context of each of the above Jehovistic claims of Jesus. Simply using the verb *eimi* would have been enough if Jesus had wanted only to draw a parallel between Himself and something else, but the addition of *ego* to this expression draws attention to emphasis. On several occasions Jesus used the expression that includes an emphatic subject and verb but failed to supply the predicate (see, for example, John 4:26; 8:58; 18:5-6,8). This was not a failure on the part of Christ to complete a sentence but rather an affirmation of His being *Jehovah* (see Exod. 3:14). On at least one occasion, His statement was understood by those who heard it in this light, for they responded by picking up stones to kill Jesus for blasphemy (see John 8:58-59). On another occasion the uttering of this name was apparently accompanied by a revelation of the Lord's glory, which caused the soldiers who had come to arrest Him to fall back under His power (18:5-8). Jesus used this expression not just to assert His claims to be *like Jehovah* but also to demonstrate that He *was Jehovah*.

CONCLUSION

Jesus is the *Jehovah* of the Old Testament. All the names of *Jehovah* in the Old Testament, therefore, may be applied legitimately to Him. Jesus is the eternal contemporary who meets our every need. G. Campbell Morgan once suggested that we could better understand experientially the name *Jehovah*, "I Am," if the verb "to be" were translated "to become." The significance of this name is that *Jehovah* (Jesus) is and will become to us exactly what we need when we feel that need. In this sense it is an intensely personal and subjective name of Jesus. What has Jesus become to you recently?

FOR DISCUSSION

1. What is important about the I Ams of the eight Jehovistic titles of Christ? How do they reflect His deity?
2. What is the purpose of bread? How does Christ fulfill this purpose for believers?
3. What did Christ mean when He described Himself as light?
4. Relate the function of a door to Christ's ministry. What does it mean to go in and out?
5. How is Christ a Good Shepherd?
6. What twofold promise is extended because of Christ's title of Resurrection and Life?
7. When Christ said "I Am . . . I Am," what did He imply?
8. What do we know about Christ because of these Jehovistic titles?

11

The Church Names of Christ

*I say also unto thee, That thou art Peter, and upon this rock I will build
my church; and the gates of hell shall not prevail against it.*
MATTHEW 16:18

Several names of Christ focus upon His unique relationship to the
Church. The Church is described with many metaphors, such as
"the Body," "a flock of sheep," "a Bride," "a temple" or "building,"
and "a garden" or "vineyard." In this connection Jesus is the Head
of the Body, the Shepherd of the sheep, the Bridegroom of the
Bride, the Cornerstone and Master Builder of the Building, and
the Vine that gives life to the branches.

The Head of the Body

One of the common images of the Church, particularly in the Epistles of Paul, is the Body of Christ. The word "body" is the key word
in 1 Corinthians 12, where the apostle sought to resolve problems
at Corinth concerning spiritual gifts. The theme of the Epistle to
the Ephesians is the Church as the Body of Christ (see Eph. 5:23).
In the Epistle to the Colossians, probably written at the same time
as the Ephesian Epistle, Paul's theme is Christ as the Head of the
Body (see Col. 1:18).

The Body is the best known and most used symbol of the
Church in Scripture. When Paul called Christ the Head of the Body,
he emphasized the authority of Christ in and over His Church.
It was a reminder of the distinctiveness and supremacy of Jesus.
To comprehend this name more fully, we must understand how
the apostle used the word "body" to describe the Church.

The Greek word *soma* is used in several ways in the New Testament. On many occasions it refers to the physical body (see Rom. 1:24; 1 Cor. 5:3; Gal. 6:17; 1 Thess. 5:23), but Paul also uses this word to identify the total personality of a person, not just his or her physical being (see Rom. 12:1; 1 Cor. 9:27; 13:3; Phil. 1:20). It is interesting to note that Paul never uses this word to describe a dead body, as is common in classical Greek and in the Septuagint.

Within this context the Church is a living organism, the Body of Christ. She has a personality and identity that is intimately related to Christ, her head. She is a living entity indwelt by Christ Himself. Although we must be careful not to make the Church more authoritative than the Scriptures (as is common in Catholic traditions), it is important that we recognize the living reality of the Church as the Body of Christ.

If the Church is the Body, then Christ Himself is the Head (see Col. 1:18; 2:19; Eph. 1:22-23; 4:15; 5:23). Just as the head is the determinative center of one's physical being, so too Christ is authoritative in the Church. He does not build His Church independent of His body but directs and controls the actions of every muscle, organ and nerve so as to accomplish His will. Part of the mystery of this name is that Christ, who is in His nature and attributes omnipotent, should voluntarily choose to limit Himself to working through human beings who, although they are members of His body, retain an independent will by which they can and too often do refuse the directives of the head.

That Christ is called the Head of the Body implies several truths concerning His relationship to the Church. First, it means that His purposes cannot be frustrated; He holds ultimate control. Even if one part of the Body is rebellious and does not respond to His directives, another will respond. Second, it suggests that no individual member within that Body can be the organic head of it. Attempts to do so will be frustrated, as in the case of Diotrephes, "who loveth to have the preeminence among them" (3 John 9). The place of preeminence in the Church belongs to Jesus alone. "And he is the head of the body, the church: who is the beginning, the firstborn from the dead; that in all things he might have the preeminence" (Col. 1:18).

The practical implication of this title of Christ relates to our submission to Jesus as the Head of the Body. He demands our obedience to His will and reverential worship of His Person. Anything less falls short of a personal acknowledgment of Jesus as the Head of the Body.

The Shepherd of the Sheep

Scripture often refers to the Church as the flock of God, so it is not surprising that the LORD should bear the title "Shepherd." When He sees the multitudes of people, He sees them "scattered abroad, as sheep having no shepherd" (Matt. 9:36). He was the Good Shepherd in His death (see John 10:11; Ps. 22), He was the Great Shepherd in His resurrection (see Heb. 13:20; Ps. 23), and He will be the Chief Shepherd in His return to this earth (see 1 Pet. 5:4; Ps. 24). Unlike the hireling, whose primary concern is himself, Jesus cares for His sheep. He has entrusted the care of parts of His flock to others called pastors, or, more literally, shepherds. Jesus the Shepherd is the model for pastors in caring for the flock. The title "Shepherd" was also one of the Jehovistic names of Jesus in the Gospel of John.

The Bridegroom of the Bride

When John the Baptist became the first to call Jesus "the bridegroom" (John 3:29), the term was already rich in meaning. The Old Testament frequently portrayed Israel as the wife of the LORD (see Isa. 54:6; Jer. 31:32; Hos. 2:1-23). As John on that occasion noted, "He that hath the bride is the bridegroom" (John 3:29). This title was to have special significance in the New Testament, not for Israel as the wife of God but rather for the Church, which is the Bride of Christ. The relation between the Bride and Bridegroom is most fully taught in a passage in which the apostle Paul addresses several principles of family living (see Eph. 5:25-27). These verses emphasize that Christ loved the Church, gave Himself for it, purposes to sanctify and cleanse it by the Word of God, and promises to take it to Himself as a perfected Bride. This work of Christ began in eternity past when He determined to die for her because of His love for her and will be consummated in the new Jerusalem when we shall with John see "the holy city, new Jerusalem, coming down from God out of heaven, prepared as a bride adorned for her husband" (Rev. 21:2).

The image of the Bride and Bridegroom serves to emphasize the need for qualitative or spiritual Church growth—that is, growth in our love for Christ. The Church was "espoused" (2 Cor. 11:2) to Christ by the apostles and should grow closer to Christ during the "engagement period" of this present age. Unfortunately, the history of the professing Church suggests she has been as unfaithful to her Groom as Israel was to her Husband.

The Cornerstone and Foundation of the Building

Jesus is called a Stone, or Rock, in three different senses in the Scriptures. To Israel He is a "stumbling stone" or "a rock of offence" (see Isa. 8:14-15; Rom. 9:32-33; 1 Cor. 1:23; 1 Pet. 2:8). To the world He is the Smiting Stone, who will destroy the antichrist kingdoms of the world (see Dan. 2:34). But to the Church, "the stone which the builders disallowed, the same is made the head of the corner" (1 Pet. 2:7). Jesus is the Cornerstone of the Church, which He is presently building.

Some of the significance of this title has been lost to the average Christian today because of changes in architectural design in the centuries since this title was first applied to Christ. The Greek word *lithos* was used of ordinary field stones that were found on the ground. It was common in the construction of first-century buildings to lean a building into itself. This meant that one part of the structure would have a greater amount of pressure on it than the rest of the structure. Over the years, the materials used in this area would wear faster. To compensate for this, builders sought for a hard field stone upon which to rest the structure. This became known as the cornerstone and was the one part of the building on which the rest of the structure depended absolutely.

When the apostles called Jesus the Cornerstone, they were not thinking of the decorative marble slab affixed to a completed building but rather to the foundational rock upon which the building would depend for its stability and strength. In the temple of God, the Church, Jesus is "the head of the corner," who gives both strength and stability to the spiritual temple of believers, who are also likened to the stones with which the rest of building is constructed (see 1 Pet. 2:5).

The True Vine and the Branches

In the Old Testament, God often used the image of a vine or a vineyard to describe the nation of Israel (see Ps. 80:8; Isa. 5:1-7; Jer. 2:21; Ezek. 15; 19:10; Hos. 10:1), but always the image was that of an unkempt vineyard that had gone wild. Jesus called Himself, in contrast, the True Vine, and He identified His disciples as the branches of that Vine (see John 15:1-8). This is perhaps the most intimate of images used in Scripture to describe the oneness of Christ and believers. Jesus is not the stem from which the branches grow but the Vine, which is the total life of the branches. The image of a vine is better suited than that of a tree, for the vine and branches grow into one another so that it is difficult to distinguish the vine from the branches. That ought also to be true of the relationship of the believer to His Lord.

This title, "the Vine," is the seventh of the Jehovistic titles of Jesus in the Gospel of John, and further aspects of this title are discussed elsewhere in this book. The practical application of this title to the Church relates to our oneness with Christ, the nature of spiritual growth, our responsibility to bear fruit consistently, and our need for occasional pruning.

Because Jesus is the Vine and we are the branches, we can accomplish nothing apart from Him. He is the supplier and sustainer of the very life of the believer, and the Christian life is lived by faith in Christ (see Gal. 2:20). As Christ lives His life through us, we will bear fruit. This fruit will consist of both converts to Christ, whom we will be instrumental in reaching, and the character of Christ, which the apostle Paul describes as the fruit of the Holy Spirit (see 5:22-23). Our primary responsibility relevant to this name of Christ is that of abiding in Him.

From time to time in our Christian lives, we encounter difficult and trying circumstances. Many times they are of the sort
that motivates us to seek spiritual reasons as to their cause. Many
Christians mistakenly conclude at such times that problems in
the Christian life are always caused by sin, and even though they
may be right with God, they are convinced that they have committed some sin that they must have forgotten about. What they
fail to realize, however, is that some troubles in the Christian life
are the result of our faithfulness. One of the forgotten promises
of Christ is that He will reward fruitfulness with pruning that
we "may bring forth more fruit" (John 15:2). By using a different
metaphor, Job expressed this same hope in the midst of his trial:
"But he knoweth the way that I take: when he hath tried me,
I shall come forth as gold" (Job 23:10).

CONCLUSION

The above titles of the LORD are significant, for they reveal who
God is in relation to His people. This emphasis is so common
in Scripture as to be taken for granted too often by Christians.
The deity of most religious systems is to be feared, served and
sacrificed to. But the LORD delights not in keeping His distance
from but in developing a greater intimacy with His people.

Although Jesus does relate individually to His disciples,
it is interesting that many of His names should relate to the
Church. During the '60s the mood of America was largely anti-
institutional, and many Christians were infected with this
spirit and rejected the Church. Things have changed to some
degree since then, but many Christians are still somewhat anti-
Church. Remember that Jesus loves the Church and gave
Himself for her and has great plans for her in the days to
come. Christians who voluntarily divorce themselves from the
Church and fail to belong to, support and pray for their local,
Bible-believing church are placing themselves in a position in
which they can hardly experience the rich reality of the Church
names of Jesus.

FOR DISCUSSION

1. Discuss the five titles for Christ mentioned in this chapter. What unique ministry is highlighted in each title?

2. How may we express our submission to Christ as the Head of the Body?

3. Discuss how Jesus the Shepherd is the model for pastors in caring for the flock.

4. As a Bridegroom, what does Christ do for those who are His Bride?

5. List several contributions that a foundation makes to a building. How do these relate to the believer's life and his or her Cornerstone, Christ?

6. Why does Jesus add the qualifying term "true" when He calls Himself a vine? How does Christ the Vine relate to believers as branches?

12

The Apocalyptic Names of Christ

The Revelation of Jesus Christ, which God gave unto him,
to shew unto his servants things which must shortly come to pass;
and he sent and signified it by his angel unto his servant John.
REVELATION 1:1

The final book of the New Testament offers the fullest revelation of Christ in Scripture. Even its divinely inspired title states its purpose as "the Revelation of Jesus Christ" (1:1). It is not therefore surprising that this book contains over 70 names and titles of Jesus. In reading the Revelation many people get sidetracked by focusing on obscure symbols or strained interpretations of things to come. But ultimately, when we look at this book, we ought to see Jesus.

Note carefully the 72 names and titles of Christ in this book: He is called "Jesus Christ" (1:1), "word of God" (v. 2), "the faithful witness," "the first begotten of the dead," "the prince of the kings of the earth" (v. 5), "Alpha and Omega," "the beginning and the ending," "the Lord," "the Almighty" (v. 8), "the first and the last" (v. 11), "the voice" (v. 12), "the Son of man" (v. 13), "he that liveth" (v. 18), "he that holdeth the seven stars," "who walketh in the midst of the seven golden candlesticks" (2:1), "who was dead, and came to life" (v. 8, *NKJV*), "he which hath the sharp sword with two edges" (v. 12), "the hidden manna" (v. 17), "the Son of God" (v. 18), "the morning star" (v. 28), "he that hath the seven Spirits of God," "the seven stars" (3:1), "he that is holy," "he that is true," "he that hath the key of David," "he that openeth, and no man shutteth" (v. 7), "my new name" (v. 12), "the Amen," "the faithful and true witness," "the beginning of the creation of God" (v. 14), "LORD God Almighty" (4:8), "worthy" (v. 11), "the Lion of the tribe of Judah," "the Root of David" (5:5), "a Lamb" (v. 6), "the Lamb that was slain" (v. 12), "Lord," "holy and true" (6:10), "him that sitteth on the throne" (v. 16), "the Lamb which is in the midst of the throne" (7:17), "him that liveth for ever and ever," "who created" (10:6), "our Lord" (11:8), "his Christ" (v. 15), "her child" (12:4), "a man child" (v. 5), "the Lamb slain from the foundation of the world" (13:8), "Jesus" (14:12), "King of saints" (15:3), "which art, and wast, and shalt be" (16:5), "which hath power over these plagues" (v. 9), "God Almighty" (v. 14), "Lord of lords," "King of kings" (17:14), "the Lord God who judgeth her" (18:8), "the Lord our God" (19:1), "God that sat on the throne" (v. 4), "Lord God omnipotent" (v. 6), "Faithful and True" (v. 11), "a name written, that no man knew" (v. 12), "The Word of God" (v. 13), "Christ" (20:4), "husband" (21:2), "God" (v. 7), "the glory of God" (v. 23), "the Lord God of the holy prophets" (22:6), "the root of David," "the offspring of David," "the bright and morning star" (v. 16), "he which testifieth these things," "Lord Jesus" (v. 20), and "our Lord Jesus Christ" (v. 21).

John was a climactic writer. Like all good writers, he developed his own style. When he wrote, he did so under inspiration and expressed himself climactically. In his Gospel he builds his case until the reader comes to the climax of the book and falls on his or her face to declare with Thomas, "Jesus is 'My LORD and my God'" (John 20:28). Climactically he wrote the last of the four Gospels. Climactically he was the last person to write Scripture. Climactically his Gospel is the greatest thesis on Christ. Climactically his book was the last to be recognized as canonical. Climactically he wrote the last book of the Bible. Climactically he wrote concerning the last things. In baseball there has to be a finisher, that is, a relief pitcher. If anyone was God's relief pitcher, it was the apostle John. It should almost be expected that John would be the one chosen of God to give such a full and rich description of Jesus in His names.

This profusion of names and titles, many highly symbolic in meaning in keeping with the nature of the book, provides a composite portrait of the Person of Christ. It is truly a "revelation of Jesus Christ" in His names. It is perhaps the fullest description in the New Testament of the majesty of His being.

Obviously, within the space limitations of this chapter, we cannot study all 72 names of Jesus in the final book of the Bible. What we shall do, however, is examine several groups or principal names of Christ in this book. An examination of these names makes us increasingly aware that Jesus can meet any and every need that we might have.

Jesus Christ

In his brief introduction to the book, John first uses the name "Jesus Christ" (1:1). This name is a composite of the personal and official names of Jesus. By the end of the first century, this name had become a common way to refer to the Lord. In a sense it represented a synthesization of the New Testament. "Jesus" is the predominant name in the Gospels and in Acts, whereas "Christ" is the predominant name in the Epistles, especially the Pauline Epistles. We examined both of these names closely in earlier chapters.

A Threefold Picture of Jesus Christ

John goes on to describe Jesus Christ as "the faithful witness, and the first begotten of the dead, and the prince of the kings of the earth" (1:5). This introduces in this book the three primary ideas concerning who Christ is. It is typical throughout the writings of John that although he writes in Greek, he thinks in Hebrew. It is not therefore surprising that the Revelation should focus on the threefold messianic office of prophet, priest and king.

Jesus Christ is first the prophet, and John identifies Him so as "the faithful witness." Jesus came to reveal the Father to mankind, and He did so perfectly (see Matt. 11:27). The Greek word translated "witness" here is *martus*, from which we get the English term "martyr." Originally *martus* meant "a witness" but came to refer to one who died because of his or her faithfulness in witnessing. It is interesting to note that Jesus Himself later applied this title to a believer in Pergamum named Antipas (see Rev. 2:13). The implication is that just as Jesus is the faithful witness of the Father to us, so too we need to be faithful witnesses of Him to the world. This title must have been very meaningful to John, who was himself exiled on Patmos because of his faithful witness of the things of God.

The second of these three titles in Revelation 1:5 emphasizes Christ's role as a priest; He is "the first begotten of the dead." In the Epistle to the Hebrews, He who arose became the high priest. Jesus was the first to rise to eternal life. Others had been raised before but had later died again. Theologians call these resuscitations as opposed to resurrections. Also unique concerning the resurrection of Jesus is the fact that He was raised not only to live forever but also to become "a quickening [or life-giving] spirit" (1 Cor. 15:45).

Third, Revelation 1:5 calls Jesus "the prince of the kings of the earth."Although not denying the sovereignty of Christ now as the authority by which kings rule (see Rom. 13:1) and the "LORD of all" (Acts 10:36), the book of Revelation emphasizes His coming dominion upon this earth. In this sense it is right for John to refer to Jesus not only as king but also as prince. A man is a prince until he formally assumes office as king. The next monarch of the British Commonwealth is scheduled to be Prince Charles. Even though he is trained to be king and will likely someday assume the throne of his mother, until Queen Elizabeth dies or surrenders the throne to her son, Charles will remain a prince. At the beginning of the book of Revelation, Jesus is called a prince of kings, but when He comes to establish His kingdom on Earth, He is called "KING OF KINGS, AND LORD OF LORDS" (19:16).

His Eternal Completeness and Sufficiency

Another significant grouping of names appears in Revelation 1:8. The first of these four titles is "Alpha and Omega." This is the Greek expression of a Hebrew idiom that implies completeness. The Jews took the first and last letters of their alphabet to emphasize and express the entirety of a thing. Alpha is the first letter of the Greek alphabet; omega is the last. As we noted earlier, a similar English expression is "everything from A to Z." In a sense this title includes all the more than 800 names and titles of Jesus.

In the second of this grouping of names, Jesus is identified as "the beginning and the ending." He is the One who not only pioneers or initiates but also perfects or finishes (see Heb. 12:2). This title serves to emphasize the absolute sovereignty of Christ over history. He is the LORD of history—its beginning, its ending and all that lies between. Although He may not yet be sitting on the throne of David in Jerusalem, nevertheless, Jesus has control and a unique way of working through others, even using tyrants and terrorists at times to accomplish His purpose (see Rom. 8:28).

Third, Revelation 1:8 describes Jesus as "the Lord, which is, and which was, and which is to come." There could be no more specific statement of the deity and eternality of Christ. This title of Christ parallels Moses' great affirmation of faith: "From everlasting to everlasting, thou art God" (Ps. 90:2). Jesus is eternally contemporary, the "I Am" of all times. The writer of the Hebrews speaks of "Jesus Christ the same yesterday, and to day, and for ever" (13:8).

Finally, Jesus here calls himself "the Almighty." This title probably was not intended to emphasize the omnipotence of Christ, although that attribute of God is certainly implied. Possibly John was thinking in the context of *El Shaddai*, an Old Testament title of God usually translated "God Almighty." Are you trusting the Almighty with your problems in life?

The Son of Man

More than any other book in the New Testament, the book of Revelation draws from the Old Testament, particularly from the messianic prophecies of the Old Testament. Much in the first three chapters of the Revelation describes a vision of the resurrected and glorified Jesus and His message to seven churches. In this context John uses many names and titles, but now John introduces Jesus as "one like unto the Son of man" (1:13). Most conservative commentators agree that this is a reference to the One whom Daniel called "the Son of man" (7:13), who received "dominion, and glory, and a kingdom" (v. 14) from the Ancient of Days.

When John turned to see the voice that spoke to him, the first things he observed were seven golden candlesticks. These candlesticks were probably not the kind that decorate homes but rather the type of candlesticks used in Jewish worship. They stood about five feet, five inches tall and weighed about 110 pounds each. They branched out on top to hold several candles; thus, many lights produced the one light of the candlestick. Jesus explains that these candlesticks represent seven local churches in Asia (see Rev. 1:20). It is interesting to note that Jesus was "in the midst of the seven candlesticks"—that is, an equal distance from each of them. He was as close to the Church in its delinquency as He was to the Church in revival. Why? Because the whole Church is His Body.

John pictured Jesus Christ here in the garment of the priest. The vivid description of Christ, as He stood glorified and trans-figured before the apostle, tends to emphasize His role as a judge. His head and hair were "white like wool, as white as snow" (v. 14), a symbol of His purity. "His eyes were as a flame of fire" (v. 14)—that is, they burned through the one whom they saw to discern accu-rately the nature of man. His feet were compared to "fine brass, as if they burned in a furnace" (v. 15). Throughout the Scripture, brass, or more correctly, bronze, is offered as a symbol of judgment. Jesus' voice is here compared to "the sound of many waters" (v. 15), emphasizing His authority. "Out of his mouth went a sharp twoedged sword" (v. 16), a symbol of the Word of God in its dis-cerning power (see Heb. 4:12). There was a brilliance about His entire countenance "as the sun shineth in his strength" (Rev. 1:16).

There in the presence of the glorified, transfigured Christ, John fell prostrate to the ground. Like the Old Testament proph-ets, John was learning experientially that if someone really wants to do something for God, it begins in the presence of Jesus Christ. Greatness always begins in the presence of God, not at a seminary or a Bible college.

This vision of Christ was significant in every detail through-out the seven epistles of Jesus to the seven churches in Revelation chapters 2 and 3. Each name that Jesus used to identify Himself represented His ability to meet the particular need of each church. As we have studied the names of Jesus together, I trust that you too have already discovered that whatever your need today, Jesus can meet that need.

The first of the seven churches that Christ addressed was the church at Ephesus. This was a commendable church in many re-spects, but it had begun to wander from its first love. The church needed leadership that would boldly direct it back to the place from which it had fallen. To that church Jesus identified Himself as "he that holdeth the seven stars in his right hand" (2:1). Earlier John had been told that the stars were the angels, or messengers—that is, the pastors of the churches (see 1:20). The senior pastor of the church at Ephesus needed to be encouraged that he was in the right hand of the Savior as he undertook to lead the flock in that city.

The church at Smyrna was a congregation under intense persecution. Many of its members had already lost their lives because of their faithfulness, and many more would do so in the days to come. They were not criticized in any way by the Lord, only encouraged to remain faithful. To encourage this church, Jesus reminded them that He was "the first and the last, which was dead, and is alive" (2:8).

Unlike the above churches, the church at Pergamum (or Pergamos) was a congregation with a mixed multitude. Some of its members gave no evidence of being saved and committed to the Lord. They were somewhat lax in their standards of personal separation, and they engaged in activities that most Christians of that day considered wrong. It was a church that was bending to social pressure to conform to the standard of the world and as a result had begun to wander away from its commitment to biblical authority. More than anything else, the church needed a back-to-the-Bible revival. To this church Jesus revealed Himself as "he which hath the sharp sword with two edges" (v. 12)—that is, the Word of God.

The church at Thyatira was one that would probably have been rejected as a legitimate church by most evangelical definitions today. A prominent woman in the church was introducing several pagan practices into the church, including immorality and idolatry. Of these two named sins, Jesus appears to have been most concerned with this woman's refusal to repent of fornication. As a result, He introduced Himself to that church as the Son of God coming in judgment with His burning eyes and bronze feet (see v. 18).

The next church Jesus addressed was the church at Sardis. It was a very reputable church, but in many respects its reputation was all it had. The church is described as dead but still possessing a believing remnant. Some commentators identify this church with the Reformation movement in the seventeenth century. In many respects, although the Reformers helped the church in its time and in subsequent generations greatly with their reemphasis upon the doctrines of grace, they failed to be as effective as they could have been because they neglected the work of the Holy Spirit. Significantly, Jesus reminded the church at Sardis that it was "he that hath the seven Spirits of God" (3:1) who addressed them.

In many respects the church at Philadelphia enjoyed the most coveted of circumstances among the seven Asian churches. Again, there is nothing about this church that Jesus chose to criticize directly. Although the church was small, it had unprecedented opportunities for service ahead of it. It was a church in the midst of revival and simply needed to be reminded not to allow the revival to degenerate into emotional fanaticism. To this church Jesus identified Himself as "he that is holy, he that is true, he that hath the key of David" (v. 7). The reference to "the key of David" originates in Isaiah 22:22 and emphasizes that Christ alone has authority to admit whom He wishes into the Kingdom. This church needed truth and holiness, but it also needed to grasp the opportunities that awaited it in reaching its world with the gospel.

The church of Laodicea has come to represent the lukewarm compromise often characteristic of many churches today. It needed to be reminded of who Jesus was as "the Amen, the faithful and true witness, the beginning of the creation of God" (Rev. 3:14). Jesus was to this church the final Word, an example that one could be both faithful and true, and a reminder that as Creator, He knew what was best for His church in Laodicea.

The Lion and Lamb

One of the most interesting contrasts of names in Revelation occurs in chapter 5, where in the same context Christ is called both the Lion of the tribe of Judah and a Lamb (vv. 5-6). If this combination sounds paradoxical in English, it is even more so in Greek. The word used here for "lamb" is a diminutive and a term of endearment. It is the sort of word a child might use to describe a cute and cuddly baby lamb. And yet this title is used here in the context of the regal majesty of the Lion of the tribe of Judah, the ruling tribe of Israel.

John here brings together two titles that have different emphases to give his readers a fuller understanding of who Jesus is. As the Lion, He was everything the Jews expected in their Messiah. He was the son of David who would rule over Caèsar. He was the One coming to establish the kingdom of God on Earth. But He was also the Messiah who had come to give His life a ransom for many. As such, He is the sacrificial yearling Lamb. But He is a Lamb with a difference: this Lamb had seven horns. A horn was a symbol of power in the Old Testament, and seven was a number of completeness in Scripture. This is the Lamb with the fullness of the strength and power of the Lion.

When Samson sought to give the Philistines a riddle they could not resolve on their own, he said, "Out of the strong came forth sweetness" (Judg. 14:14). Even today it is uncommon to find strength and sweetness, or beauty, in the same thing or being. But Jesus manifested both strength and beauty. As we survey the many names and titles of Christ, we note that some emphasize His strength while at the same time others tend to emphasize His gentleness. This is evident in Revelation, which emphasizes the fact that God still sits on the throne and will ultimately triumph over the world system: yet 26 times we learn that this God is Jesus the Lamb. The predominant name of Jesus in Revelation is "the Lamb."

The Coming Conqueror

The plot of the book of Revelation, particularly from chapter 4 to the end, shows forth Jesus as the legitimate One to possess the title-deed of the world and notes the preparations in heaven and the events on Earth that are necessary for Jesus to claim what is rightfully His and to establish His kingdom. This plot reaches a climax in chapter 19, in which the second coming of Christ in glory is described. In that passage Christ is identified by five significant names (see 19:11-16).

The first of these conquering names of Christ is "Faithful and True" (v. 11). Faith, or faithfulness, and truth are constant themes in the writings of John. Jesus is identified by these names earlier in Revelation, but for emphasis the compound name appears here at the climax. Right to the end Jesus is faithful. Right to the end Jesus is true. This is a tremendous encouragement in time of trial and in those hours in which even the finest of Christians begins to wonder, "Is it really worth all this?" Regardless of our circumstances, regardless of our situation, regardless of how long our circumstances and situation have been the way they are, Jesus will prove Himself to be faithful and true right to the end.

The second name John records in this passage is "a name written, that no man knew, but he himself" (v. 12). This may be one of the most fascinating of all the names of Jesus. Several years ago I became interested in discovering the names of Jesus in Scripture. Originally I compiled a listing of about 250 names, and I thought I had exhausted the topic. Yet as I continued to read and study the Scripture, I came across names that were not on my list. I had heard someone once say that there were 365 names of Christ, one for each day of the year, and I wondered whether that was so. To date I have found over 800 names of Christ, and I am no longer convinced that even this longer list is exhaustive. Each time I discover a new name, I am impressed again by another attribute or aspect of the work of Christ that a name suggests.

As much as I want to know all the names of Jesus, I realize that even at the return of Christ there will be an element of mystery about at least one of His names. When we consider all that is involved in each of the names we have examined, it is clear that there is no limit to all that Jesus is in regard to His names. It would be futile even to try to speculate as to the particular significance of this unknown name in Revelation 19:12. Its presence in Scripture reminds us again that Jesus has a name for every need, even if we don't know the name specifically.

Third, Jesus is called "The Word of God" (v. 13). He is the idea or expression of God Himself. This is also one of the birth names of Jesus, and I have dealt more fully with the significance of the *Logos* in my chapter on birth names. A fourth name mentioned in this passage is "Almighty God" (v. 15), which may refer to *El Shaddai* or, in this context, the omnipotence of God, which is an attribute of Jesus.

Finally, John notes the published name embroidered into Jesus' garment, "KING OF KINGS, AND LORD OF LORDS" (v. 16). With this title Christ comes, followed by the armies of heaven, which may be an angelic host or more probably the raptured saints. Although I am not much of a rider on horseback today, I hope someday to ride in that heavenly cavalry behind the King of kings and LORD of lords. This title of "Christ" emphasizes the absolute sovereignty of Jesus.

The Root and Offspring of David

In the closing verses of this book, Jesus identifies Himself as "the root and offspring of David" (Rev. 22:16). This name suggests two ideas in Christ's relationship with David. The first is that of an old root buried in the ground that from time to time sends up shoots, or "suckers," as they are sometimes called. The sucker draws all the strength and nourishment from the root. Those in charge of orchards are continually watching for these new shoots and pruning them back so that the original fruit tree is not robbed of any nourishment that the root might otherwise supply to it. Jesus was David's source of strength and nourishment, just as a root supplies the shoot with its strength and nourishment. What was true in David's experience with Christ is also true in the experience of believers today: we derive everything we need from Christ.

But Jesus was not only the source of David but also the seed of David. As the offspring of David, He was the legitimate heir to the throne of his father David. He was the qualified candidate in which all the messianic prophecies concerning David's greater Son were or shall be fulfilled. He was the Son of David and also David's LORD (see Mark 12:35-37). This title was rich in Jewish heritage, for David was considered the model king of Israel.

The Bright and Morning Star

Again, in identifying another title of Jesus, the Scriptures refer to an image of light. Jesus calls Himself "the bright and morning star" (Rev. 22:16). This star is so named because it appears on the horizon just before sunrise. The appearance of the morning star tells us that the Dayspring from on High is almost here. It is the star of hope for those who are tired of the long night of darkness. And with the apostle John, we are encouraged by this star to pray, "Even so, come, LORD Jesus" (v. 20).

CONCLUSION

If Jesus were to come to you today and ask, "What could I do for you?" how would you respond? Actually, the question is not hypothetical. He is here and asking. He wants to become more meaningful in your life by revealing Himself in His names to you. I trust that you have learned something new about the LORD Jesus Christ in this study of His names, but I hope even more that your new knowledge of Jesus goes beyond the intellect. The names and titles of Jesus in Scripture become ever clearer in the context of your experience with the Lord. Don't be the barrier that prevents Jesus from doing for you what He wants to do in order to make His names a meaningful part of your Christian experience.

FOR DISCUSSION

1. Why does the last book in the Bible, Revelation, contain perhaps more names of Jesus than any other? What is the main theme of this book?
2. Why is Revelation called a climactic book?
3. What is the threefold picture of Jesus in Revelation? Relate it to His threefold anointed offices.
4. Note the contrasting descriptions of Christ as a Lion and a Lamb. How do these titles carry out the theme of Revelation? What do these titles tell us about Christ?
5. Name the titles in Revelation that describe Christ as a conqueror. What do these titles tell us about Christ?
6. Explain how Christ is the root and offspring of David.
7. What is something new that you have learned about the Lord?

BOOK THREE

The Names of the Holy Spirit

UNDERSTANDING THE NAMES OF THE HOLY SPIRIT AND HOW THEY CAN HELP YOU KNOW GOD MORE INTIMATELY

ELMER L. TOWNS

Introduction

I have been fascinated with names all my life, perhaps because my name—Elmer—is not a common one. I have both liked and disliked my name since I was a small boy. I remember some friends making fun of my name when I was in the first grade. It seems that there was a comedy character on radio named Elmer at whom people laughed—he was considered dumb. When I asked my mother why I had that name, she told me, "Because I loved your father." I was named after him. So I liked the name after that, no matter what others said.

My fascination with names led me to write *The Names of Jesus*. In my research on the names of Jesus, I discovered more than 800 names, titles and references to Jesus.

Then I wrote *My Father's Names*, primarily analyzing the names of God in the Old Testament, and I found more than 100 of His names and titles.

Because the Holy Spirit is the third Person of the Trinity, I naturally wanted to write a book on His name. This book finishes the trilogy. In my study for this volume, I uncovered more than 100 names, descriptive phrases and titles for the Holy Spirit. In this study, however, you will learn more than the Spirit's names. You will also learn about His personality and what He does for you today. This book is, therefore, more than a doctrinal study of the names of the Holy Spirit. I want you to learn about Him, to know Him and to experience Him in your life.

People usually do not think of the term "Holy Spirit" as a name. Instead, they think of the phrase as a description. Maybe this is because they do not think of the Spirit as a person. People think of Him as an influence and give Him a title just as they give a title to boats, cars or hurricanes. They think of Him as an influence, like "the spirit of democracy" or "the spirit of the Yankees."

Because people pray to "our Father in heaven," or they pray, "Dear Jesus," they know of the Father and the Son as persons. But most people never pray to the Holy Spirit, perhaps because they do not think of Him as a person. Some do think the command "Pray the Lord of the harvest" (Matt. 9:38, *NKJV*) is directed to the Holy Spirit; also, "the Lord is the Spirit" (2 Cor. 3:17, *NKJV*). And Scripture shows examples of prayer to the Lord as the Spirit present among His people—instances in which the Spirit responds to the prayers being offered (see Luke 2:25-29; Acts 10:9,13-15,19; 11:5,7,8,12; 13:2; 15:28).

I can't write about the names of the Holy Spirit and not write about the Trinity. When describing the Trinity, I like to use the statement written by the Early Church fathers in the Athanasian Creed: "We worship one God in Trinity and Trinity in unity, neither confounding the persons, nor dividing the substance."

To explain how the doctrine of the Trinity works, I have used the following statement: "The members of the Trinity are equal in nature, separate in Person but submissive in duty." In this book, therefore, I have emphasized three things.

First, this book equally emphasizes the deity of the Holy Spirit along with God the Father and God the Son—they all have the same nature, attributes and character.

Second, this book separates the personality of the Holy Spirit from the personality of the Father and the personality of the Son—the Godhead consists of three separate persons.

Third, this book emphasizes the duties of the Holy Spirit, who was sent by the Father and the Son to carry out the work of God in the world.

When I asked several authorities to read this book, most of them were surprised. They indicated that they had never seen all these names for the Holy Spirit gathered in one place. I taught this series in the Pastor's Bible Class at Thomas Road Baptist Church in Lynchburg, Virginia, where approximately 1,000 people gather weekly to study Scripture. Just as with my two previous books, *The Names of Jesus* and *My Father's Names*, the congregation was fascinated with the content, wanting to know more. I feel that my best books have been hammered out in the arena of a class's receptivity before being offered to the publisher.

This book is aimed beyond the study of Bible facts. I want you to feel the Holy Spirit living through you. I wrote this book to do more than fill academic curiosity. It should help you live successfully for God. Each chapter, therefore, concludes by offering principles to be applied to life.

One name or title is missing in this study: the term "ghost," as in "Holy Ghost." The original *King James Version* (1611) translated the word *pneuma* "ghost" as in, "Ye shall be baptized with the Holy Ghost" (Acts 1:5) and "after that the Holy Ghost is come upon you" (1:8). This has resulted in confusion in some minds.

Some think the word "ghost" refers to a phantom, as in the ghosts of Halloween. But the word *pneuma* should be translated "spirit." The word "ghost" had a different meaning in 1611 than it does today, and this difference blurs the personality of the third Person of the Trinity for some. The solution to this confusion is simple. Every time the term "Holy Ghost" is found in the original *King James Version,* it should be translated "Holy Spirit." If you prefer to use the name "Holy Ghost," do so, as long as you understand the meaning of the name you are using. For the Holy Spirit is the furthest thing from a phantom. He is very real.

His primary name, Holy Spirit, has a twofold implication. First, when we take the Holy Spirit into our lives, He should make us holy, as His name implies. "Do you not know that your body is the temple of the Holy Spirit who is in you, whom you have from God, and you are not your own?" (1 Cor. 6:19, *NKJV*). Second, when we live by the principles of the Holy Spirit, He will make us spiritual, because we will become like Him. We should become holy and spiritual as we study the Holy Spirit.

I want to thank the many people who have helped me understand the Holy Spirit. My theology of the Holy Spirit was transformed by reading *He That Is Spiritual* by Lewis S. Chafer, founder of Dallas Theological Seminary. Before this I was afraid of the Holy Spirit because of some extremes I had seen in some churches. I had an unfortunate experience as a young believer and was turned off to any emphasis on the Holy Spirit throughout my life.

I also want to recognize John R. Rice for convincing me that power in service comes from the Holy Spirit. He urged me to seek His power. I appreciate how Larry Gilbert clarified my thinking about the gifts of the Holy Spirit. Dr. Douglas Porter, a former student and a graduate of Liberty Baptist Theological Seminary, challenged me to think about the many names of God. We discussed these matters for hours, and he helped in the research for this book.

Many have contributed to my thinking about the Holy Spirit, but in the last analysis, we are all a product of our teachers and friends. Just as every tub must sit on its own bottom, so I must take responsibility for all the weaknesses and omissions of this volume.

May God make you more holy and more spiritual as you study these terms for His Holy Spirit.

Elmer L. Towns
Lynchburg, Virginia
Summer, 1994

PART 1

Jesus and the Holy Spirit

1

The Helper: Jesus' Favorite Name for the Holy Spirit

The Ministry of the Helper

His Pre-conversion Ministry	
1. The Helper as prosecuting attorney	His role in convicting us of sin
2. The Helper as crossing guard	His role in restraining us from sin

His Ministry at Conversion	
1. The Helper as interior decorator	His role in renewing spiritual life
2. The Helper as apartment manager	His role in indwelling the believer
3. The Helper as notary public	His role in guaranteeing our salvation

His Post-conversion Ministry	
1. The Helper as administrative assistant	His role in filling us for service
2. The Helper as search committee	His role in setting us apart to God
3. The Helper as teacher	His role in explaining spiritual truth to the believer
4. The Helper as lawyer	His role in presenting our prayers to the Father

"What is Jesus' favorite name for the Holy Spirit?" I asked a minister as I was writing this chapter.

"I never thought about it before," my pastor friend responded. I then explained this book and what I wanted to accomplish with it. My friend said to me, "I think Jesus' favorite name is 'Holy Spirit.'"

Obviously he thought of the third Person of the Trinity as the Holy Spirit because of His title. But is a title the same thing as a name? The title "Father" for the first Person of the Trinity is designated a name (see John 17:1). This was Jesus' favorite name for God. The second Person of the Trinity is Jesus: "You shall call His name JESUS" (Matt. 1:21, *NKJV*). Yet Jesus' favorite name for Himself was "Son of man," a title that He used more than any other.

The name or title "Spirit" is used approximately 500 times in Scripture in reference to the third Person, and the combined term "Holy Spirit" is used approximately 100 times. The expression "Holy Ghost," used 91 times in the *King James Version,* should be translated "Holy Spirit."

My name is Elmer, but when I first had children, their favorite name for me was Dad. My wife calls me Sweetheart. That could be her favorite title for me.

My minister friend told me that Jesus' favorite name for the third Person of the Trinity is "Holy Spirit." He thought so because it is used so many times in Scripture. But I disagree.

Jesus' favorite name for the Holy Spirit was probably "Helper." Of all the things the Holy Spirit does, He helps us obtain the personal salvation that was accomplished for us on the cross. In the *King James Version*, the name "Helper" is translated "Comforter." Jesus promised, "And I will pray the Father, and He will give you another Helper, that He may abide with you forever" (John 14:16, *NKJV*). The Greek word for "helper" is *parakletos* and may be translated "helper," "comforter," "advocate" or "one called alongside." This term is related to the compound verb with the prefix *para,* meaning "alongside," and the verbal base *kaleo,* meaning "to call."

Although the name "Helper" for the Holy Spirit occurs only four times in Scripture, I think it is Jesus' favorite name because it best identifies what the Holy Spirit does. Each time this name is used in Scripture, it is used by Jesus Christ (see John 14:16, 26; 15:26; 16:7, *NKJV*). Jesus repeated the name "Helper" during the Upper Room discourse, perhaps the most intimate of all the recorded sermons of

Christ. I think it is Jesus' favorite name for the Holy Spirit because it relates to salvation.

After I asked my friend the question "What is Jesus' favorite name for the Holy Spirit?" he later came back to me and said, "I hadn't thought of the Holy Spirit as having a name."

Why We Don't Recognize His Names

My friend is similar to a lot of people who think of the Holy Spirit as an influence, an attitude or a corporate opinion. Some of the titles for the Holy Spirit in the *King James Version* have contributed to misinformation about the Holy Spirit's name. The name "Holy Ghost" makes people think of Him as a Halloween spook, and the name "Comforter" makes people think of Him as a quilt on a bed or as someone who comes and comforts people at a funeral.

Perhaps people do not recognize the names of the Holy Spirit because of certain implications in Scripture. First, Jesus promised that the Holy Spirit would come, but He also emphasized that a major thrust of His ministry would be glorifying Christ (see John 16:14). Because the Holy Spirit talks more about Jesus than Himself, many Christians have concluded they should not glorify the Holy Spirit. They do not speak to Him and do not know Him. But as the third Person of the Godhead, the Holy Spirit should receive glory just as much as the Father and the Son do.

Another reason that people do not recognize the Holy Spirit's name is because of His task. The Father initiates the process of salvation, and the Son carries it out on Calvary. But the Holy Spirit works in the heart of the believer to effect that which the Son has done.

This work of the Spirit can be compared to the construction of a large building. The owners of the building, who initiate its construction, are typically remembered, as are the engineer and the architects. But most people do not remember the workers who do the actual building. In a similar way, most people do not give attention to the Holy Spirit who actually applies salvation in our hearts.

Another reason the Holy Spirit is not recognized is because He did not come in the flesh. No one doubts that Jesus was a person or that He had a corporeal body on Earth. The most obvious physical manifestation that we see of the Holy Spirit is of Him descending as a dove upon Jesus at the Lord's baptism (see Mark 1:10) and as tongues of fire on the Day of Pentecost (see Acts 2:3).

In the Old Testament, however, the Holy Spirit is identified with the pillar of cloud and fire by which the Lord guided the Israelites at the Exodus and in their wilderness wanderings (see Exod. 13:21; 19:16-19; Isa. 63:11-14; Heb. 12:29).

Also, Paul identifies the Spirit of the Lord as the source of the glory and radiance seen on Moses' face after he had entered the Lord's presence in the cloud covering Sinai (see Exod. 19:9; Deut. 31:15; Ps. 99:6-7; 2 Cor. 3:17-18). Ezekiel shows the Spirit of God manifesting Himself in glory, radiance and fire (see 1:27–2:2).

As you read this book, ask for "Holy Spirit eyes" so that you will be able to see Him in Scripture. In my research I have discovered more than 100 references to the names, titles and descriptions of the Holy Spirit. One person said to me, "Wow! I didn't know that He had that many names." Perhaps that is because we are not accustomed to looking for them. Many Christians have "Holy Spirit blindness." They are blinded to the Holy Spirit because of the nature of His task or because of some bias that grows out of their experience.

Stop before continuing to read, and breathe this prayer:

> Lord, give me eyes to see the Holy Spirit in my life and in the Scriptures, in Jesus' name. Amen.

Why a Favorite Name?

Most of us like the name that best describes us. Certain women like to be called Mom because they see their main task as raising children. When I first began preaching, I pastored the Westminster Presbyterian Church in Savannah, Georgia, during my sophomore and junior years in Bible college. Obviously I was too young for the scriptural titles that describe a pastor, such as "elder," "bishop" or "minister." I was not ordained, so I could not be called Reverend. Everybody in the church called me Preacher. Because I liked to preach, and because I thought I did a pretty good job, I liked to be called Preacher.

After graduating from seminary, I became a professor of Christian education at Midwest Bible College in St. Louis, Missouri. Again, I love to teach. All my students called me Prof. I enjoyed that title because it described what I enjoyed doing. When people call us by names that reflect what we do best, we usually enjoy the designation.

A certain salesman was transferred from Chicago to Atlanta, and because he considered himself a good salesman, he decided to sell his house without the aid of a real-estate company. He advertised and got a few people to come and walk through his house. The salesman gave a strong sales pitch to each prospect. But his hard-sell tactics produced no sales. After six frustrating months and the loss of time and money, he finally listed his house with a real-estate agent.

What the salesman did not realize was that an agent counsels customers before showing them a home. The agent whom the salesman hired first qualified customers so that he showed the salesman's home only to those who had the financial ability to purchase it. Also, the agent found customers who had a desire for a home similar to the salesman's home. Once he had shown the home, the agent could continue to point out its advantages and answer people's questions.

The work of the Holy Spirit in salvation is similar to that of the real-estate agent. The Holy Spirit works conviction in the hearts of the unconverted long before they come to a gospel service. He witnesses to the person the positive reasons for salvation and warns against procrastination. The Holy Spirit is the Helper (*paraclete*) who gets a decision and seals the contract. Although this analogy cannot be pushed to every aspect of the Holy Spirit's work in salvation, it is illustrative of the process.

The Holy Spirit Helps Us in Salvation

Pre-conversion	Conversion	Post-conversion
1. Reproves, or convicts (see John 16:7-10)	1. Regenerates (see Titus 3:5)	1. Fills (see Eph. 5:18)
2. Restrains (see 2 Thess. 2:7)	2. Indwells (see 1 Cor. 6:19)	2. Sanctifies (see 2 Cor. 3:18)
	3. Seals (see Eph. 4:30)	3. Illuminates (see 1 Cor. 2:12)
		4. Helps us pray (see Rom. 8:26-27)

The Helper in Our Conversion

Before returning to the Father, Jesus promised that He would send "another Comforter" (John 14:16), using the Greek word *allos* for "other," which means "another of the same kind." Jesus could have used the word *heteros* for "other," meaning another of a different kind. But Jesus used the word *allos,* which means that the Holy Spirit is another Helper just like Jesus is our Helper.

Pre-conversion Ministries

"The Holy Spirit Helps Us in Salvation" chart shows nine helping ministries of the Holy Spirit. First, He reproves sin (see John 16:7-10), which means that He is like a prosecuting attorney who helps the state prove a case of wrongdoing. Second, the Holy Spirit is the restrainer (see 2 Thess. 2:7), which means that He is like the crossing guard who protects children on their way to elementary school. He helps by holding us back from harm and danger.

Conversion Ministries

In His conversion ministry the Holy Spirit regenerates (see Titus 3:5), which means that He is like an interior decorator who renews an old room, making it new. Then the Holy Spirit indwells us (see 1 Cor. 6:19), which means that He is like an apartment manager, one who comes to live in the complex to protect it, making sure that all the equipment is functioning. Finally, the Holy Spirit is our seal (see Eph. 4:30), which means that He is like a notary public. He helps to guarantee the accuracy of the signature, and if necessary, He will testify in court.

Post-conversion Names

In His post-conversion ministry, the Holy Spirit fills the person (see Eph. 5:18). He is like an administrative assistant who comes in to help get the job done. Next, He is the sanctifier (see 2 Cor. 3:18), serving as a search-committee chairman who helps the group select a leader, set the leader apart and put that person in a place of prominence. The Holy Spirit is the illuminator (see 1 Cor. 2:12), like the teacher who helps believers to understand and apply the Word of God to their lives. Then the Holy Spirit helps believers to pray (see Rom. 8:26-27), just as a lawyer helps people by presenting their cases before a magistrate.

How the Holy Spirit Helps

The Helper as Prosecuting Attorney

The Holy Spirit is sent to help people become Christians. Before they can become saved, however, they must realize that they are lost. The Holy Spirit helps unsaved people by revealing their sin to them. In this role the Holy Spirit could be called our Convicter, or Reprover. Like a prosecuting attorney, He convicts people of their sin, enabling them to seek salvation.

As a prosecuting attorney, the Holy Spirit helps to convict people of sin in three ways. First, He helps people see their sin. Jesus said that the Holy Spirit would help convict people "of sin, because they do not believe in Me" (John 16:9, *NKJV*). Before salvation people can have difficulty believing in God. Jesus said, "He who believes in Him [the Son] is not condemned; but he who does not believe is condemned already, because he has not believed in the name of the only begotten Son of God" (3:18, *NKJV*). Therefore, the Holy Spirit helps people accept salvation by pointing out unbelief and bringing them to Christ.

Second, the Holy Spirit helps prosecute people concerning righteousness. Jesus said that the Holy Spirit would convict "of righteousness, because I go to My Father and you see Me no more" (16:10, *NKJV*). Hence, the Holy Spirit helps people see themselves in relationship to Jesus Christ. People do not measure up to Jesus Christ, who is God's righteous standard, so the Holy Spirit helps them see their shortcomings.

Third, the Holy Spirit helps people come to Christ by convicting them "of judgment, because the ruler of this world is judged" (16:11, *NKJV*). This judgment does not refer to the coming judgment of all believers at the Great White Throne but to the judgment of Satan and sin at the cross of Christ (see 12:31, *NKJV*).

The Helper as Crossing Guard

As bad as things are in the world, they are not as terrible as they might be if the Holy Spirit were not present in the world to restrict the persuasive influence of sin. In the role of restrainer of sin, the Holy Spirit is like a crossing guard who restrains children from running into the path of traffic. He helps the children by protecting them from harm. As the Restrainer, or crossing guard, "He who now restrains will do so until He is taken out of the way [at the return of Christ]" (2 Thess. 2:7, *NKJV*).

The Helper as Interior Decorator

The Holy Spirit helps us with our new life when we are saved. The Greek word translated "regeneration" is used only once in the Bible in the context of salvation, and it relates to the ministry of the Holy Spirit: "Not by works of righteousness which we have done, but according to His mercy He saved us, through the washing of regeneration and renewing of the Holy Spirit" (Titus 3:5, *NKJV*). "Regeneration" is the theological word for being "born again." Jesus told Nicodemus, "Unless one is born of water and the Spirit, he cannot enter the kingdom of God" (John 3:5, *NKJV*). This regeneration of the Holy Spirit gives us new life, makes us part of God's family and gives us eternal life. This is not just life unending; it is a new quality of life (that is,

God's life). The Holy Spirit is like an interior decorator who takes a shabby old house and renovates it, making it like new.

The Helper as Apartment Manager

The indwelling of the Holy Spirit is like the manager of an apartment building. He lives in the building to tend to problems, to make sure the building is not damaged, and to help people enjoy the apartment complex.

One of God's purposes from the very beginning was to live with His creatures. He walked with Adam in the garden, lived in the Tabernacle among the children of Israel in the wilderness, and came to dwell in Solomon's temple. Likewise, the Holy Spirit comes to dwell in Christians to help us live the Christian life: "Do you not know that your body is the temple of the Holy Spirit who is in you, whom you have from God, and you are not your own?" (1 Cor. 6:19, *NKJV*). The Holy Spirit uses our body as a temple. This indwelling is the basis on which He helps us in every other area of our lives.

When we realize that the Holy Spirit indwells us as our Helper, we should first yield our bodies to God (see Rom. 12:1). Second, we must then assist Him by properly caring for our physical bodies, keeping them pure and clean. Third, we should glorify God in our bodies by doing those things that please Him.

The Helper as Notary Public

The Holy Spirit seals us with Himself to guarantee our salvation. The Bible teaches that the Holy Spirit is more than One who seals us; He *is* our seal: "You were sealed with the Holy Spirit of promise, who is the guarantee of our inheritance until the redemption of the purchased possession" (Eph. 1:13-14, *NKJV*).

Our lives consist of many seals. When a man and woman agree to marry, the man usually gives the woman an engagement ring, which is the seal of his commitment to her. Paul used a first-century custom to tell how the Holy Spirit is our Seal. In the ancient world a person would seal a letter with candle wax, then place his signet ring into the melted wax as the seal. When the recipient got the letter, the unbroken seal in the hardened wax guaranteed that the content was genuine.

In like manner, the Holy Spirit is our notary public in that He guarantees God's "signature." He seals the salvation that God has given to us against the day when we fully experience it in heaven. It is important that we "do not grieve the Holy Spirit of God, by whom [we] were sealed for the day of redemption" (Eph. 4:30, *NKJV*).

The Helper as Administrative Assistant

The Holy Spirit comes on us every time we ask Him to fill us for service, just as an administrative assistant is available to perform a job until it is completed. The Holy Spirit dwells in us, and, when we will allow Him, He will help us in our Christian lives and service. The Bible calls this the filling of the Holy Spirit (at other places in this book it is called the anointing). Paul encourages, "Do not be drunk with wine, in which is dissipation; but be filled with the Spirit" (Eph. 5:18, *NKJV*). This imperative is in the present tense, which means that God commands us to be continually filled with the Holy Spirit for effective service.

Many people think that being filled with the Spirit is like taking an empty glass to the sink and filling it up. In one sense, of course, we already have the Holy Spirit in our lives because of His indwelling in the experience of conversion. But the filling of the Holy Spirit means that He fills us with His grace and power. In other words, He fills us with His ability to accomplish much for God. Jesus promised His disciples the power to witness (see Acts 1:8), and on the day of Pentecost they were filled with the Spirit (see 2:4). On another occasion Peter needed filling (see 4:8). And later, in a prayer meeting, the building shook when the people were filled with the Holy Spirit (see 4:31). These verses indicate that we can be filled many times.

The Helper as Search Committee

The Holy Spirit is our Sanctifier, which means that He helps us become holy. Actually, the word "sanctify" means "to set apart." A twofold action occurs when the Holy Spirit sanctifies. First, He sets us apart from sin. In this action He works in our hearts to motivate us to repent of and to turn from sin. In the second action the Holy Spirit sets us apart to God. We are motivated to seek God and His righteousness.

The Helper as a search committee actually does the work of searching us out, just as a pulpit search committee seeks the proper person for a pastoral position. When the committee finds the person it believes should be hired, it recommends him or her and prepares the way for the candidate to get the position. The Holy Spirit, like a search committee, works *internally* in our lives to make us holy and *externally* in heaven to secure our position, or standing, before God. In heaven we are declared righteous (justified), standing perfect before God.

The Helper as Teacher

The Holy Spirit illuminates the believer to see spiritual truth. In this role He is the teacher of spiritual truth. "The god of this age has blinded [those] who do not believe" (2 Cor. 4:4, *NKJV*). This means that the unsaved person cannot understand spiritual truth. But when a person is converted, the Holy Spirit becomes the Helper to teach or illuminate the person so that he or she can understand spiritual truth.

The job of teaching or illuminating the believer has several names in the New Testament. At one place it is called the anointing: "But the anointing which you have received from Him abides in you, and you do not need that anyone teach you" (1 John 2:27, *NKJV*). This does not mean that the believer should not have human teachers but rather that the Holy Spirit is the Teacher who causes the believer to understand, whether or not a human teacher is involved in the learning process. The apostle Paul noted, "The natural man does not receive the things of the Spirit of God . . . because they are spiritually discerned" (1 Cor. 2:14, *NKJV*). In contrast, "We have received, not the spirit of the world, but the Spirit who is from God, that we might know the things that have been freely given to us by God" (2:12, *NKJV*).

Returning to the illustration of the Helper as a Teacher, John the apostle puts these two together: "But the Helper, the Holy spirit, whom the Father will send in My name, He will teach you all things, and bring to your remembrance all things that I said to you" (John 14:26, *NKJV*).

The Helper as Lawyer

The Holy Spirit is our attorney who presents our case before the judge. A lawyer is usually hired by a defendant because the lawyer knows the law, knows the legal system, and has the ability to argue (logically present) the matter before the judge.

The Holy Spirit also is the Intercessor who prays for the believer and with the believer and in the place of the believer. Why? "For we do not know what we should pray for as we ought, but the Spirit Himself makes intercession for us with groanings which cannot be uttered" (Rom. 8:26, *NKJV*).

We are not always aware of the perfect way to approach God in prayer. Perhaps we come begging when we should be worshiping Him. We are human, and God is infinite. So the Holy Spirit makes sure that the believer always prays properly. That means that no matter how the believer prays or what the believer prays, the Holy Spirit makes the words come out accurately when presented to the Father in heaven. "The Spirit also helps in our weaknesses ... [making] intercession for us with groanings which cannot be uttered" (8:26, *NKJV*). What is the result of the Holy Spirit's work as our lawyer? "He makes intercession for the saints according to the will of God" (8:27, *NKJV*).

Living with the Complete Godhead

Often after we have known someone for some time, there are times when we see that person in a new setting and learn something new about our friend. Perhaps we discover a new common interest or a shared experience or a similarity in certain skills in the process of the growing friendship. Our new knowledge helps us to better understand our friend and may contribute to a better relationship.

Many who have known God and walked with God are ignorant of the Holy Spirit and how He can make their lives complete. Knowing about the Holy Spirit is the first step to knowing Him and allowing Him to work in our life.

Many Christians limit their understanding of the Holy Spirit to a single experience that they have had with the Holy Spirit or to a particular work of the Holy Spirit. This person may emphasize the gifts of the Holy Spirit, the filling of the Holy Spirit or the illumination of the Holy Spirit. Obviously this is a narrow understanding of the Holy Spirit.

The Principle of God's Dwelling Place

As the Spirit of the LORD, the Holy Spirit is the key to our having a vital relationship with God. From the beginning of time, it has been God's desire to dwell with people and to have fellowship with them. Originally He prepared a garden in which He apparently met with Adam and Eve on a regular basis. Later He gave Moses the plans for the Tabernacle, and His glory rested in the Holy Place in the center of His people. When the Tabernacle wore out with age, Solomon built a temple, which again was filled with the glory of God. Then, in the fullness of time, "The Word became flesh and dwelt among us" (John 1:14, *NKJV*). As Jesus prepared to return to heaven, He promised His followers that He would send another Helper. In this age the Holy Spirit is the means by which God dwells in and among people.

The name "Spirit of the LORD" occurs 25 times in the Old Testament. In every case, a relationship between the Holy Spirit and a specific person is either clearly stated or strongly implied. The use of this name for the Holy Spirit illustrates the desire of God to have a meaningful place among His people.

The Principle of Insight for Living

A second principle implied by the names of the Holy Spirit is that He imparts insight for living. The description of the Helper as Teacher suggests that the Holy Spirit is willing to give us insight and to help us make decisions. Also, this name implies the guidance and leading of the Holy Spirit in our lives.

At times Christians find it difficult to discern God's will concerning a particular decision. God directs Christians in two primary ways in making decisions. "A man's heart plans his way, but the LORD directs his steps" (Prov. 16:9, *NKJV*). First, God leads in our decision making by giving us the ability to think through the issues and come to a conclusion.

Second, God reserves the right to intervene in our circumstances, either through counsel with others or in some other way to redirect our steps toward a better decision. In both cases the Holy Spirit living within the Christian helps the Christian discern God's will.

The Principle of Power for Service

The principle of power for service is implied in the name "spirit of power" (see 2 Tim. 1:7). Someone has said, "You can't do the work of God with the power of man. You do the work of God with the power of God." Unfortunately, many Christians know by experience that they can in fact witness, teach Sunday School and engage in other forms of ministry without possessing a sense of God's power upon their lives. But ministry done for God in the flesh does not produce the kind of results that could otherwise be anticipated, nor is it as personally fulfilling as ministry done in the power of the Holy Spirit. The Helper as administrative assistant reminds us of the power for ministry that is available in the daily filling of the Holy Spirit.

This principle of power for service is also implied in the Helper being a search committee. The 25 occurrences of the title "the Spirit of the LORD" in the Old Testament describe the work that people do for God when they have the Holy Spirit. Usually the Bible describes the Spirit of the LORD coming upon people and enabling them to do a work for God. Spiritual power results from the sanctification and filling of the Holy Spirit.

The Principle of Reverence for God

The Helper as our apartment manager pictures for us the indwelling of the Holy Spirit in us. Then the Helper as lawyer is His work for us. Although the Scriptures say much about developing personal intimacy with God (that is, knowing God), in a certain sense we must stand in awe of Him. This principle of reverence will influence our faith in God, our prayer life and our worship; as a matter of fact, it will influence everything we do. Having proper reverence for God will help us see Him in His majesty. We will see His greatness as One who is both trustworthy and worthy of our worship.

The principle of reverence for God will also help us understand ourselves better. Throughout the Scriptures, whenever a person or group of people gained a clearer understanding of the nature of God, they gained a more realistic understanding of themselves. Because men and women are made in the image of God, when a person can better see the primary object (God), he or she will better understand the reflection in the mirror. Usually this understanding can be accompanied by personal repentance or a revitalization of the spiritual life. Reverence for God results in us understanding who we are.

This principle of reverence for God will also change the way we live. The New Testament makes it clear that the Holy Spirit lives within the believer. When we have reverence toward the Holy Spirit of God, we will be careful about what we do with and where we take our body, His temple. Many Christians would change their language, actions and the places they go if they had an inner consciousness of reverence for the indwelling Holy Spirit.

PART 2

The Ministry of the Holy Spirit in the Believer

2

The Atonement Terms for the Holy Spirit

The Atonement Terms for the Holy Spirit

Providing Salvation	
1.The Eternal Spirit	His priestly role in intercession for the unsaved
2. The Gift of God	His gift of eternal life to the unsaved
3. The Spirit of Him Who Raised Jesus from the Dead	His role in resurrection

Effecting Salvation	
1. The Spirit of Grace	He accepts the sinner for salvation.
2. The Same Spirit of Faith	He enables the sinner to believe.
3. A New Spirit	He gives the repentant sinner a new nature.
4. The Spirit of Life	He makes the convert alive to God.
5. The Spirit of Adoption	He makes us heirs of God.

The Scriptures were given that people may come to faith in Christ and experience salvation. John explained, "These are written that you may believe that Jesus is the Christ, the Son of God, and that believing you may have life in His name" (20:31, *NKJV*). The previous chapter emphasized the role of the Holy Spirit as Helper in our conversion. Conversion is what enables a person to receive eternal life. But the door of salvation has two sides: man's side and God's side. This chapter describes the role of the Holy Spirit in providing salvation. This is God's side of the door. This chapter describes several names and titles of the Holy Spirit as He does His work in the atonement wrought by Christ.

The Holy Spirit in the Work of Atonement

The Holy Spirit is involved in two aspects of the atonement. First, the Spirit was involved in the atoning death of Christ, which made salvation possible (see Heb. 9:14). Second, He is involved in drawing people to faith in Christ (see John 16:8-11) and applying the results of salvation.

In light of the multifaceted role of the Holy Spirit in salvation, many of His names describe aspects of His saving ministries. These names include "the Eternal Spirit," "the Gift of God," "a New Spirit," "the Same Spirit of Faith," the Seal names, "the Spirit of Adoption," "the Spirit of Grace," "the Spirit of Him Who Raised Jesus," "the Spirit of Life" and "My Witness."

The first involvement of the Holy Spirit in salvation is His role in making salvation possible. Although the focus of the Scriptures is on what Christ did in His atoning death, a closer examination of the biblical teaching makes it clear that providing salvation was a trinitarian ministry (that is, involving all three members of the Trinity). Three names are used to relate the Holy Spirit to the sacrificial nature of Christ's death, His descent into hell and His victorious resurrection to life.

Names of the Holy Spirit Related to the Atonement

1. The Eternal Spirit
2. The Gift of God
3. The Spirit of Him Who Raised Jesus

The Eternal Spirit
In the Old Testament the priest would take the blood of a sacrificial animal and offer it to God for atonement. In the sacrificial

death of Christ, the Eternal Spirit apparently acted in this priestly role. The writer of the Epistle to the Hebrews asks,

> If the blood of bulls and goats and the ashes of a heifer, sprinkling the unclean, sanctifies for the purifying of the flesh, how much more shall the blood of Christ, who through the eternal Spirit offered Himself without spot to God, cleanse your conscience from dead works to serve the living God? (Heb. 9:13-14, *NKJV*).

The Holy Spirit was the (active) agent who offered the (passive) Lamb to God.

The Gift of God

Between the death and resurrection of Jesus, the Bible describes Jesus descending into Hades. This was done to release the Old Testament saints from the captivity of Hades that they might enjoy the presence of God (see Ps. 68:18; Eph. 4:8). In the context of describing this work, it is also noted that Christ gave gifts to men. Although this statement has some reference to the gifts of the Holy Spirit (see Eph. 4:11), it probably also refers to the gift of eternal life (see Rom. 6:23). All these gifts are linked to the ultimate "gift of God" (John 4:10; Acts 8:20), the Holy Spirit. All these gifts are in Him—the Holy Spirit—and to get Him is to get them. Without this Gift of God, it would be impossible for Christians to enjoy spiritual gifts, eternal life or any of the other gifts and blessings of God in the Christian life.

The Spirit of Him Who Raised Jesus

In describing the Holy Spirit as "the Spirit of Him who raised Jesus" (Rom. 8:11, *NKJV*), Paul linked the Holy Spirit with the resurrection of Jesus to life. Earlier in Romans this linkage was also made through the use of another name, "the Spirit of holiness." In his opening remarks Paul described Jesus as "declared to be the Son of God with power, according to the Spirit of holiness, by the resurrection from the dead" (1:4, *NKJV*). These two names imply some measure of the Holy Spirit's involvement in the resurrection of Jesus.

274 The Ultimate Guide to the Names of God

The Holy Spirit Applying the Work of Atonement

The Holy Spirit was not only involved in securing the means by which salvation is possible; He is also actively involved in effecting that salvation in the lives of those who respond to the gospel. The atonement names of the Holy Spirit tend to emphasize this aspect of His ministry.

Names of the Holy Spirit Effecting Salvation

1. The Spirit of Grace
2. The Same Spirit of Faith
3. A New Spirit
4. The Spirit of Life
5. The Spirit of Adoption

Because salvation is all of grace (see Eph. 2:5,8), it should not be surprising that one of the saving names of the Holy Spirit is "the Spirit of grace" (Zech. 12:10). Grace is the unmerited favor of God toward the repentant sinner. Grace has been described through the use of an acrostic: **G**od's **R**iches **A**t **C**hrist's **E**xpense. The Spirit of Grace is the channel through which God's unmerited favor is applied to the believer at conversion.

Grace
God's **R**iches **A**t Christ's **E**xpense

The Same Spirit of Faith

Paul also described the Holy Spirit as "the same spirit of faith" (2 Cor. 4:13). The Bible teaches that people could not be saved without faith (see Eph. 2:8-9). Some teachers maintain that this gift of grace is sovereignly given. Others hold that God has already given to everyone the ability to exercise saving faith in Christ in response to the gospel (see John 1:12). Regardless of one's belief about the extent of this aspect of the Holy Spirit's ministry, the title "Spirit of Faith" suggests the involvement of the Holy Spirit in a person's response to salvation. Also implied in this name is one means by which we may grow in our faith in God. As we develop our relationship with the Spirit of Faith, we will increase in our faith as we live by the faith of God (see Rom. 1:17; Gal. 2:20).

A New Spirit
The prophet Ezekiel spoke of a time when God would save Israel by giving them "a new spirit" (Ezek. 11:19). When a person is saved today, he or she also receives a New Spirit. In the act of salvation, God makes each of us a new creation and helps us live the Christian life:

> Then I will give them one heart, and I will put a new spirit within them, and take the stony heart out of their flesh, and give them a heart of flesh, that they may walk in My statutes and keep My judgments and do them; and they shall be My people, and I will be their God (Ezek. 11:19-20, *NKJV*).

The new Spirit makes a person a "new creation" (2 Cor. 5:17, *NKJV*).

The Spirit of Life
Another saving name of the Holy Spirit describing His role in effecting salvation is "the Spirit of Life." Paul explained, "The law of the Spirit of life in Christ Jesus has made me free from the law of sin and death" (Rom. 8:2, *NKJV*). Before salvation people are described as "dead in trespasses and sins" (Eph. 2:1, *NKJV*), but when they are converted, they are "alive to God in Christ Jesus our Lord" (Rom. 6:11, *NKJV*). The difference is effected by the ministry of the Spirit of Life in salvation.

The Spirit of Adoption
The Spirit of Adoption refers to the ministry of the Holy Spirit in appointing us as heirs within the family of God. "For you did not receive the spirit of bondage again to fear, but you received the Spirit of adoption by whom we cry out, 'Abba, Father'" (Rom. 8:15, *NKJV*).

In the first century, adoption was a common means of legally placing a child in a family as an heir. Although the work of the Holy Spirit in regeneration makes us a part of the family of God, the work of the Holy Spirit in adoption guarantees our position in the family as heirs. By regeneration the Holy Spirit gives the believer a new nature and a new spiritual desire toward God. By adoption the Spirit guarantees us all the rights and privileges of belonging to the family of God. This also implies that we have a responsibility to live up to that honor.

Regeneration	Adoption
We are born again.	We are placed as sons.
We become a child.	We become a son.
It is experiential.	It is legal.
We receive God's nature.	We receive rights as heir.

Enjoying the Atonement Names of the Holy Spirit

The atonement names of the Holy Spirit serve as a reminder of the greatness of God's provision of salvation. Salvation is a gift of God, something He intends for us to enjoy rather than to work for. So the saving names of the Holy Spirit should be a source of enjoyment in our lives. This is more likely to be the case when we understand and apply four principles arising out of these saving names.

The Principle of Complete Provision

When a young boy goes to camp, he will find the experience more enjoyable when he realizes his mother has packed everything he needs to have a great trip there and a great experience at camp. The saving names of the Holy Spirit remind us that God's provision in salvation is complete. The Father has packed complete provisions for every emergency on life's journey.

The Bible uses at least 131 different expressions to describe the salvation experience. Why are so many expressions used? One reason is that there are many aspects involved in God's complete provision for us, which we call salvation. Just as the supply checklist on a trip to camp may include many things that could be summarized as necessary supplies, so too God's salvation checklist contains many individual expressions of salvation that are summarized in the word "salvation."

Consider some of the provisions of the Holy Spirit in salvation. For our guilt, He offers forgiveness (see Eph. 1:7). For our sense of rejection, He offers acceptance (see v. 6). For our alienation, He brings us close to God (see 2:13). He replaces our deadness with life (see v. 1). Our bondage is exchanged for liberty (see Gal. 5:1). Our poverty is replaced by His riches (see Eph. 1:3). And the list continues to meet every human need. Certainly much is to be enjoyed in the Holy Spirit's complete provision of salvation.

The Principle of Family Security

A second principle implied in the saving names of the Holy Spirit is the principle of family security. These names indicate the Holy Spirit's ability to complete the good work of salvation that He has begun in every believer (see Phil. 1:6) and His power over anything that would threaten the believer (see John 17:2). Our spiritual assurance is guaranteed by the Person and work of God. If God were to take away eternal life from anyone, it would be a denial of His nature and work. God is true and just. He cannot deny Himself. Therefore anyone who has eternal life has it forever. Beyond the nature of God, Christians have the promise that nothing can separate us from the love of God (see Rom. 8:33-39).

When my children were growing up, I often motivated them to good behavior by telling them, "You're a Towns." I reminded them that their grandmother had often motivated me with the same admonition. Some object to the doctrine of our eternal position in the family of God, fearing that it may lead some into sinful lifestyles. Actually, just the reverse can be true. Most people do not actively live to dishonor their family. They know that they have the family name and would not want to drag it through the mud. Family honor is a motivating factor, encouraging people to live up to the family name. So an understanding of our position in the family of God ought to motivate us to live up to the honor of that great family.

The Principle of Family Identity

Also implied by these names is the principle of family identity. Many people have searched out their family tree to discover that they are distantly related to some important ancestor. When they learn this, they may change their lifestyle as they subconsciously begin to live as that famous ancestor lived. The saving names of the Holy Spirit refer to our being brought into the family of God and our identification with the Son of God. In at least one sense, the Christian life is simply letting Jesus live His life through us (see Gal. 2:20).

The Principle of Continuing Support

The final principle arising from the saving names of the Holy Spirit is that of continuing support. Although many of these names relate to various aspects of salvation, some of them, such as the name "Helper," indicate that what the Spirit has begun in salvation He will continue in His teaching and maturing ministries in our lives. These ministries of the Holy Spirit are considered in greater detail in the next chapters, but they are introduced in the saving names of the Holy Spirit.

3

Terms for the Maturing Work of the Holy Spirit

Terms for the Maturing Work of the Holy Spirit

Indwelling Names of the Spirit	
1. A New Spirit	He gives the believer the Spirit-filled life.
2. A Spirit of Grace	He helps the believer walk by grace, not law.
3. Spirit of Supplication	He motivates the believer to pray.
4. My Witness	He bears witness of the believer's salvation.
5. My Helper	He helps the believer grow in Christ.

The Life of God in Human Lives	
1. Union with God	He puts the believer in God.
2. Communion with God	He helps the believer's fellowship with God.

God's purpose in our lives as Christians is that we might be transformed into the image of Christ (see Rom. 8:29). This change in our character and life is accomplished through the maturing ministry of the Holy Spirit. As we have seen in other ministries of the Holy Spirit, several names tend to describe this work. Each of these names emphasizes the ministry of the indwelling Holy Spirit in the process of sanctification.

The word "sanctification" means "to be set apart." When Bible teachers use this word to describe the ministry of the Holy Spirit, they are referring to His attempts to make the Christian set apart from the world as well as spiritual (to reflect the character of God).

Three Tenses of Sanctification

Past	Present	Future
Position	Experience	Consummation
Positional sanctification	Progressive sanctification	Prospective sanctification
I have been sanctified.	I am now being sanctified.	I shall be sanctified.
Hebrews 3:1	1 Thessalonians 5:28	1 John 3:2

The word "sanctification" is used in three tenses. First, Christians *have been* sanctified in that they were forgiven and set apart to God in salvation. Second, Christians are constantly *being* set apart from sin through the work of the Holy Spirit in their lives. Third, Christians *will be* completely sanctified at the rapture or when they enter God's presence through death, when they will be completely free from sin. The maturing names of the Holy Spirit are those names that draw attention to the fact that the Holy Spirit indwells Christians and makes them mature. The word "mature" means to be whole, complete or well rounded. Although many aspects of the maturing process are evident in the Christian life, the key to Christian living is the life of God living through human lives. This intimacy with God is experienced by the Christian as he or she comes to understand the Holy Spirit's indwelling of the believer.

The Indwelling Names of the Holy Spirit

One of the results of the Holy Spirit in our conversion is that He indwells us. Several names of the Holy Spirit emphasize this aspect of His ministry, including "a New Spirit" (Ezek. 11:19), "the Spirit of Grace" (Heb. 10:29), "the Spirit of Supplication" (see Zech. 12:10, *NKJV*), "My Witness" (Job 16:19; see also Heb. 10:15), and "the Helper" (John 14:26, *NKJV*).

A New Spirit

When a person becomes a Christian, God puts within that person "a New Spirit" (Ezek. 11:19) who then effects other changes in his or her life. All growth toward maturity in the Christian life is the result of the New Spirit living His life through the Christian. This new life is sometimes called the victorious life, or the Spirit-filled life. The Christian should yield to the control of the New Spirit. When this is done, the believer will grow toward maturity.

Spirit of Grace

Another maturing name of the Holy Spirit is "the Spirit of Grace" (Heb. 10:29). The Scriptures describe salvation as being all of grace (see Eph. 2:8), and the Spirit of Grace is the means by which the grace of God is communicated to people (see Heb. 10:29). But the maturing process in the Christian life is also dependent upon the ministry of the Spirit of Grace. Paul challenged the Galatians, "Are you so foolish? Having begun in the Spirit, are you now being made perfect by the flesh?" (Gal. 3:3). In this way he reminded them that the same Spirit of Grace who brought them salvation was also the key to the maturity they were seeking.

Spirit of Supplication

The term "Spirit of Supplication" (see Zech. 12:10) reminds the Christian of the importance of prayer in the maturing process in the Christian life. Many Bible teachers have described personal Bible study and prayer as the two absolute essentials in the process of spiritual growth. The teaching names of the Holy Spirit help us grow as we read the Scriptures and as the Spirit of Supplication helps us grow in our prayer life. Sometimes the Spirit of Supplication prays for us when we do not know how to pray. "For we do not know what we should pray for as we ought, but the Spirit Himself makes intercession for us with groanings which cannot be uttered" (Rom. 8:26, *NKJV*).

My Witness

A fourth maturing name of the Holy Spirit is "My Witness" (Job 16:19; see also Heb. 10:15). Together with the Father and the Son, the Holy Spirit consistently bears witness in heaven (see 1 John 5:7). The Holy Spirit bears witness of our salvation because of what Christ has done. But the Holy Spirit also bears witness on Earth by using the testimony of our salvation to speak to unsaved people (see 1 John 5:8-10).

The Helper

The fifth maturing name of the Holy Spirit is "the Helper" (see John 14:26, *NKJV*). As we have already noticed, Jesus used this term to describe the multifaceted ministry of the Holy Spirit. Part of that ministry involves helping us grow to become all God intended us to be. Whenever we face a new challenge to grow spiritually, we can be confident of the ministry of the indwelling Helper to assist us in our adjustments and to guide us in our decisions.

The Life of God in Human Lives

At the very heart of the Christian life are the union and communion of the Christian with God. Union with God refers to that relationship of salvation between God and the Christian that happens at the moment of conversion. Communion with God refers to our continuing experience of recognizing and enjoying fellowship with God. In both union and communion, the Holy Spirit is involved in helping us mature in Christ.

Union with God

The Christian's standing, or his new position, in heaven is described in Scripture by the phrase "in Christ." This expression is used 172 times in the New Testament in connection with virtually every aspect of Christian experience. The experience of being placed in Christ occurs at conversion as the Holy Spirit puts us into the Lord Jesus Christ and we enjoy the perfection of Christ in the heavenlies. It is usually not until long after conversion, however, that many Christians experience the reality of this truth.

Being in Christ is a description of the Christian not only at conversion but also throughout his or her Christian life. In identifying the believer's position in Christ, Paul hints at the intimacy that exists between the Christian and Christ. Just as the child in its mother's womb is an individual personality while being very much a part of its mother, so too the Christian retains his or her individual personality while being in Christ. This expression describes the intimacy of the Christ-Christian relationship more than any other biblical expression or illustration of that relationship.

Communion with God

Communion with God is like the tide—it comes and goes. It is another term for fellowship with God. At times a Christian may sense a deeper communion with God than at other times. Although all Christians are united with God, relatively few experience the communion, or fellowship, with Christ that is characteristic of the deeper Christian life. Our union with God is an accomplished act at conversion, but our communion with God is an experience that usually involves many steps. The following six steps to fellowship, or communion, are suggestive of how this experience occurs.

The first step in experiencing communion with Christ is *knowledge*. The apostle Paul often used the "know ye not" formula when introducing some aspect of Christian experience (see Rom. 6:3). For some, merely understanding aspects of the believer's union with God is the beginning of a deeper communion with Christ. One cannot fully appreciate any truth that is not at least partially understood intellectually.

Repentance of known sin is a second step for entering into a deeper communion. Repentance involves turning from sin and being cleansed from sin. In repenting the Christian (1) searches his or her heart for sin that blocks fellowship with God, (2) begs forgiveness for sin (see 1 John 1:9), (3) asks God to forgive on the basis of the blood of Jesus Christ (see 1:7), and (4) promises to learn lessons from the experience so that the sinful behavior does not happen again.

A third step in enjoying communion with God is a *step of faith*. Often, entering into communion is a matter of acting on the Word of God. Christians appropriate the deeper life of communion by faith, just as one appropriates the eternal life of salvation by faith.

The fourth step in the process is that of *surrendering, or yielding, completely to God*. Yielding is a once-and-for-all response to God that governs all future responses to God. The initial yielding of our life to God is followed by a daily outworking of that yielding through obedience to the promptings of the Holy Spirit in our life. This has been characterized as telling God one big *YES!* followed by daily telling God yes.

Step five is expressed in *obedience.* The attitude of yielding to God is expressed in active obedience to the known and revealed will of God. Christians sometimes use yielding as an excuse for their passive attitude toward working for God, but those who truly yield to God will want to work for Him.

The sixth step in experiencing communion with God is *crucifying oneself, or taking up one's cross.* The Bible teaches that the old nature was crucified with Christ (see Gal. 2:20). Now the Christian must act on what has happened. Thus, when tempted to sin, we should respond as a dead person; but when prompted by the Spirit, we should show that we are alive to His leading (see Rom. 6:11).

How the Holy Spirit Works in Maturing the Christian

The maturing names of the Holy Spirit emphasize the Holy Spirit's work in making us more like Jesus. But how does the Holy Spirit accomplish this work? He matures the Christian by supporting the processes that lead to growth, just as parents contribute to the physical growth of their children by feeding them, insisting they get sufficient rest, encouraging them in physical activities, and so on. Although the Holy Spirit may do many specific things in an individual Christian's life to help the maturing process, a few general principles show us how He helps us become more like Jesus.

The Principle of Tree Growth

The principle of tree growth recognizes that growth begins on the inside and works its way out. The psalmist noted, "The righteous shall flourish like a palm tree: he shall grow like a cedar in Lebanon" (Ps. 92:12). The comparison between these trees and the Christian emphasizes that growth in the Christian finds its origins in the inner life rather than from some external circumstances.

Palm trees can withstand many adversities and still continue to experience growth, but if the inner core of the palm is corrupted, it begins to wither and die.

The principle of tree growth is also mentioned in the New Testament. Jesus warned His disciples, "By their fruits you will know them" (Matt. 7:20, *NKJV*). By this Jesus meant that they could discern between true and false teachers by the fruit those teachers produced in their lives. Later Jesus used the image of a vine and branches to urge His disciples to bear fruit (see John 15:1-8). The apostle Paul also described Christian character as the fruit of the Holy Spirit (see Gal. 5:22-23).

The Holy Spirit matures Christians according to the principle of tree growth by being that life within that produces spiritual fruit in believers' outer lives. When we allow the Holy Spirit to live through us, spiritual fruit in the form of Christian character will result. When other influences become more dominant in our lives, a different kind of fruit will soon become evident.

The Principle of Grace as Needed

A second principle governing the Holy Spirit's maturing ministry is the principle of grace as needed. Many Christians may wish they could have some instantaneous experience with the Holy Spirit that would eliminate all sin and immaturity in their lives. Many would like instant maturity, but that is not how the Holy Spirit has chosen to accomplish His work. Rather, the Spirit of Grace constantly gives us grace as needed for each step in our maturing process.

A parent would not bring a newborn baby home from the hospital and give it several bags of food at one time and expect the child to be fully mature within a week. Maturing of children takes many years; some parents may wonder if they will ever accomplish that task. Similarly, God does not expect Christians to become spiritual giants overnight. Rather, the Holy Spirit gives Christians grace as needed, day by day, throughout many years as He matures them.

The Principle of Glory to Glory

When Paul wrote to the Corinthians about the maturing ministry of the Holy Spirit, he noted,

But we all, with unveiled face, beholding as in a mirror the glory of the Lord, are being transformed into the same image from glory to glory, just as by the Spirit of the Lord (2 Cor. 3:18, *NKJV*).

The principle of glory to glory recognizes one of the processes used by the Holy Spirit in maturing believers. Apparently maturity was not a one-time experience with the Holy Spirit that instantaneously transformed carnal Christians into spiritual, Christlike giants. Rather, it was a process by which Christians became increasingly more Christlike by focusing their attention on the glory of the Lord.

Paul also refers to this principle in his Epistle to the Philippians. There he expressed his confidence in "this very thing, that He who has begun a good work in you will complete it until the day of Jesus Christ" (Phil. 1:6, *NKJV*). This practical spiritual growth to maturity is part of God's will for every Christian (see 1 Thess. 4:3). These changes toward greater Christlikeness could not be accomplished apart from the maturing ministry of the Holy Spirit.

The Principle of Encouragement Through Confirmation

A fourth maturing principle used by the Holy Spirit is the principle of encouragement through confirmation. When a student struggles to master some new skill, the teacher will often draw the student's attention to the progress that has already been made. The teacher measures the progress of growth to motivate the student to continue mastering new skills. In the same way, the Holy Spirit encourages us to become more like Christ by occasionally causing us to realize how much we have already changed.

This is an important principle to remember as we struggle to break harmful habits or to develop healthy spiritual disciplines in our lives. Sometimes recognizing the enormity of a significant change that needs to be made in our lives can overwhelm and discourage us in our spiritual growth. At those times especially we need to pause and realize what the Holy Spirit has already done in this work of making us more like Jesus. In most cases, the big challenge before us becomes more realistic when we recognize the bigger change that has already been made.

The Principle of Available Assistance

The fifth maturing principle governing this aspect of the Holy Spirit's ministry is the principle of available assistance. No Christian ever needs to feel that he or she must struggle alone against the world, the flesh and the devil. The Holy Spirit lives within every Christian and is constantly working to help us become like Jesus. Paul reminded the Corinthians,

> No temptation has overtaken you except such as is common to man; but God is faithful, who will not allow you to be tempted beyond what you are able, but with the temptation will also make the way of escape, that you may be able to bear it (1 Cor. 10:13, *NKJV*).

This verse illustrates two ways in which the principle of available assistance is at work in our lives. First, the Holy Spirit has set reasonable limits on problems that He will allow to come into our lives. This is illustrated in the Old Testament experience of Job, who was protected by God (see 1:10). Even when God allowed Satan to introduce problems into Job's life, He set limits, knowing how much Job could handle (see 1:12; 2:6).

Second, the Holy Spirit will also offer solutions to any problems He allows to come into our lives. Whenever we encounter a problem that seems overwhelming, we can be confident that the Holy Spirit has already prepared a way of escape to make the problem more bearable.

The maturing names of the Holy Spirit emphasize our responsibility as Christians to continue to grow in grace. In the Old Testament the prophets often called Israel to look back to their origins and realize how much God had done for them as a nation. This is a good practice for Christians today. As you conclude this chapter, take a few minutes to make a list of the evidences of growth in your life as you review the maturing ministry of the Holy Spirit in you since you became a Christian.

4

Terms for the Teaching Ministry of the Holy Spirit

The Teaching Names of the Holy Spirit

1. The Anointing	He removes spiritual blindness.
2. The Spirit of Revelation	He reveals spiritual truth.
3. The Spirit of Truth	He communicates the content of truth.
4. The Spirit of Knowledge	He makes believers know facts about God.
5. The Spirit of a Sound Mind	He takes away fear and enables rational thought.

When you read the Scriptures and a verse seems to leap off the page and you see a truth that you have never seen before, that is the ministry of the Holy Spirit causing you to see that truth. At other times you may be listening to a sermon or Bible lesson, and a light flashes on. You see Christ clearly. That is the work of the Holy Spirit. The Holy Spirit is the Illuminator, the Teacher, the One removing your spiritual blindness.

When you pray, "Open my eyes, that I may see wondrous things from Your law" (Ps. 119:18, *NKJV*), you are asking the Holy Spirit to show you new things from the Bible.

The Holy Spirit is your Helper. Just as a kindergarten teacher helps students recognize the letters of the alphabet or helps them add two and two, so too the Holy Spirit helps babes in Christ recognize basic Christian truth and helps mature believers understand the deeper Christian life.

The Holy Spirit is our Teacher. Jesus promised to send the Spirit, adding, "He will teach you all things, and bring to your remembrance all things that I said to you" (John 14:26, *NKJV*). Although this reference may relate directly to the disciples, it surely applies to us today. Then Jesus promised that the Teacher would "guide [us] into all truth" (16:13, *NKJV*).

Paul also identified the teaching ministry of the Holy Spirit when he reminded the Corinthians, "These things we also speak, not in words which man's wisdom teaches but which the Holy Spirit teaches, comparing spiritual things with spiritual" (1 Cor. 2:13, *NKJV*). Later John also emphasized the teaching ministry of the Holy Spirit, reminding Christians,

> But the anointing which you have received from Him abides in you, and you do not need that anyone teach you; but as the same anointing teaches you concerning all things, and is true, and is not a lie, and just as it has taught you, you will abide in Him (1 John 2:27, *NKJV*).

In this passage "the anointing" occurs when the Holy Spirit comes upon a believer and anoints the believer with Himself. The believer receives the Holy Spirit, who teaches the believer spiritual things.

We usually think of Jesus as a teacher; this was the title used to address Him more than any other. The title "Teacher" is apparently never used to describe the Holy Spirit in the way it is used to describe Jesus, but the Holy Spirit performs all the duties a teacher does: He guides, reveals, teaches, tells, shows, leads and, even as a human teacher will do, reproves, corrects and convicts.

The Holy Spirit as Teacher

This chapter will describe the Holy Spirit in His teaching ministry by using several terms:

The Teaching Names of the Holy Spirit

1. The Anointing (see 1 John 2:27)
2. The Spirit of Revelation (see Eph. 1:17)
3. The Spirit of Truth (see John 14:17)

The Anointing

When John described the Holy Spirit as "the anointing" (1 John 2:27), he emphasized His direct teaching ministry. Some have taken this statement to justify their refusal to learn from human teachers. Actually, John did not say it is wrong to learn from human teachers (he himself was teaching others as he wrote these words) but only that teachers were not absolutely necessary to help Christians distinguish the truth from error. Most Bible teachers agree that John wrote this epistle to warn Christians about the false teachings of heretical teachers. In doing so he reminded his readers that the Anointing teaches truth, not lies, and therefore could be relied upon more consistently than human teachers who may or may not teach the truth.

Often the Holy Spirit has prevented new Christians from becoming involved in a religious cult by making them aware of some error in the teaching of the cult. Sometimes they do not fully understand this direct ministry of the Anointing until they look back years later and realize how the Holy Spirit helped them discern between truth and error as they studied the Scriptures.

In addition to protection from negative lessons, the Holy Spirit will teach with His anointing. The Holy Spirit comes and removes spiritual blindness from those "whose minds the god of this age has blinded" (2 Cor. 4:4, *NKJV*). Being worldly minded blinds us to God's plan and keeps us from understanding the principles of salvation. The Holy Spirit is the Teacher who shows us the meaning of the Cross.

As Teacher, the Holy Spirit also teaches us about Jesus Christ. Some were blinded "lest the light of the gospel of the glory of Christ, who is the image of God, should shine on them" (4:4, *NKJV*). The Holy Spirit magnifies Jesus Christ so that we can see Him. Jesus explained, "He will not speak on His own authority. . . . He will glorify Me" (John 16:13-14, *NKJV*). The main topic in the Holy Spirit's curriculum is the Lord Jesus Christ.

The Spirit of Revelation

When Paul prayed that the Ephesians might have "the Spirit of Revelation" (Eph. 1:17), he emphasized the teaching ministry of the Holy Spirit in showing us things that we could not otherwise know apart from His ministry. A good teacher communicates not only the facts of a lesson but also insights that help the student understand and appreciate the relationships that tie those facts together. The Spirit of Revelation teaches Christians insights about life, helping them understand the forces at work in their lives. Those believers who learn under the Holy Spirit's teaching ministry will have a better idea of what God is doing in and through their lives.

The Spirit of Truth

Another teaching name of the Holy Spirit that emphasizes the character of His teaching is the title "Spirit of Truth" (John 14:17). As the Spirit of Truth, all that the Holy Spirit teaches is characterized by truth. This means the lessons of the Holy Spirit are accurate, and His students can have complete confidence in what they are taught.

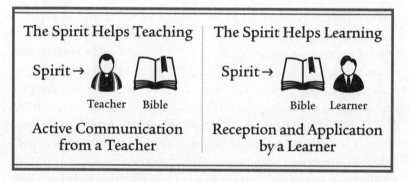

The Spirit Helps Teaching	The Spirit Helps Learning
Spirit → Teacher Bible	Spirit → Bible Learner
Active Communication from a Teacher	**Reception and Application by a Learner**

I have taught in Christian colleges and seminaries for 33 years. I wish that I could say that I have never made a mistake, but I can't. Just the other day I pointed to a pronoun in a verse and told the class that it was a reference to Paul when it was a reference to Christ. I backed up, corrected myself and went on. But the Holy Spirit is accurate and never contradicts Himself, because He is the Spirit of Truth.

The Holy Spirit's Learning Names

1. The Spirit of Knowledge (see Isa. 11:2)
2. The Spirit of a Sound Mind (see 2 Tim. 1:7)
3. The Spirit of Understanding (see Isa. 11:2)
4. The Spirit of Wisdom (see Exod. 28:3)

The Holy Spirit's Role in Learning

In the previous section the Holy Spirit as Teacher was emphasized. Here we should note that some of the teaching names of
the Holy Spirit apparently emphasize learning rather than teaching. The goal of all teaching is learning. I have defined teaching as
"the guidance of learning activities." No teacher has really taught
until the student has learned the lesson. Here are some of the
terms applied to the Holy Spirit that emphasize learning:

The Spirit of Knowledge

As "the Spirit of Knowledge" (Isa. 11:2, *NKJV*), the Holy Spirit
enables His students to understand basic facts about God and
His world. These spiritual lessons become the basis of the rest
of His teaching ministry in our lives. The primary thrust of the
teaching ministry of the Holy Spirit is to enhance our experiential knowledge of God.

For example, we know that lying is wrong, but the Holy Spirit
reveals the true nature of our "fibs," as we like to call them. Then
we are horrified by what we have said. We have theoretical knowledge about our actions until the Holy Spirit reveals their actual
nature. The same can be said of positive truth. Someone knows
about Jesus from seeing a Christmas or Easter movie. They hear
a sermon or read a Christian book, but they have no experiential relationship with Jesus Christ. Then the Holy Spirit reveals
Jesus Christ to this person, who is miserable because of sin. This
ministry is of the Holy Spirit as Teacher, who is also the Spirit
of Knowledge.

From our perspective as the Holy Spirit's students, we
should rely upon the Holy Spirit to teach us to have both a greater intellectual understanding of Jesus and a deeper communion
with Him.

The Holy Spirit does not whisper in our ears during an exam
when we pray for an answer that we have never memorized.
The Holy Spirit illuminates the Scripture as we study and learn
the Word of God. He helps us learn and retain knowledge about
spiritual things. The Holy Spirit works hand in glove with our
abilities so that we will have spiritual illumination.

The Spirit of a Sound Mind

Sometimes Christians have behaved irrationally while claiming to be under the influence of the Holy Spirit. The Bible, however, promises that God has given us "a spirit of . . . a sound mind" (2 Tim. 1:7). This soundness is communicated to our spirits by the Holy Spirit. He keeps us from fear or other emotional pressures that would cause us to do dumb things or make foolish decisions. He works with our own spirits to give us confidence.

When people are converted to Christ, the Holy Spirit's ministry in their lives often results in an enhanced ability to think rationally, without their minds being clouded by the effects of drugs, alcohol, pornography, and so on. Perhaps you have experienced the ministry of the Holy Spirit in your own life in a way that involved a new direction that surprised you. At other times the Spirit of a Sound Mind enables us to learn through the rational application of truth that we already know. The Holy Spirit expects us to think through the issues involved and to come to a conclusion, much as a college student does in an independent research course. This is both a learning experience for the Christian and the teaching ministry of the Holy Spirit.

The Spirit of Understanding

A third step in the learning process involves gaining insights from "the Spirit of understanding" (Isa. 11:2, *NKJV*). Understanding is the ability to discern the subtle differences involved between two or more options. We can't always simply look at a problem and seek to come to a rational conclusion on the basis of what is known. We can rely upon the Spirit of Understanding to give us insights that we might not otherwise have. The Holy Spirit might have taught us former lessons, so at the point of making a decision, He helps us to make the correct choice.

The Spirit of Wisdom

As "the spirit of wisdom" (Exod. 28:3), the Holy Spirit teaches us to view life from God's perspective. Wisdom is the ability to correctly apply all the facts or knowledge that we have learned. A young Ph.D. may have a lot of knowledge, but the scholar may not have the wisdom of his or her father who never attended college. The wise father knows how to apply the facts that he knows.

As the Spirit of Knowledge, the Holy Spirit takes the facts that He teaches and, as the Spirit of Understanding, He helps the believer apply them to life. The thesis of the book of Proverbs may be paraphrased as, "My son, give yourself to knowledge that you may gain wisdom." When Christians find themselves in a situation in which they do not know what to do, they should pray for increased wisdom (see Jas. 1:5). One of the ways that God will answer such a prayer is through the ministry of the Spirit of Wisdom.

How the Holy Spirit Teaches

All good teachers realize that certain laws of teaching and learning will enhance their teaching ministry if consistently applied. Likewise, the Holy Spirit teaches us the truths of God according to certain principles. Although many teaching principles may be drawn from the teaching names of the Holy Spirit, the following illustrate how the Holy Spirit teaches us and how we can more effectively teach others.

The Principle of Readiness

Readiness as a principle in the teaching ministry of the Holy Spirit is illustrated in the way that He revealed God's will to the human writers of Scripture. The Holy Spirit used 40 writers over a period of some 1,600 years to complete the 66 books of the Bible. The finished product can be read by the average reader in about 80 hours. Certainly a book the size of the Bible could have been written in less than the 1,600-plus years it took for the Holy Spirit to write it. After all, the Bible itself claims that God's Word is forever "settled in heaven" (Ps. 119:89). Presumably the Holy Spirit could have dictated the settled Word of God to an efficient typist who could have transcribed it in a matter of weeks or months rather than centuries.

One reason the Holy Spirit took His time in teaching generations of people the Scriptures relates to the principle of readiness. Before He could teach the heart of the Scriptures, which is the salvation provided by Christ on the cross, the Holy Spirit first needed to teach people the Old Testament law that showed them the need for salvation. The lessons He taught through the prophets served to reinforce our inability to keep the law. This helped make other generations ready for the message of the gospel. After teaching the means whereby we could be saved, the Holy Spirit then taught through the apostles how to live the Christian life. In every instance a lesson was not taught until readiness had been established.

If you have been a Christian for some time, you realize that the Holy Spirit teaches you best when you are ready to learn new truth. Have you ever read a familiar passage of Scripture and learned something new that you could apply to your life? Why didn't the Holy Spirit teach you that principle when you first read that passage? One reason may be that you were not ready to learn the principle. In our response to the teaching ministry of the Holy Spirit, we need to maintain an openness to His instruction and the readiness to learn all that He wants to teach us.

The Principle of Variety
The Holy Spirit revealed truth to the writers of the Scriptures in a variety of ways, including through dreams, verbal conversations, historical events and rational thinking processes. On some occasions the Spirit wrote or dictated the message directly. He did not simply rely upon one proven method of teaching and use it until it became ineffective.

In His teaching ministry in your own life, have you noticed the various ways in which the Holy Spirit seeks to teach you truth? Often He teaches as we read the Scriptures or hear a lesson taught or a sermon preached. On other occasions He may allow certain circumstances in life to teach us important lessons. Sometimes He speaks through the formal or informal counsel of others as they share what they have been taught by the Holy Spirit. On yet another occasion the Holy Spirit may use Christian literature, radio or television to teach us what He wants us to know. We should not be surprised by the many creative ways in which the Holy Spirit seeks to teach us important lessons.

An important lesson can be learned here for those of us who seek to teach our children or others what the Holy Spirit has taught us. We should not rely upon a single means of teaching to communicate to others but rather realize that varying our teaching methods will make our teaching more interesting and will usually result in better or increased learning in those we teach.

The Principle of Life Response
A third principle implied in the teaching names of the Holy Spirit is the principle of life response. The Holy Spirit does not teach us simply to expand our knowledge, but rather He communicates truth for us to apply to our lives. When He teaches, He expects to see a life response in His students.

From time to time, it is good for Christians to evaluate how well they are applying the lessons that the Holy Spirit has taught them. In the past six months, what new lessons has the Holy Spirit taught you? What difference have those lessons made in your life? What difference could those lessons make in your life if you were more responsive to the Holy Spirit's teaching?

This is also a principle that should characterize our teaching ministry. When we teach others, our primary concern should be to change their lives through truth rather than simply to communicate content as an end in itself. This is especially true when we teach the Bible, which was written "that the man of God may be complete, thoroughly equipped for every good work" (2 Tim. 3:17, NKJV).

The Principle of Review
Many verses in the Holy Spirit's textbook, the Bible, teach the importance of review as a teaching principle. The Holy Spirit's repetitious style of teaching may be illustrated when phrases are repeated to emphasize a point: "Precept upon precept, precept upon precept; line upon line, line upon line; here a little, and there a little" (Isa. 28:13). Repetition and review are the key to learning.

The Holy Spirit's use of review in His teaching ministry is readily apparent in the Christian life. Certain things taught to us by the Holy Spirit early in our Christian lives are often repeated periodically throughout the Christian life. Most Christians learn early that they need to pray regularly. But it is a lesson we often forget. So we need to be constantly reminded of this lesson if we are to have an effective prayer life. The same is true of personal Bible study, sharing our faith with others and a host of other lessons the Holy Spirit has to repeat for our edification.

A good teacher will periodically take time to review previous lessons. These former lessons serve as the foundation upon which new truth is taught as well. If the foundation of a structure is weakened, the whole structure will fall. Therefore, teachers should review basic lessons with their students to ensure that these foundational truths are well learned.

The Principle of New Frontiers

Finally, the principle of new frontiers reminds us that the teaching ministry of the Holy Spirit is unending throughout our lives. The Holy Spirit always can and will teach us something new if we are open to Him. Learning ought to constantly push out our frontiers.

Good teachers realize that their students need to be constantly challenged with new truth. Although review is important, to constantly repeat the basics without moving on to something else will eventually frustrate students in their learning and often lead to discipline problems in the educational environment (whether the home, school, church or elsewhere). But when students are challenged with new frontiers, they respond enthusiastically to learning.

The teaching names of the Holy Spirit remind us of a significant ministry of the Holy Spirit in our lives today. Our response to these names ought to be twofold.

First, if the Holy Spirit is teaching, we ought to be eager to learn. Learning the lessons He has to teach us results in a changed life.

Second, understanding that the Holy Spirit often teaches indirectly through others, we ought to be willing to be a part of His teaching ministry in the lives of others. One reason the Holy Spirit teaches us lessons is to equip us to communicate these lessons to others (see 2 Cor. 1:4; 2 Tim. 2:2). The teaching names of the Holy Spirit are both an invitation for us to learn for ourselves and a motivation for us to teach others.

PART 3

The Nature of the Holy Spirit

5

Terms Describing the Identity of the Holy Spirit

The Identity of the Holy Spirit

The Holy Spirit Is a Person	
1. The pronoun "He"	He is a Person.
2. The Love of the Spirit	He has emotions.
3. The Same Spirit	He makes independent choices.

The Holy Spirit Is God	
1. The Spirit as *Elohim*	He is God of the Old Testament.
2. The Spirit as *Jehovah*	He is LORD in the Old Testament.
3. The Spirit as *Shekinah*	He is the glory of God.
4. The Spirit as *Shaddai*	He is strong to nourish the believer.
5. The Spirit as *El Elyon*	He is the possessor of heaven and Earth.

Throughout the Scriptures, one of the ways in which God reveals Himself to mankind is by assigning meaningful names to Himself. In two of my previous books, *My Father's Names* and *The Names of Jesus*, selected names of God and Jesus were considered to learn what they taught about the identity of the first and second Persons of the Trinity. We can also learn more about the nature and identity of the Holy Spirit by examining the names that Scripture ascribes to Him, the th... Person of the Trinity.

Two mistakes are commonly made in considering the identity of the Holy Spirit. First, some tend to think of the Holy Spirit as some sort of influence or concept rather than as a distinct Person. Second, some tend to think of the Holy Spirit as significant but as something or someone less than God the Father and Jesus. Although many arguments may be used to dispute these false views of the Holy Spirit, understanding the identity names of the Holy Spirit will help Christians understand the Holy Spirit. In a sense, every name ascribed to the Holy Spirit in Scripture is an identity name, but the names considered here particularly identify the personality and deity of the Holy Spirit.

The Holy Spirit Is a Person

A confused understanding of the unique personality of the Holy Spirit is accepted by at least two distinct groups of teachers today. First, some liberal theologians will acknowledge that the Holy Spirit may be a reality, but their failure to accept the Scriptures as the inspired and inerrant Word of God leads them to think of the Holy Spirit as a mythological being.

Second, some radical cults, such as the Jehovah's Witnesses, deny the personality of the Holy Spirit and refer to Him as a mere influence. Unfortunately, some otherwise conservative Christians who do not know what the Bible teaches about the Holy Spirit tend to believe similar views about the personality of the Holy Spirit.

The primary identity term of the Holy Spirit that emphasizes His personality is the pronoun "He" (see John 14:17; 16:13, *NKJV*). Normally, special recognition would not be given to a personal pronoun as a significant name. But the use of the masculine pronoun is significant in reference to the Holy Spirit. The New Testament was originally written in the Greek language, which has three genders: masculine, feminine and neuter. The word "spirit" is a neuter noun, so when it is used apart from the Holy Spirit, the neuter pronoun "it" should be used.

Twice the Greek neuter pronoun *auto* is used to identify the Holy Spirit (see Rom. 8:16,26). This form of the pronoun is used to agree with the article that it shares with the word *pneuma* (spirit).

When the translators of the *King James Version* translated this word, they suggested the translation "the Spirit itself." This is the correct meaning of the neuter pronoun of the Greek, but it suggests something different in English than was probably intended by Paul when he wrote the epistle in Greek. Paul used this form of the pronoun to make it clear that he was talking about the Holy Spirit, not to suggest that He was an "it" or less than a person. More recent translations have overcome this problem by translating the phrase "the Spirit Himself," which captures the apostle's meaning without suggesting something that was never intended.

The Bible says "when He has come" in identifying the Holy Spirit in John 16:8. John's decision to use the masculine pronoun *ekeinos* when referring to the Holy Spirit and the use of the translation "He" rather than the neuter pronoun "it" demonstrates an effort to reflect the apostolic emphasis on the personality of the Holy Spirit. If the Holy Spirit were just an influence, the neuter pronoun could be used. But because the Holy Spirit is a person, the masculine pronoun is used of Him just as it is used of God the Father and of Jesus. When John used this pronoun to describe the Holy Spirit, it was not just a slip of the pen. The Holy Spirit is a person as demonstrated throughout the Scriptures. The various attributes and actions of personality are attributed to the Holy Spirit.

Personality implies the existence of certain attributes: intellect, emotion or sensibility, and volition or willpower. Paul emphasized the intellectual ability of the Holy Spirit to know things: "For what man knows the things of a man except the spirit of the man which is in him? Even so no one knows the things of God except the Spirit of God" (1 Cor. 2:11, *NKJV*). Paul further understood that the rational capacity of the Holy Spirit included wisdom and communication when he prayed "that the God of our Lord Jesus Christ, the Father of glory, may give to [us] the spirit of wisdom and revelation in the knowledge of Him" (Eph. 1:17, *NKJV*).

The emotional aspect of the Holy Spirit is also evident in the Scriptures. Paul described the positive emotions of the Holy Spirit when he referred to "the love of the Spirit" (Rom. 15:30). He also spoke of the Spirit's ability to empathize with our inner emotional struggles:

> Likewise the Spirit also helps in our weaknesses. For we do not know what we should pray for as we ought, but the Spirit Himself makes intercession for us with groanings which cannot be uttered (Rom. 8:26, *NKJV*).

One of the negative emotions of the Holy Spirit is His ability to be grieved: "Do not grieve the Holy Spirit of God" (Eph. 4:30, *NKJV*). Isaiah cited an example of how Israel "rebelled and grieved [the LORD's] Holy Spirit" (Isa. 63:10, *NKJV*). The Holy Spirit has the ability to respond emotionally to the ideas and experiences that He encounters.

The Holy Spirit has the faculty of will and the ability to make decisions. In his discussion of spiritual gifts in the church at Corinth, Paul used the title "the same Spirit" five times (1 Cor. 12:4-11) in describing the Spirit's independent choice to impart different gifts to different believers. When the Greek word *autos* is preceded by an article, it is translated "the same" and is distinguished from being a personal or reflexive pronoun, whether or not it is followed by a noun. It is also interesting to note that Paul may have been using this form to identify the other distinct Persons of the Godhead in this context, although the terms "the same Lord" and "the same God" may also be names of the Holy Spirit (1 Cor. 12:5-6).

Elsewhere in the Scriptures the Holy Spirit is also described as teaching (see John 14:26), testifying (see 15:26), guiding (see Rom. 8:4), speaking (see 1 Cor. 2:13), enlightening (see John 16:13), striving (see Gen. 6:3), commanding (see Acts 8:29), interceding (see Rom. 8:26), sending workers (see Acts 13:4), calling (see Rev. 22:17), comforting (see John 16:7), and working (see 1 Cor. 12:11). These actions cannot be accomplished by a mere influence or force. Only a rational, emotional, active person could do all that the Scriptures teach that the Holy Spirit accomplishes.

The Holy Spirit Is God

The identity names of the Holy Spirit also reveal the Spirit's divine nature. Names ascribed to the Holy Spirit such as "God," "Spirit of

God," "the Breath of the Almighty," "the Voice of God," "the Spirit who Is from God," "Lord," "Spirit of the Lord" and "the Glory of the Lord" all tend to emphasize the deity of the Holy Spirit. These are only a few of the various identity names of the Holy Spirit that emphasize aspects of His deity.

The Old Testament Names of the Holy Spirit

1. *Elohim*
2. *Jehovah*
3. *Shekinah*
4. *Shaddai*
5. *El Elyon*

The Holy Spirit as *Elohim* (God)

Some of the identity names of the Holy Spirit link Him to *Elohim,* an Old Testament name for God. These names include "the Breath of God" (see Job 27:3), "the Finger of God" (Luke 11:20), "the Fullness of God" (Eph. 3:19, *NKJV*), "the Gift of God" (Acts 8:20), "God" (5:4), "the Seal of God" (Rev. 9:4), "the Seal of the Living God" (7:2), "the Seven Spirits of God" (3:1), "the Seven Spirits of God Sent Out into All the Earth" (Rev. 5:6), "the Spirit of God" (Gen 1:2; 1 Pet. 4:14), "the Spirit of Our God" (1 Cor. 6:11), "the Spirit Who Is from God" (1 Cor. 2:12, *NKJV*), "the Spirit of the Holy God" (Dan. 4:8, *NKJV*), "the Spirit of the Living God" (2 Cor. 3:3), and "the Spirit of the Lord GOD" (Isa. 61:1).

The Old Testament name *Elohim,* usually translated "God," is by far the most common name for God in Scripture. This name is derived from the Hebrew word *El,* meaning "Strong One." Therefore, *Elohim* is the Strong One who manifests Himself by His Word. This name is used more than 2,500 times in the Old Testament, often to remind the reader of the strength or faithfulness of God. It is the name used in the first (see Gen. 1:1) and last (see Rev. 22:19) references to God in Scripture and is often used in connection with God's rule over His creation.

The various identity names of the Holy Spirit that link the Holy Spirit with *Elohim* tend to emphasize His divine nature, particularly

306 The Ultimate Guide to the Names of God

as it is manifested in the strength and faithfulness of His Word. Because the Holy Spirit is the divine Author of the Scriptures, these names of the Holy Spirit remind us of the faithfulness of the Scriptures. Also implied in these names is the ability of the Holy Spirit to accomplish His work in our lives and to honor the promises of the Scriptures.

The Holy Spirit as *Jehovah* (Lord)

Some of the identity terms of the Holy Spirit link Him to the name *Jehovah,* another Old Testament name for God. These terms include "the Breath of the LORD" (Isa. 40:7, *NKJV*), "the Lord" (2 Cor. 3:17), "the Spirit of the LORD" (Judg. 3:10), "the Spirit of the Lord GOD" (Isa. 61:1), and "the Voice of the LORD" (see Ps. 29:3-5,7-9). Several other references to the Holy Spirit are given in a context that suggests a relationship to *Jehovah*, although the name *Jehovah* is not a specific part of the title.

The name *Jehovah*, printed "LORD" in many Bible translations,* means "Self-existent One" according to many scholars. It is derived from the verb "to be" repeated twice. *Jehovah* identifies Himself as "I AM THAT I AM" (Exod. 3:14), implying both His self-existence and His eternity.

The name *Jehovah* for God is used about 4,000 times in the Bible,* usually in association with His people. It has been called "the covenant name of God" because it is often used to identify God in His covenants with mankind (see Gen. 2:15-17; 3:14-19; 4:15; 12:1-3). If *Elohim* ("God") is the primary name of God in Scripture, then *Jehovah* ("LORD") might be called the personal name of God in Scripture.

When the identity names of the Holy Spirit are associated with *Jehovah*, we are reminded of the role that the Holy Spirit has in our relationship with God. The very name implies His desire to relate closely to His people. In the Old Testament it was the Spirit of the LORD who repeatedly came upon the judges as God brought deliverance to His people (see Judg. 3:10; 6:34; 11:29; 13:25; 14:6,19; 15:14).

In the New Testament the liberty of the Christian is linked to the Spirit of the Lord. "Now the Lord is the Spirit; and where the Spirit of the Lord is, there is liberty" (2 Cor. 3:17, *NKJV*).

The Holy Spirit as *Shekinah* (Glory)

Two identity names of the Holy Spirit link Him to the *Shekinah* glory that was manifest in the wilderness wanderings, in the Tabernacle and in the first Temple of Israel. In this regard the Spirit is identified as "the glory of the Lord" (2 Cor. 3:18) and "the Spirit of glory" (see 1 Pet. 4:14, *NKJV*). Other references such as "divided tongues, as of fire" (Acts 2:3), "the seven lamps of fire burning before the throne" (Rev. 4:5), "the spirit of burning" (Isa. 4:4) and "the voice of Your thunder" (Ps. 77:18, *NKJV*) might also be related to manifestations of the *Shekinah* glory of God.

The *Shekinah* glory of God was a self-revelation of the presence of God in the midst of His people. Originally the pillar of fire by night and cloud by day were the means by which God led Israel through the wilderness and protected His people from the Egyptians. When the *Shekinah* glory filled the Temple built by Solomon, those who had come to praise and worship the Lord could do little more than stand back silently in awe of God's unique presence among them. Throughout history revivals of the Church have been described as God manifesting His glory among His people.

When the identity names of the Holy Spirit link the Spirit with the *Shekinah* glory of God, it is again a reminder of His divine nature. Also implied in these terms are the leading and protecting ministries of the Holy Spirit in the life of the believer. Personal and corporate revival comes when we recognize the Holy Spirit as God, repent of those sins that He brings to our attention and yield to His leading by obeying the known will of God.

The Holy Spirit as *Shaddai* (Almighty)

The Breath of the Almighty (see Job 32:8; 33:4) and the Voice of the Almighty (see Ezek. 1:24) are identity terms of the Holy Spirit that link the Spirit to the Old Testament name of God, *Shaddai*. This name means "rest" or "nourisher." Although the Old Testament name of God *El Shaddai* is usually translated "the Almighty God" (see Gen. 17:1-2), it also means "the All-sufficient God." The characteristic of strength and the ability to supply our needs are tied to the name *Shaddai*.

When the name *Shaddai* is used of the Holy Spirit in Scripture, it is a reminder that the Holy Spirit is sufficient to meet the needs in our lives. It is interesting to note that this title of the Holy Spirit is given in the context of people who needed to be encouraged, comforted and strengthened by reminding them of the all-sufficiency of the Holy Spirit. Elihu reminded Job that the Breath of the Almighty would give him both understanding (see Job 32:8) and life (see 33:4). Ezekiel must have been discouraged as he was taken among the captives to Babylon. Yet young Ezekiel heard the Voice of the Almighty (see Ezek. 1:24). Likewise, when we are feeling down in our Christian life, recognizing the all-sufficient ministry of the Holy Spirit in our lives should be a source of encouragement.

The Holy Spirit as *El Elyon* (Most High)

Twice in Scripture an identity term is ascribed to the Holy Spirit linking Him with *El Elyon that is* usually translated "the Most High God." The reference to "his voice" (Ps. 18:13) by the psalmist implies that he is talking about the Voice of the Most High. In the New Testament, Gabriel referred to "the power of the Highest" (Luke 1:35) to describe the Holy Spirit when he explained to Mary how she would bear a son and remain a virgin.

El Elyon is used primarily in the context of convincing Gentiles that the true God of Israel was above all the false gods of the Gentiles. The first reference of this title in Scripture occurs in the context of Abraham's meeting with Melchizedek (see Gen. 14:18). On that occasion the meaning of this name is linked with the idea of God's rightful ownership over all He created (see v. 22). Prior to that meeting the name was also used by Lucifer in his quest to challenge God's authority in heaven and to "be like the most High" (Isa. 14:14). Perhaps because of the significance of this name in the beginning of their continuing rebellion against God, the name *El Elyon* appears to be the preferred name of God used by demons in addressing Jesus (see Mark 5:7).

The identity names of the Holy Spirit that link the Spirit with *El Elyon* emphasize the rightful authority of the Holy Spirit over all His creation. Also implied in these names is the idea that the power of the Holy Spirit is supreme over whatever power may be associated with other spiritual beings. A third implication of these names of the Holy Spirit is a reminder to Christians that we are part of an ongoing spiritual conflict between God and the devil. This conflict began with the devil's refusal to recognize the rightful authority of *El Elyon* over all creation, and it will end with the devil's realization of the supreme power of *El Elyon*.

Developing Your Relationship with the Holy Spirit

When we understand the terms for the Holy Spirit that emphasize His identity, personality and deity, we should work to develop our relationship with Him. Just as Christians are "called into the fellowship of His Son, Jesus Christ our Lord" (1 Cor. 1:9, *NKJV*), we to are called into the "fellowship of the Spirit" (Phil 2:1, *NKJV*). Paul's final recorded prayer for the church at Corinth was, "The grace of the Lord Jesus Christ, and the love of God, and the communion of the Holy Spirit be with you all. Amen" (2 Cor. 13:14, *NKJV*).

The Principle of Integrity

An important part of building any relationship is to be honest and up front in your dealings with the other person. Lying about yourself, your attitudes or your actions will hinder the development of open lines of communication that are so essential in building interpersonal relationships.

The Bible records the story of two disciples who offended the Holy Spirit when they attempted to lie to Him (see Acts 5:3). Ananias and Sapphira were not required to give the proceeds of the sale of their property to God, so under normal circumstances anything they gave would have been appreciated. But their decision to lie about what they were doing had severe consequences, and it cost them their lives. Christians today who are committed to developing their relationship with the Holy Spirit should be careful to be honest before God in all they do.

The Principle of Openness

A second important part of developing a relationship with other people is that of openness to their ideas. When others sense consistent resistance to their ideas, they will soon abandon any efforts to build the relationship. In his address before the Sanhedrin, Stephen rebuked the religious leaders for resisting the Holy Spirit: "You stiffnecked and uncircumcised in heart and ears! You always resist the Holy Spirit; as your fathers did, so do you" (Acts 7:51, *NKJV*). Christians today need to guard against resisting the Holy Spirit in their lives.

The early Christians understood this principle of openness and were eager to obey the directives of the Holy Spirit. Peter obeyed the Holy Spirit when he was commanded to go to Cornelius's household (see 10:19-20). Philip followed the leading of the Holy Spirit in his ministry (see 8:39). Against his better judgment Ananias came to Saul, obeying what the Holy Spirit had revealed to him (see 9:10-17). Later Paul and Silas were led by the Holy Spirit in their ministry (see 16:7-10).

The Principle of Consideration

A third important element involved in developing a relationship with another person is being considerate of the values, interests and preferences of the other person. If a man understands that his wife prefers a particular type of flower, he contributes to their relationship when he buys that kind of flower for his wife rather than a flower he may prefer. Many relationships are eroded and eventually destroyed when couples refuse to consider their partner's values relating to finances or child rearing or when they consistently neglect each other's interests when planning vacations or even meals.

Being inconsiderate can also hinder our relationship with the Holy Spirit. Jesus warned about the sin of blaspheming the Holy Spirit (see Matt. 12:31). Many Bible teachers believe that the "unpardonable sin" of blaspheming the Holy Spirit involved ascribing the works of Jesus to Satan and could only be committed by those who witnessed the public ministry of Jesus while He was on Earth. But Christians may insult or offend the Holy Spirit in other ways today. Paul warned the Ephesians, "Do not grieve the Holy Spirit of God" (Eph. 4:30, *NKJV*). He then added some specific ways to avoid this sin against the Holy Spirit: "Let all bitterness, wrath, anger, clamor, and evil speaking be put away from you, with all malice.

And be kind to one another, tenderhearted, forgiving one another, even as God in Christ forgave you" (vv. 31-32, *NKJV*).

The Principle of Commitment
A meaningful relationship cannot be developed without a commitment on the part of both persons to each other and a commitment to their relationship. Several of the identity terms for the Holy Spirit emphasize His commitment to us and to our relationship with Him. When we recognize this, we should respond in like manner, committing ourselves to developing a healthy relationship with the Holy Spirit.

The Principle of Reverence
The identity names of the Holy Spirit reveal His divine nature. Thus, as God, the Holy Spirit should be treated with all the reverence and respect one would give the Father or Jesus. Treating the Holy Spirit as anything less than God in our response to His leading in our lives, in our thanksgiving for His gifts or in our worship of His Person demonstrates our failure to understand the implications of the identity names of the Holy Spirit.

The Principle of Sufficiency
When we are developing a relationship with another person, it is much easier to respond to that person positively if he or she is sufficiently meeting our personal needs. The identity names of the Holy Spirit are a reminder of the all-sufficiency of the Holy Spirit in His ministry in our lives. Some Christians find it helpful to take inventory occasionally and to identify specific needs that God has met in their lives. We can come to a deeper appreciation of the value of our relationship with the Holy Spirit by reviewing how God has answered prayer, healed inner hurts, enabled us to minister effectively to others, and helped us lead others to salvation.

---

* The original pronunciation for *Jehovah* may have been *Yahweh*. The word comes from four Hebrew consonants transliterated YHWH. Originally Hebrew was written without vowels. Later the vowels from *Adonai*, Hebrew for "Lord," were inserted. Hence, the term "LORD" (capital and small capitals) denotes the name *Jehovah*.

6

Descriptions Given by God the Father

Descriptions of the Spirit Given by the Father

1. The Promise of the Father	He would fulfill salvation.
2. The Procession of the Holy Spirit	He was sent to the world.
3. The Spirit of Your Father	He is identical in nature to the Father.

In any close relationship such as those within a family, people tend to be called by nicknames given them by other members of the family. Sometimes those names remain unknown to others outside the family and have special meaning only in the context of the relationship in which they were first assigned. Because this sort of thing often happens in human relationships, such as among families, athletic teams, fraternal organizations and churches, it should not be surprising that both God the Father and Jesus have special names by which they address the Holy Spirit. Also, certain names of the Holy Spirit tend to emphasize the Spirit's relationship with the other two members of the Trinity. This chapter will consider some of the terms that relate the Holy Spirit to God the Father.

At least a dozen names of the Holy Spirit are used to describe His relationship to the Father. (Some are included here for full reference but were discussed earlier in the book; hence, they will not be discussed here.) These names include "the promise of the Father" (Acts 1:4), "Spirit of God" (Gen. 1:2), "Spirit of the LORD" (Luke 4:18), "Spirit of our God" (1 Cor. 6:11), "his Spirit" (Num. 11:29), "Spirit of the Lord GOD" (Isa. 61:1), "Your Spirit" (Ps. 104:30, *NKJV*), "Your Holy Spirit" (51:11, *NKJV*), "Spirit of Your Father" (Matt. 10:20), "Spirit of the living God" (2 Cor. 3:3), "My

Spirit" (Gen. 6:3), and "the Spirit of Him who raised Jesus" (Rom. 8:11, *NKJV*). In addition, variations of these names may also imply a relationship between God the Father and the Holy Spirit.

In seeking to analyze descriptive terms for the Holy Spirit, it quickly becomes obvious that many may belong to more than one grouping. This is true in part because of the nature of the terms. As the Author of Scripture, it was never the intent of the Holy Spirit to magnify Himself. Rather, His commitment was to magnify Christ (see John 16:13-15).

Two consequences of this commitment are usually apparent. First, many more names for Jesus appear in Scripture than do names for the Holy Spirit—between seven and eight times as many. Second, many of the names of the Holy Spirit are used in more than one context. Thus, a single term might be described as an identity name, be related to the Father and/or the Son, reveal something of His character, and also describe an aspect of His ministry.

When the names of the Holy Spirit are examined in relationship to other members of the Trinity, it should not be concluded that the Holy Spirit is less than God. The Bible recognizes three Persons in the Godhead who are equal in nature, separate in person, yet submissive in duties.

Members of the Trinity

Equal in Nature
Separate in Person
Submissive in Duties

When people describe the Holy Spirit as a possession of the Father, they err. The names of the Father and the Holy Spirit express a relationship between two equals, just as two brothers may use the possessive pronoun to describe their relationship to each other. For one to speak of the other as "my brother" does not imply inferiority. They are equal in nature (that is, they are both boys). Yet they are separate persons. In most cases one will submit to the other's expertise, insight or perceived authority in the relationship. In this sense one might be described as subservient in duty to the other, at least in certain areas. Although this illustration shows how the Holy Spirit is separate from the Father and Jesus, the illustration does not show the unity of the Godhead: they are One.

The Promise of the Father

Jesus described the Holy Spirit as "the promise of my Father" (Luke 24:49) and "the promise of the Father" (Acts 1:4). In both cases the Holy Spirit is described in the context of prophetic teaching about the coming of the Holy Spirit in this age. On the Day of Pentecost, Peter abbreviated this title of the Holy Spirit and told his listeners, "The promise is to you and to your children, and to all who are afar off, as many as the Lord our God will call" (Acts 2:39, *NKJV*).

This promise of the Holy Spirit was significant in the Old Testament context in which it was given (see Joel 2:28). The ministry of the Holy Spirit was largely preparatory in the Old Testament. Only in the New Testament era has the reality of the abiding presence of the Holy Spirit and His continuing ministry in the life of believers been realized.

This does not mean that the Holy Spirit did not have a ministry in the Old Testament. Actually, His work in the Old Testament was similar in several respects to His work today. First, He enabled people to become spiritual and to serve God. Second, He was active in restraining sin in the Old Testament just as He is in the New Testament (see Gen. 6:3; 2 Thess. 2:7).

As similar as the Old and New Testament ministries of the Holy Spirit are, some significant differences are also evident. The Old Testament ministry of the Holy Spirit was limited in its purpose, effect and quality. Relatively few people prior to Pentecost had an awareness of the ministry of the Holy Spirit in their lives. Those who did were not guaranteed of its continuity. On at least one occasion, David prayed, "Do not take Your Holy Spirit from me" (Ps. 51:11, *NKJV*).

As the Promise of the Father, the Holy Spirit came on the Day of Pentecost, which marked the beginning of a new era in human history, particularly as it relates to the relationship between the Christian and the Holy Spirit. When a person becomes a Christian, he or she is regenerated, indwelt, filled and sealed by the Holy Spirit. (These various ministries of the Holy Spirit are examined more closely in chapter 2.)

As these ministries relate to the title "the Promise of the Father," they indicate a continuation of the Holy Spirit's Old Testament ministry into the New Testament but in a much broader and more consistent manner. The New Testament Christian never needs to share David's fear that the Promise of the Father may depart. This Gift of God (see John 4:10; Acts 8:20) is given to Christians when they are converted and abides with them forever.

The Procession of the Holy Spirit

When Jesus taught His disciples about the coming of the Holy Spirit, He told them, "But when the Helper comes, whom I shall send to you from the Father, the Spirit of truth who proceeds from the Father, He will testify of Me" (John 15:26, *NKJV*). Many of the names of the Holy Spirit include the use of a possessive pronoun, indicating a relationship between the Father and the Holy Spirit. Among other things the use of these pronouns by the Father may imply what has been called the Procession of the Holy Spirit, which refers to the order, or sequence, of the Spirit's work.

Theologians have used the term "procession" for centuries to explain how the Father and Jesus relate to the Holy Spirit. The Greek word *ekporeuomai,* translated "proceeds," means "in the process" or "continually proceeding." This has resulted in the expression "the eternal procession" to describe the Holy Spirit as eternally coming rather than just His coming at one time in history. Although Jesus only spoke specifically of the Holy Spirit proceeding from the Father, He suggested that the Spirit also proceeded from the Son when He described the Helper as the One "whom I shall send to you" (John 15:26, *NKJV*).

The Holy Spirit is continually proceeding in order to minister to specific needs in our lives. This procession of the Holy Spirit demonstrates the compassionate concern our heavenly Father has for His children. Just as a human father constantly gives time, money and guidance to help his children grow to maturity, so too our heavenly Father constantly gives the Holy Spirit to help us grow to spiritual maturity. The eternal procession of the Holy Spirit ought to be a constant reminder to Christians of the eternal compassion of the Father.

The Spirit of Your Father

The Holy Spirit is also described by the title "the Spirit of your Father" (Matt. 10:20). This description, along with other terms for the Holy Spirit that include the possessive pronoun, tends to emphasize the similarity of character between the Holy Spirit and God the Father. Just as people today may use the expression "the spirit of liberty" to describe something that is characteristically the same as liberty, so too the term "the Spirit of your Father" describes the Holy Spirit as One whose nature is like that of God the Father. All that is true of the essential character of God the Father is also true of the Spirit of your Father.

What is God the Father like? The Bible describes God the Father as One who gives life to His children (see John 1:13), loves His children (see Rom. 8:15), protects His children (see 8:31), provides good things for His family (see Jas. 1:17), and teaches and trains His children (see John 14:26).

Likewise, the Holy Spirit is portrayed in Scripture as giving new life to the Christian (see 3:8), expressing love in and through the Christian (see Gal. 5:22), protecting Christians by offering to lead them away from unnecessary danger (see Acts 20:23), giving spiritual gifts to Christians to equip them for effective ministry (see 1 Cor. 12:11), and teaching and training Christians (John 14:26). Everything that God the Father does for the family of God, the Spirit of your Father also does for the believer.

Responding to the Father's Holy Spirit

The names of the Holy Spirit that are related to God the Father imply several principles in the Christian life. As we consider the Holy Spirit as the Promise of the Father, the coming of the Spirit on the Day of Pentecost is a reminder of the reliability of the other promises of God in Scripture. The nature of the Holy Spirit's relationship to Christians in this age ought to help us feel more secure in our relationship with God. The eternal procession of the Holy Spirit demonstrates the consistent concern that God has for us. The similarity between the Spirit of your Father and God the Father is a reminder that we too need to be like our heavenly Father (see Matt. 5:48). This similarity between the Christian and God the Father ought to extend to several areas of life and is only possible as the Spirit of your Father perfects His work in us (see Phil. 1:6).

The Principle of Reliable Promises

When Joshua called on Moses to rebuke two men because they had not gone outside the camp to prophesy as they had been instructed, Moses responded, "Oh, that all the LORD's people were prophets and that the LORD would put His Spirit upon them!" (Num. 11:29, NKJV).

Throughout the entire Old Testament, this longing for a fuller relationship with the Holy Spirit was felt by those in Israel who walked with God. The highlight of the prophecy of Joel was the promise,

> It shall come to pass afterward that I will pour out My Spirit on all flesh; your sons and your daughters shall prophesy, your old men shall dream dreams, your young men shall see visions (2:28, NKJV).

This promise was considered so significant that Jewish scribes usually isolated the five verses containing it as a separate chapter in the brief prophecy of Joel.

Peter stood on the Day of Pentecost and announced, "This [pouring out of the Spirit] is what was spoken by the prophet Joel" (Acts 2:16, NKJV). Many Jews may have wondered if the longing of Moses and the prophecy of Joel would ever become a reality in the life of the nation. But despite the apparent delay, the Promise of the Father did come in God's perfect timing. Once again the promises of God proved reliable.

Many Christians can identify with the Jews' longing for the promised Holy Spirit. Like them we sometimes find ourselves wondering if God's promise will ever be honored as we continue to seek the Holy Spirit's power. Sometimes we need to be reminded, "For all the promises of God in Him are Yes, and in Him Amen, to the glory of God through us" (2 Cor. 1:20, *NKJV*). Every Christian has the Holy Spirit, who is called the Promise of the Father. His indwelling is a constant reminder that God honors His promises in His perfect timing.

But are we, who are indwelt by the Promise of the Father, as reliable in our word as He is? Sometimes circumstances over which we have no control may prevent our fulfilling all that we promised to do. When that happens, we want people to be understanding and not to blame us. But what about the other times when for other less compelling reasons we forget or fail to do all that we promised? That practice becoming a pattern in our lives indicates that the Promise of the Father is not being allowed to do His work in our lives. Jesus warned His disciples about making commitments beyond their ability and urged them, "Let your 'Yes' be 'Yes,' and your 'No,' 'No.' For whatever is more than these is from the evil one" (Matt. 5:37, *NKJV*).

The Principle of a Secure Relationship

The Christian today does not have to pray like David, "Do not take Your Holy Spirit from me" (Ps. 51:11, *NKJV*). The coming of the Promise of the Father on the Day of Pentecost marked a new era in the work of the Holy Spirit in the believer. Today we can be secure in our relationship with the Holy Spirit, knowing that He has taken up residence in our lives.

Understanding the security of our relationship with the Holy Spirit ought to influence our living for and our service to God. If we constantly had to please God in order to maintain our relationship with Him, that pressure would drain our energy, and very soon our service would be marred by personal frustrations. But when we know our relationship with Him is secure, we are free to serve God out of a heart of gratitude. The result of this inner assurance is a motivation to do more for God.

One of the greatest hindrances to developing a healthy interpersonal relationship with another person is the pressure to live up to unreasonable expectations. When we base our concern for others on the condition of their meeting our expectations, we apply pressure that will inevitably destroy any relationship with them. Rather, we would do well to follow the example of the Holy Spirit to love others unconditionally. Then, as others feel secure in that relationship, we can be the kind of friend who helps them develop to their potential.

The Principle of Demonstrated, Consistent Concern

The eternal procession of the Holy Spirit demonstrates God's consistent concern for us. We recall that Jesus referred to the Spirit as the *parakletos*, meaning "one called along side to help." The Holy Spirit is our constant Helper who is ready, able and willing to assist us in every area of our lives. God the Father not only loves His children, but He has also demonstrated His love by sending His Spirit to help us.

Again, we can learn something about dealing with other people from our relationship with the Holy Spirit. People will tend not to be convinced of our love for them until they see our consistent concern demonstrated in some practical way. As we do things for others and assist them whenever and wherever possible, we give them the opportunity to experience the love of God flowing through our lives. In the process we also establish credibility for our witness. Then, as we explain the love of God as revealed in the gospel, others are more open to responding to Christ as Savior because they have experienced the consistent concern of a Christian. This is the most effective means of reaching some people with the gospel. That may be why Jude called on the Early Church to demonstrate their consistent concern for others: "On some have compassion, making a distinction" (Jude 22, *NKJV*).

The Principle of Father-Son Likeness

As a boy matures in his family, it is not unusual for him to develop the habits and mannerisms he sees modeled by his father in the home. The same principle of father-son likeness ought to be at work in the family of God. Just as the Spirit of the Father is like God the Father, so too Christians ought to become like their

heavenly Father. Jesus called on His disciples, "You shall be perfect, just as your Father in heaven is perfect" (Matt. 5:48, *NKJV*).
The word translated "perfect" means perfect in the sense of complete, rather than perfect in the sense of being without sin.

From time to time, every Christian should take inventory of
his or her progress in becoming like God the Father. The Bible
describes various moral characteristics of God, including integrity
(see Num. 23:19), zeal (see Nah. 1:2), mercy (see Ps. 116:5), goodness (see 73:1), holiness (see 99:9), impartiality (see Acts 10:34),
faithfulness (see 1 Cor. 1:9), righteousness (see Heb. 6:10), love (see
1 John 4:8), longsuffering (see Num. 14:18), graciousness (see Ps.
111:4; 1 Pet. 2:3), and compassion (Ps. 145:8).

Although many other attributes of God are identified in
Scripture, the list above would be a good starting point to determine if you are allowing the Spirit of your Father to develop the
character of God the Father in your life.

7

References to the Spirit and Jesus

The Spirit and Jesus

The Spirit of Jesus Christ	
1. The Spirit of His Son	He has the same nature as Jesus.
2. The Spirit of Jesus	He does the work of salvation.
3. The Spirit of Christ	He assists in the threefold anointed office of the Son.
4. The Spirit of Jesus Christ	He assists in the balanced ministry of the Son.

The Helper in the Life of Jesus Christ	
1. The Spirit was involved ...	in Jesus' virgin birth.
	in Jesus' growth.
	in Jesus' ministry.
	in strengthening Jesus during the temptation.
	in Jesus' miracles.
	in Jesus' atoning work.
	in raising Jesus from the dead.
	in Jesus' Ascension.

The Helper in the Life of Jesus Christ	
1. The Holy Spirit is involved ...	in Christ's ministry to believers.

Just as certain ways of referring to the Holy Spirit emphasize the Spirit's relationship to God the Father, so too other terms for Him tend to describe His relationship with Jesus. Some of these names or descriptions were given to the Holy Spirit by Jesus. Others were used by the apostles to describe the relationship between Jesus and the Holy Spirit. These references include "the Spirit of Christ," "the Spirit of Jesus," "the Spirit of Jesus Christ," "the Spirit of His Son" and "the Helper."

We have noticed that the name "Helper" is perhaps the best-known name Jesus gave to the Holy Spirit (see John 14:16,26). In some respects all the names of the Holy Spirit given by Jesus may be summarized in this name.

The Holy Spirit may be considered the Helper in three senses. First, He is called "another Helper" (John 14:16, *NKJV*) in that He follows Jesus, to whom this same name is applied ("Advocate," see 1 John 2:1). Second, He demonstrated Himself to be a faithful Helper throughout the life of Jesus on Earth. Third, He is promised as the Helper who helps us today in our Christian life.

The Holy Spirit as Helper

1. Another Helper like Jesus
2. The faithful Helper in the life of Jesus
3. The promised Helper for Christians today

The Spirit of Jesus Christ

As we have said, when Jesus spoke of the Holy Spirit as *another* Helper, He used the Greek word *allos*, which means "another of the same kind or sort." This word is used in Scripture, for example, to refer to different bodies of flesh or different celestial bodies (see 1 Cor. 15:39-41)—things or people who are of the same sort. Thus, when this adjective is used to describe the Holy Spirit, it affirms that He and Jesus are of the same nature. Jesus is the first Helper to be sent, and the Holy Spirit is the second. Several other titles of the Holy Spirit are used in Scripture to help remind Christians of the similarities between the second and third Persons of the Trinity.

The Spirit of His Son

The title "the Spirit of His Son" for the Holy Spirit stresses the complete unity of nature in the Trinity. The expressions "son of" and "spirit of" are used in the Bible to describe similarity of nature. When Jesus is called the Son of God, this implies that He is by nature God. When the Holy Spirit is described as "the Spirit of His Son" (Gal. 4:6, *NKJV*), the title implies that the Holy Spirit has the same nature as the Son, who has the same nature as God the Father. This is the most trinitarian name of God in Scripture applied to any individual Person of the Godhead. This title summarizes the teaching of Scripture on the equality and unity of nature in God.

Although I believe that the name "the Spirit of His Son" refers to the Holy Spirit, I am also aware that many Bible teachers interpret the title to be a description of the nonphysical nature of Jesus Christ. Just as a person has body, soul and spirit, some interpret this phrase to mean "the spirit that belongs to Jesus," not the Holy Spirit. They would interpret the names "the Spirit of Jesus," "the Spirit of Christ" and "the Spirit of Jesus Christ" in the same manner.

The Spirit of Jesus

When the title "Spirit of . . ." is used to describe the Holy Spirit, the word following the preposition is often the key to understanding the meaning of that particular name. The meaning of the title "the Spirit of Jesus" (Acts 16:7, *NIV*) is wrapped up in the meaning of the name "Jesus." "Jesus" means "*Jehovah* is Savior." It is used to describe the second Person of the Trinity primarily in the context of His saving work (see Matt. 1:21).

The Spirit of Christ

The term "the Spirit of Christ" (Rom. 8:9) needs to be understood in the context of both the Old and New Testaments. The word "Christ" means "the anointed one" and was used to describe the threefold anointed office (that is, those anointed to serve in the office of prophet, priest or king). When the title "Christ" is applied to Jesus, it affirms that Jesus was the fulfillment of each of these three Old Testament offices. In this context the Spirit of Christ implies that the Holy Spirit also has this threefold anointed ministry. It is a prophetic ministry in that it reveals the message of God to humanity (see 2 Pet. 1:21), a priestly ministry in that it offers an acceptable sacrifice for sin (see Heb. 9:14) and a regal ministry in that He rules in the broader kingdom of God (see Rom. 8:2).

In the New Testament the expression "in Christ" is often used to describe the Christian's relationship to Jesus as one of union and communion. Again, this aspect of the meaning of the title Christ is also implied in the title "the Spirit of Christ." The union and communion with God enjoyed by Christians are possible because of the indwelling Holy Spirit (see 1 Cor. 6:19). This means that the Holy Spirit is the member of the Trinity with whom Christians tend to relate most directly in their union and communion with God.

The Spirit of Jesus Christ

Just as the title "Jesus Christ" is used in Scripture to illustrate the balance between His saving and His messianic ministry, so too is the title "the Spirit of Jesus Christ" (Phil. 1:19). Paul used this title to emphasize the full provision and supply of Jesus Christ in his Christian life and ministry.

The Helper in the Life of Jesus Christ

The Holy Spirit was involved in at least seven aspects of the earthly life and public ministry of Jesus. First, the Holy Spirit was involved in Jesus' virgin birth (see Luke 1:35). Second, the Spirit was involved in the maturing process of Jesus as He grew into manhood (see 2:40,45). Third, the public ministry of Jesus began with the descent of the Holy Spirit upon Him at His baptism (see 3:21-22), after which the Holy Spirit led Jesus into the wilderness and filled Him so that He could face temptation (see 4:1). Fourth, Jesus ministered in the power and anointing of the Holy Spirit (see vv. 14,18). Fifth, Jesus attributed His miracles to the work of the Holy Spirit (see Matt. 12:28). In His death the Holy Spirit assisted Jesus in His atoning work (see Heb. 9:14). Sixth, Jesus was raised from the dead by the Holy Spirit (see Rom. 8:11). Finally, the Holy Spirit is involved in the post-resurrection glorification of Jesus (see John 16:14).

The New Testament uses five different expressions describing the relationship between Jesus and the Holy Spirit during Jesus' ministry. First, Jesus was led by the Spirit (see Luke 4:1). Second, He was filled with the Holy Spirit (see Luke 4:1; John 3:34-35). Third, He was anointed by the Spirit (see Luke 4:18; Acts 10:38; Heb. 1:9). Fourth, He was empowered by the Holy Spirit (see Matt. 12:18). Finally, He rejoiced in the Spirit (see Luke 10:21). Each of these expressions implies a helping relationship with the Holy Spirit.

When Bible teachers seek to explain how Jesus became a man, they use the word *kenosis* to describe the self-emptying of Jesus in taking on human flesh (see Phil. 2:7). This emptying included submitting to the limitations of humanity. Although Jesus never ceased to be God during His life on Earth, He was nevertheless dependent upon the third Person of the Trinity to accomplish much of the work of God. Although not denying the deity of Jesus, this truth illustrates His humanity.

The Helper in the Christian's Life

The Holy Spirit is active in the world today. Although at times one may wonder if anything is going right and think that the world is in total chaos, things are never as bad as they would be if the Holy Spirit were removed from the world. The Spirit is working to restrain sin in the world and to reprove sin in the unbeliever.

The moment someone is saved, a number of things take place in that person's life. The person is born again by the Holy Spirit, indwelt by the Holy Spirit, sealed with the Spirit, and a host of other things—almost too many to list. Many times Christians are not aware of all that takes place when they are saved until years afterward, but these things happen the moment they trust Christ as personal Savior. The Holy Spirit is the agent of regeneration.

The ministry of the Holy Spirit in our lives does not end at conversion but continues beyond. He fills Christians as they yield to Him and allow Him to control their lives. He leads them and sheds light on the Scriptures, helping them to learn better the things of God. He gives them the fruit of the Spirit for character and the gifts of the Holy Spirit for Christian service.

How the Holy Spirit Helps Us Live for God

In other chapters of this book, some of these present ministries of the Holy Spirit are discussed as they relate to other specific names, titles and emblems of the Holy Spirit. The names of the Holy Spirit given by Jesus imply a number of principles that will help us cooperate with the Holy Spirit as He helps us live for God.

The Principle of Modeling Character

One way the Holy Spirit helps us live for God is by modeling the character He wants to develop in our lives. As noted in the previous chapter, a number of the moral attributes of God are characteristic of the Holy Spirit. These are also character traits Christians need to develop in the Christian life. The Bible also calls these the fruit of the Holy Spirit (see Gal. 5:22-24) because they are character traits that are not only modeled by the Holy Spirit but are also developed by the Holy Spirit in our lives. This is one of the helping ministries of the Holy Spirit.

The Principle of Eye-Opening Conviction

One aspect of the Holy Spirit's helping ministry in our lives is conviction. The word "conviction" is derived from two Latin terms meaning "cause to see." Conviction is the means by which the Holy Spirit opens our eyes to see what is right and wrong in our lives. When Jesus taught His disciples about the coming Helper, He noted, "When He has come, He will convict the world of sin, and of righteousness, and of judgment" (John 16:8, *NKJV*).

The sin that keeps people out of heaven is the sin of unbelief. All sin can be forgiven, but sin is not forgiven apart from faith. People who refuse to believe God are attacking His character, and God cannot save them in their unbelief. The Holy Spirit opens people's eyes so that they can see their sin of unbelief "because they do not believe in [Jesus]" (16:9, *NKJV*).

Jesus also taught that the Holy Spirit would cause people to see righteousness, because He would be going to His Father and we would see Him no more (see 16:10). When Jesus was on Earth, He stood as an example and reflection of the righteousness of God. His sinless life convicted people who saw their own unrighteousness. Today it is the Holy Spirit who causes people to see themselves in relation to the righteousness of God. When that occurs in our lives, we will respond like Isaiah, who cried, "Woe is me, for I am undone! Because I am a man of unclean lips, and I dwell in the midst of a people of unclean lips" (6:5, *NKJV*).

The Holy Spirit also causes us to see the judgment that is a consequence of our sin "because the ruler of this world is judged" (John 16:11, *NKJV*). Sometimes we tend to classify certain sins as more evil than others. Depending upon our cultural values, some sins may be more acceptable than others, but all sin is repulsive to God. Not everyone commits the same sins, but the Holy Spirit convicts people of sin of which they are guilty and causes them to see that their sin has been judged already. In this way He shows them their need of a Savior and draws them to the place of salvation.

The Principle of Inner Fulfillment

A third way that the Holy Spirit helps us in our Christian life and ministry is through inner fulfillment. This fulfillment is experienced by the Christian because of two aspects of the helping ministry of the Holy Spirit. First, the indwelling ministry of the Holy Spirit enables us to experience and appreciate our union with God. As God's "Spirit who dwells in [us]" (Rom. 8:11, *NKJV*), the Holy Spirit unites God and the Christian into a mysterious union. Our union with God is the basis of every aspect of our Christian life and ministry, which may be defined as God living and ministering His life through us.

The second helping ministry of the Holy Spirit is implied in the phrase "the Spirit of Christ." The Spirit of Christ enables us to enjoy communion with Christ. God made people to worship Him and enjoy Him forever. This means that people will have a greater sense of personal fulfillment in life when they are enjoying communion with God. This is realized as Christians are filled with the Holy Spirit and walk in the Spirit. To experience the fullness of the Holy Spirit, the Christian needs to repent of sin and yield to God. As we have fellowship with God through His Holy Spirit, we enjoy the communion with God that He intended humanity to experience from the beginning.

The Principle of Availability

Have you ever experienced the frustration of calling a government office to get information only to be put on hold or be transferred from person to person and to end up talking to someone in the wrong department or talking to one who is not sure of the answer to your question? These descriptions of the Holy Spirit given by Jesus emphasize His availability as needed in our lives. When we turn to the Holy Spirit for help, we are never put on hold or transferred. Also, the help provided by the Helper is always just what we need to resolve the problem that we face.

One of the characteristics of the Holy Spirit is that He is always and everywhere present at all times. When David asked, "Where can I go from Your Spirit? Or where can I flee from Your presence?" (Ps. 139:7, *NKJV*), he had to conclude that the Holy Spirit was present everywhere (see vv. 8-12). This attribute of the Holy Spirit guarantees that the Helper Jesus sent to help us is always at our side to assist as needed. In this regard the Holy Spirit fulfills one of the chief prerequisites of a helper. He is available to help when needed.

The Principle of Personal Power

The Holy Spirit helps us by providing spiritual power to enable us in ministry. We are most effective in ministry when we use the gifts the Holy Spirit has given to us. These gifts are given us to do the work He has entrusted to us in the power He makes available to us. Jesus did not commission His disciples to begin the task of world evangelism before they were endued or clothed with the power of the Holy Spirit (see Luke 24:49).

Sometimes children receive toys marked with three words that promise problems ahead: "batteries not included." Without batteries to energize these toys, they will not do what they were designed to do. Although they may look like the picture on the box, they fail to function like the toy our children see in the television commercial.

Like the toy without its batteries, many Christians fail to rise to their potential effectiveness, because they are not energized with the power of the Holy Spirit. They may look like a Christian should look, but they fail to perform as a Christian should perform. They lack the power of the Holy Spirit to overcome sin in their lives and increase their effectiveness in ministry. Only as they yield more completely to God and allow the Holy Spirit to exercise greater control in their lives can they be energized by the power He offers.

8

Descriptions of the Spirit's Character

Designations that Reveal the Character of the Spirit

Character Unique to God	
1. The Breath of Life	His role in giving life to His creatures
2. The Eternal Spirit	His role in giving eternal life
3. The Spirit of Judgment	His role to discern

Character Reproduced in Believers	
1. Your Generous Spirit	His giving nature
2. Your Good Spirit	His attribute of goodness
3. Holy Spirit	His holy nature
4. Spirit of Grace	His nature to forgive and to bestow blessings
5. Spirit of Truth	His truthful nature
6. Spirit of Wisdom	His omniscience
7. Steadfast Spirit	His immutability

One reason parents choose certain names for their children is based on their expectation or desire of what they hope their child will become. The meaning of a certain name may emphasize a particular character trait that they would like to see developed in their child's life. Sometimes a Christian parent will select a biblical name for their child, hoping that the child will mature to become a man or woman of God just like the one after whom he or she is named. Even when a child is given a family name, the particular name chosen is often selected because of some admirable characteristic in the life of the relative after whom the child is named.

When my first granddaughter was born, I was only 45 years old and felt I was too young to be called Grandpa or Grandfather by anyone, including my daughter and wife. "No one is going to call me Gramps—or any other name for old people," I announced vigorously.

My daughter taught my granddaughter to call me Dr. Towns, obviously because that is what I was called by my students at Liberty University. The first few times she attempted to call me Dr. Towns, people smiled or laughed. Because she was sensitive, she became self-conscious about addressing me at all.

My son-in-law calls me "Doc," and that is fine. Without any help my granddaughter started calling me Poppa Doc, and the name stuck. The name reveals my occupation and character, yet it shows the affection of a granddaughter.

Also, naming people on the basis of discernible character traits often leads to nicknames. When a coach begins calling a certain player Bulldog, he does so to draw out that player's tenacity. In a church a lady who is particularly hospitable to others might earn the nickname "Miss Hospitality." At work a certain person's creativity in dealing with problems on the job may be recognized when others refer to him or her as the in-house troubleshooter.

Many of the names of the Holy Spirit are names that draw our attention to His character or attributes. These names answer the question "What is the Holy Spirit like?" The character names of the Holy Spirit include "Breath of Life," "the Eternal Spirit," "Your Generous Spirit," "Your Good Spirit," "the Holy Spirit," "the Spirit of Grace," "the Spirit of Holiness," "the Spirit of Judgment," "the Spirit of Knowledge," "the Spirit of Life," "the Spirit of Love," "the Spirit of Might," "the Spirit of Power," "the Spirit of Truth," "the Spirit of Understanding," "the Spirit of Wisdom" and "the Steadfast Spirit."

These character descriptions may be further broken into two classes. First, some of the character names of the Holy Spirit draw attention to attributes that belong exclusively to God—for example, eternity. Second, many character names of the Holy Spirit describe some characteristic of God that should be reproduced to some degree in the life of the Christian. The character described by this second group of names is sometimes called "the fruit of the Spirit" because it is the character that is developed in the life of the Christian by the Holy Spirit.

Character that Is Unique to God

When the various character names of the Holy Spirit are used in Scripture, they focus attention upon one part of the personality of the Holy Spirit. In order to fully understand who the Holy Spirit is, it is important to realize that although a name may isolate a particular characteristic, the Spirit Himself possesses all these character traits interwoven together. Thus, when we consider the Holy Spirit as the Breath of Life, it should not be forgotten that that life is also characterized by eternity, holiness, love, goodness and all the other characteristics identified in the character names of the Holy Spirit.

The Breath of Life

When the Holy Spirit is described as "the breath of life" (Rev. 11:11, *NKJV*) or "the Spirit of life" (Rom. 8:2), these titles emphasize the nature of God in His self-existence. Only God is able to live by Himself, independent of other life-support systems. Although people possess life, our life differs from that of God because its continuance is dependent upon the availability of oxygen in the atmosphere, the nutrients in the food we eat and the continued health of the body to digest that food and fight off disease. But when the Bible describes the Holy Spirit as possessing life, that life is sustained in itself and represents a quality of life unique to the members of the Trinity.

The Eternal Spirit

The name "eternal Spirit" (Heb. 9:14) signifies that as God, the Holy Spirit is without beginning and ending. Because we live within the limitations of time and space, our finite minds have a difficult time comprehending the nature of eternity. All other things had a beginning, and most things have an end. Even the "everlasting life" we possess as Christians had a beginning in our experience, although it will be unending. God alone is "from everlasting to everlasting" (Ps. 90:2).

The Spirit of Judgment

The title "spirit of judgment" (Isa. 4:4) also identifies a characteristic of the Holy Spirit exclusive to God: the ability to make independent judgments. Several different words are used in Scripture to describe various kinds of judgments. People may exercise discernment and make judgments in some areas, but the ability to judge is severely limited. When we make judgments, they are valid only on the basis of some external standard (that is, a law, biblical principle or precedent). Also, although we may be able to discern certain things, judging a person's motives is beyond our ability and is the exclusive prerogative of God. But the Holy Spirit of Judgment can make right decisions in judgment without relying upon an external standard.

Character that Is Reproduced in the Christian

Some of the Holy Spirit's character designations identify characteristics that apply to God in their most complete sense but also represent character that is reproduced to some degree in the life of the Christian. Understanding each of these seven descriptions of the Holy Spirit will result in a better understanding of the primary work of the Holy Spirit in transforming our character (see Phil. 1:6).

Your Generous Spirit

The Holy Spirit is called "Your generous Spirit" in Psalm 51:12 (*NKJV*). Generosity is one of the character traits the Spirit seeks to develop in our lives. To be generous is to be liberal in our giving or sharing (see Rom. 12:8). Through His generous Spirit, God "freely give[s] us all things" (8:32). As the Holy Spirit produces this character in us, we will also become increasingly generous in our willingness to give of ourselves and our resources to help others in need.

Your Good Spirit

The phrase "Your good Spirit" (Neh. 9:20, *NKJV*) draws attention to the Holy Spirit's goodness. Although only God is good in the most complete sense of the word, goodness is the only character trait that appears on both of the biblical lists of the fruit of the Holy Spirit (see Gal. 5:21-22; Eph. 5:9). This suggests that goodness is something that the Holy Spirit is committed to reproducing in our Christian lives.

The Holy Spirit

The name "Holy Spirit" is the most often used character name of the Holy Spirit in Scripture, occurring some 94 times in the Old and New Testaments. In addition, the holy character of the Spirit is emphasized in the name "Spirit of holiness" (Rom. 1:4, *NKJV*).

Because the root meaning of holiness is "to separate or to cut off," holiness implies separation. In the context of our lives, this includes both separation *from* sin and separation *to* God. Holiness is the most communicable of all God's attributes. We can become holy because we were made in the image and likeness of God (see Gen. 1:26-27). We can only become holy as the Holy Spirit lives out His life through us.

The Spirit of Grace

A fourth transferable characteristic of the Holy Spirit is graciousness, a trait that is emphasized in the term "Spirit of grace" (Zech. 12:10, *NKJV*). It is only by the grace, or unmerited favor, of God that people become Christians, so it is reasonable that Christians should respond by treating others graciously. When God and Christians treat others graciously, they do for others what is desirable yet undeserved. Only God is the complete personification of grace, but Christians should speak in such a way "that it may impart grace to the hearers" (Eph. 4:29, *NKJV*).

The Spirit of Truth

"The Spirit of truth" (John 14:17) identifies truth, or integrity, as another characteristic of the Holy Spirit that He is committed to developing in our lives. Truth is listed as an aspect of the fruit of the Holy Spirit (see Eph. 5:9). "The Spirit of Truth" is the title given to the Holy Spirit in the context of leading the apostles into truth as they wrote the New Testament. One of the authenticating marks of the Scriptures is truth. In turn, truth and integrity ought also to be authenticating marks in the Epistles that the Holy Spirit is currently writing in our lives (see 2 Cor. 3:3).

The Spirit of Wisdom

The descriptions "Spirit of understanding" (Isa. 11:2, *NKJV*) and "spirit of wisdom" (Exod. 28:3) emphasize the depth of wisdom and understanding that is characteristic of the Holy Spirit. Wisdom is seeing things from God's point of view and involves applying known truth. The beginning of wisdom is the fear of the LORD (see Prov. 1:7), but we can also grow in wisdom through prayer. "If any of you lacks wisdom, let him ask of God, who gives to all liberally and without reproach, and it will be given to him" (Jas. 1:5, *NKJV*). Wisdom is also developed in our lives as a result of the work of the Holy Spirit of Wisdom and the Spirit of Understanding as He leads us and guides us in our everyday life.

The Steadfast Spirit

In Psalm 51:10 David prayed for a steadfast spirit on the grounds of the steadfastness of the Holy Spirit. This points to the stability that is characteristic of the Spirit. Those converted on the Day of Pentecost "continued steadfastly in the apostles' doctrine and fellowship, in the breaking of bread, and in prayers" (Acts 2:42, *NKJV*). Christians today also need to develop stability in their commitment to biblical teaching, fellowship with one another, the observance of church ordinances, and their personal and corporate prayer life. This stability is developed through the ministry of the steadfast Spirit reproducing Himself in our lives.

Harvesting the Fruit of the Spirit

When Christians use the expression "the fruit of the Holy Spirit," they are usually referring to nine specific character traits listed by Paul and called the fruit of the Spirit (see Gal. 5:22-23). Actually, Paul also used this descriptive expression to identify another list of three character traits produced by the Holy Spirit in the life of the Christian (see Eph. 5:9). When the two lists are compared, only one character trait, goodness, appears on both lists.

The word "fruit" is used throughout the Scripture to describe that which is produced by some living entity. The fruit of the vine is the grape that is produced in a healthy vineyard. The fruit of the womb is used to describe a child. In this analogy the expression "fruit of the Holy Spirit" includes all the character produced by the Holy Spirit in the Christian life, not just the nine or eleven character traits specifically mentioned by Paul.

Paul's use of the word "fruit" to describe Christian character suggests a relationship between developing character and harvesting produce in an orchard, farm or garden. The application of five specific gardening principles to the character names of the Holy Spirit will help us harvest the fruit of the Holy Spirit in our lives.

The Principle of Like Produces Like

In the very beginning God created life on Earth that has the ability to reproduce life. But that ability is limited. A plant or animal can only reproduce "according to its kind" (Gen. 1:12,24, *NKJV*). The gardener who plants seed in the garden knows what will grow, because one of the laws of nature dictates that a plant can only reproduce according to its kind. As a result, only potatoes will grow from potatoes and melons from the seeds of a melon.

This law of reproduction in nature also has application in harvesting the fruit of the Holy Spirit. If like produces like, then only the Holy Spirit can produce spiritual fruit in our lives. This means that we need to yield to the controlling influence of the Holy Spirit in our lives and resist the influence of the world, the flesh and the devil. The fruit we produce in our lives will be like the seed we sow—that is, the one to whom we yield to obey (see Rom. 6:16).

The Principle of Soil Composition

In the parable of the sower and the seed, Jesus noted a relationship between the fruit-bearing of the seed sown and the soil in which the seed was planted (see Matt. 13:8). Home gardeners know that certain plants grow better in certain kinds of soil. A cactus might be planted in a soil mixture composed largely of ashes and sand, but those who grow African violets use only the richest loam.

Just as a plant produces fruit as it draws what it needs from the soil in which it is planted, so too Christians produce fruit as they draw what they need from Christ in whom they abide (see John 15:5-7) and from the Holy Spirit as they walk in the Spirit (see Gal. 5:16). When we fail to abide in Christ and walk in the Spirit, we become like the plant that is uprooted from its ideal soil environment. If the plant remains in that condition long, it will wither and die. If it remains in the right soil, it will blossom and produce fruit. So we produce the fruit of the Holy Spirit as we remain planted in the Holy Spirit.

The Principle of the Early and Latter Rain
To illustrate the need for patience, James reminded His readers, "See how the farmer waits for the precious fruit of the earth, waiting patiently for it until it receives the early and latter rain" (Jas. 5:7, *NKJV*). The principle of the early and latter rain teaches that fruit is produced throughout a growing season that includes times of rain and sunshine. If it rains all the time, plants rot in the field. If it is always warm and sunny, they dry up and die. But the balance of rain and sun at different periods in the growing season results in a fruitful plant and an abundant harvest.

The principle of the early and latter rain helps us understand how God uses various seasons in our lives, some apparently good and others apparently bad, to produce the spiritual character that He is developing in our lives (see Rom. 8:28-29). If most Christians had their way, they would order a life to be lived in the sunny seasons when everything seems to be going well. Most of us become easily frustrated during the drippy, rainy seasons of life. When the outlook is overcast, we seem to get bogged down in the muck and mire of the mundane details of life. But the Holy Spirit knows just what seasons we need to mature and produce spiritual fruit. Just as a greenhouse farmer may darken the greenhouse if there is too much sun or turn on the sprinkler system to water the plants, so too the Holy Spirit controls our environment to produce spiritual fruit in our lives.

The Principle of Weeding
When Jesus told the parable of the sower and the seed, He noted that some seeds failed to mature into fruit-bearing plants because they

were choked by the weeds that grew up around them (see Matt. 13:7). Every successful home gardener knows that it is necessary to constantly weed the garden throughout the growing season if the full harvest is to be realized. When weeds begin to dominate the garden, it is unlikely that any of the vegetables planted will become as strong as they would be otherwise.

In the parable of the sower and the seed, Jesus compared the weeds to "the cares of this world and the deceitfulness of riches" (v. 22, NKJV). In another parable, Jesus spoke of tares that were sown by the enemy (see vv. 24-30,36-43). Christians who desire to harvest the fruit of the Holy Spirit in their lives should take care to weed their lives periodically of the anxiety, deceit and other sins that may hinder the development of Christian character.

The Principle of Pruning

An ongoing task in a vineyard or orchard is that of pruning. This involves cutting away the parts of the plant that do not produce fruit so that the remaining plant will produce more fruit or stronger fruit. When Jesus described the relationship between Himself and His disciples in the context of a vine, He noted that the Father would prune the vine periodically to increase the productivity of its branches (see John 15:2). The primary sense in which the word "fruit" is used in this context is that of winning people to Christ, but a secondary meaning can be applied in harvesting the fruit of the Holy Spirit.

God may prune parts of your life to help you develop the kind of character He wants you to possess. James reminded the early Christians, "The testing of your faith produces patience" (Jas. 1:3, NKJV). During these difficult times of pruning, we would do well to follow James's advice and "let patience have its perfect work, that [we] may be perfect and complete, lacking nothing" (1:4, NKJV).

PART 4

The General Work of the Holy Spirit

9

The Bible Authorship Names of the Holy Spirit

The Holy Spirit and the Bible

How the Spirit Revealed and Inspired Scripture	
1. The Spirit of the Holy God	His revelation in dreams and visions
2. The Spirit of Revelation	His revelation of truth
3. The Wind	His energy in inspiration
4. The Spirits of the Prophets	His energy in the writing process
5. The Spirit of Prophecy	His insurance of the message
6. The Spirit of Truth	His revelation of content in Scripture

How the Spirit Helps Us Understand Scripture	
1. The Anointing	He removes spiritual blindness.
2. The Fullness of God	He helps us understand.

The Bible is unique in the history of religious literature. It claims to be eternal in content and to offer the way of eternal life to those who believe its message. The Bible claims to be the actual words of God and thus to be perfect, without error. Paul writes, "All Scripture is given by inspiration of God" (2 Tim. 3:16, *NKJV*). The word translated "inspired" is *theopneustos*, which means "God-breathed," and it describes the divine action of "out-breathing." The words of Scripture are "breathed out" by God.

What is the result of God's breathing out, or inspiring, the words of the Bible? A low view of inspiration claims that the authors were lifted by God to write beyond their ability, just as Shakespeare wrote in the spirit of inspiration and produced works that are among the greatest of all time. A high view of inspiration claims that the message of the Bible and the words used by the authors are accurate and without error. After all, because God is perfect and can do no wrong, wouldn't He write a perfect book? The answer is yes.

The Holy Spirit is described as the Breath of God and the Wind of God. As such, when God inspired the Bible, He was merging the Holy Spirit with the spirits and words of the Bible writers. When we read the Bible, we have access to a perfect message of history and doctrine. When we read the Bible, we do more than take its message into our minds. We take the Holy Spirit into our hearts, because the Bible's words are the words of God and of His Spirit.

Addressing the relationship between the divine and human authors of Scripture, Peter explained, "Prophecy never came by the will of man, but holy men of God spoke as they were moved by the Holy Spirit" (2 Pet. 1:21, *NKJV*). The phrase "moved by the Holy Spirit" means to be borne along or to be picked up and carried by the Holy Spirit. When the authors wrote, they were writing words that the Holy Spirit wanted to be written.

Humans would not have written the Bible if they could have, and humans could not have written the Bible if they would have. Humans *would* not have written the Bible, for in doing so they would have created a message of the perfect Son of God who condemns all, including themselves. Because God will judge sin, no rational people would have written a book that would condemn themselves to hell. Rather, average people would have written a book that reinforces the way that they live. So no thinking person would have written the Bible if he or she could have.

In the second place, humans *could* not have written a Bible if they would have. Because of the limitations of imperfect humanity, it would have been impossible for an imperfect human having limited rational ability to conceive of an unlimited God who is all-powerful and eternal in attributes. Therefore, people could not have written the Bible if they had been given the ability, nor would they have written the Bible if they had been given the opportunity.

How the Holy Spirit Authored the Scriptures

Various names of the Holy Spirit help explain how He produced the Scriptures. These names are directly related to what Bible teachers call revelation and inspiration. Revelation is the act whereby God gives people knowledge about Himself that they could not otherwise know. Inspiration is the supernatural guidance of the writers of Scripture by the Holy Spirit whereby they wrote the divine Word of God, transcribing it accurately and reliably. In both cases these acts of God were primarily accomplished by the Holy Spirit.

Names Associated with Writing Scripture

1. The Spirit of the Holy God
2. The Spirit of Revelation
3. The Wind
4. The Spirits of the Prophets
5. The Spirit of Prophecy
6. The Spirit of truth

The Spirit of the Holy God

Nebuchadnezzar called the Spirit who revealed truth to Daniel "the Spirit of the Holy God" (Dan. 4:8, *NKJV*). The Spirit of the Holy God revealed to Daniel the meaning of visions and dreams that could not be understood through means of divination or appeals to false gods. Nebuchadnezzar affirmed his confidence in Daniel's interpretive abilities when he said, "I know that the Spirit of the Holy God is in you, and no secret troubles you" (4:9, *NKJV*). More than 50 years after he said this, on the eve of Babylon's destruction, another Babylonian King, Belshazzar, was reminded,

> There is a man in your kingdom in whom is the Spirit of the Holy God. And in the days of your father, light and

understanding and wisdom, like the wisdom of the gods, were found in him; and King Nebuchadnezzar your father—your father the king—made him chief of the magicians, astrologers, Chaldeans, and soothsayers (5:11, *NKJV*).

Once again Daniel was called upon to interpret the meaning of God's revelation—this time the handwriting on the wall.

The Spirit of Revelation

A second authorship name of the Holy Spirit is "the spirit of revelation" (Eph. 1:17). The Holy Spirit is the Spirit of Revelation in that He revealed truth to the apostles and prophets as they, with Him, wrote the Scripture. The word for "revelation" means an "uncovering." When Paul prayed that the Ephesians be given the Spirit of Revelation, he was requesting that the same Holy Spirit who revealed truth to him as he wrote would help the reader "uncover" or understand the message that was being written.

The Wind

A third authorship name of the Holy Spirit is the emblem or picture of the Holy Spirit as "the Wind." When Peter spoke of the authors of Scripture being "moved by the Holy Spirit" (2 Pet. 1:21, *NKJV*), he used a word that pictured a ship being moved along the waves by catching the wind in its sails. Just as the wind blows leaves or a kite in a certain direction, so too the Holy Spirit "blew" the human writers of the books of the Bible in certain directions as they wrote. The result of this influence of the Holy Spirit was that the words written by the human authors were the very words that God would have written had He chosen to take the pen Himself and not involve human personalities in the writing process.

The Spirits of the Prophets

God did not opt to exclude human personalities in the writing process but rather used people to communicate His Word for us to read. One of the guiding principles of revelation is expressed in the biblical statement, "The spirits of the prophets are subject to the prophets" (1 Cor. 14:32). This statement probably indicates that the Holy Spirit's ministry of revealing truth and inspiring Scripture was always subject to the personality of the human author of Scripture.

Some may interpret this verse to mean that the human spirit in the prophets was subject to the control of the prophets. As several commentators point out, however, it is more likely that the phrase "spirits of the prophets" means "the prophetic Spirit in the prophets." The verse implies that the Holy Spirit indwelling each prophet allowed the prophet some control. In writing Scripture the Spirit supernaturally guided each human author to write the Word of God accurately and without error, but He allowed the writing style of the human author to shine through that Word. This explains how the four human authors of the four Gospels could describe an event, such as the feeding of the 5,000, and each one contribute differently to our understanding of that event. All four accounts are equally inspired and perfectly harmonious, but the personalities of the different authors caused them to treat the same event differently as they wrote what had been revealed to them by the Holy Spirit.

The Spirit of Prophecy

The title "the Spirit of Prophecy" emphasizes the role of the Holy Spirit beyond His guiding of the human authors to His ensuring that the message itself was inspired. One of the governing motives of the Holy Spirit is to glorify Christ (see John 16:14); therefore, "the testimony of Jesus is the spirit of prophecy" (Rev. 19:10). As we read the Scriptures, we should read to learn what they teach about Jesus (see Luke 24:44).

The Spirit of Truth

When Jesus explained to His disciples the work of the Holy Spirit in helping some of them contribute to the writing of the Scriptures, He said, "However, when He, the Spirit of truth, has come, He will guide you into all truth" (John 16:13, *NKJV*). This title of the Holy Spirit emphasizes the inerrancy and integrity of the Scriptures. Because the Spirit of Truth led the human writers into all truth, Christians can read and study their Bibles today, confident that what they are reading is accurate and free from error.

How the Holy Spirit Helps Us Understand the Scriptures

The Holy Spirit has not only written the Bible, but He is also involved in helping us understand what He has written. Bible teachers call this ministry of the Holy Spirit illumination. Illumination is the ministry of the Holy Spirit that enables us to understand and apply the spiritual message of the Scriptures. When a Christian opens the Bible and begins to discover the truths of Scripture, this ministry of the Holy Spirit enables him or her to understand the message of Scripture.

Names Referring to the Spirit's Help in Understanding the Scriptures

1. The Anointing
2. The Fullness of God

The Anointing

The title "the Anointing" is used in a context that emphasizes the assistance of the Holy Spirit in helping us understand the Bible: "But you have an anointing from the Holy One, and you know all things" (1 John 2:20, *NKJV*). Some Bible teachers believe that this title applies to the Holy Spirit in a twofold sense. First, we have an anointing of the Holy Spirit at conversion when we receive Him (see chapter 8). Second, we may have subsequent anointings of the Holy Spirit during times of personal revival (see chapter 11). In both cases, the ministry of the Holy Spirit as the Anointing helps us in our understanding of the truth of the Scriptures.

The Fullness of God

The Holy Spirit is also described as "the fullness of God" (Eph. 3:19, *NKJV*). In this sense, the Holy Spirit helps us understand the Scriptures at the experiential level. By applying good study habits to reading and studying the Bible, anyone can draw out its truths and make conclusions concerning the meaning of what is written. But that does not necessarily result in any change in our Christian lives. Change takes place as the Holy Spirit applies the Scriptures to our Christian experience. When God makes the Word of God real in the lives of Christians, we begin to understand the Scriptures experientially. This can only be accomplished by the Fullness of God.

How to Read and Understand the Holy Spirit's Book

How people read and comprehend a book often depends upon their preconceived ideas about its author. If they have read another book by the same author, they tend to read the book with certain specific expectations. Rather than judging the second book on its own merits, they inevitably compare it with the previous one. They conclude, "The first book was much better," or, "The second book is much improved over the first." Readers tend to make judgments quickly about authors based upon a single one of the author's books that they have read. As a result, authors are soon cast into a mold that few of them are able to break, such as, "She is a mystery writer," or, "He is a Christian life writer," or, "A book by that author must be science fiction."

As Christians, our understanding of the authorship names of the Holy Spirit will influence the way we approach His book, the Bible. But unlike many human authors, the Holy Spirit is not restricted in His book to a single writing style or subject content. The Bible contains something of interest and value for everyone. Four principles relating to our appreciation of the author will influence the way we read and understand the Bible.

1. The Principle of the Author as God

The first guiding principle in reading the Bible is to consider the author, who is, of course, God. Because the Holy Spirit is also God, the Bible that He inspired is nothing short of the Word of God. Those who appreciate the Bible as the Word of God will approach the Bible differently from those who view it merely as a piece of English literature or another religious book. When authors write a book, they invest something of themselves in that book. When God the Holy Spirit wrote the Bible, He invested something of Himself in that book. As a result, the Bible is a unique book that must be spiritually discerned.

In reading and studying this spiritual book, the Bible, Christians should approach it in a spiritual frame of reference. Before seeking to hear from God, take a moment to consciously and intentionally yield yourself to God. Ask Him to make what you are about to read become real in your life. Pray with the psalmist, "Open my eyes, that I may see wondrous things from Your law" (Ps. 119:18, *NKJV*). Then, as you read the Bible as a yielded Christian, listen carefully to the voice of God through the Scriptures. Let God speak to you as you read His Word, and let it accomplish its objectives in your life (see 2 Tim. 3:16).

2. The Principle of the Author as Teacher

Many books are written today by those who teach and who have compiled their notes on a particular subject into a textbook that they use in the classroom. When students take a course in which the teacher has written the textbook, they read the book differently than they might had they just picked the book up off a newsstand. When they are reading their teacher's book, they read every word thoughtfully, eager to understand all that has been by the author, their teacher. When possible, they may read reviews of the book or articles by others explaining it, but they will read the book first in light of what the teacher is teaching in the class.

The principle of the author as teacher suggests that Christians should read the Bible much as students read their teacher's textbook. This implies four things that should affect the way the Bible is read. First, read the Bible before reading books *about* the Bible. Studying other religious books is not wrong, unless they are books containing false teaching. But study the Bible first to get a foundation upon which the insights of other writers can be added later.

Second, read by having your whole attention on the Bible. Meditate on the words of Scripture, and allow them to become a part of you (see Ps. 119:15). When a man asked R. A. Torrey to tell him in one word how he studied the Bible, Torrey responded, "Thoughtfully." Just as a student reads the textbook in the context of what the teacher is teaching in the classroom, so too the Christian should read the Bible thoughtfully, carefully considering what the Holy Spirit has been teaching him or her in other areas of life.

Third, pay close attention to the words the Holy Spirit used to write His book. If God inspired the very words of Scripture, the very words of Scripture are very important. The Bereans "searched the Scriptures" (Acts 17:11, *NKJV*). The word "search" means "to investigate, inquire, scrutinize or sift." Originally, the word "search" referred to the sifting of chaff from the grain. As we study the Bible, we should separate every word and study every word carefully and individually.

Fourth, read the Bible to understand what the Bible is saying. Do not read the Bible to find a proof text for a particular theological system. Rather, be diligent in your study of Scripture to let the Bible speak for itself (see 2 Tim. 2:15). Someone once said, "The Bible is 21—it can speak for itself."

3. The Principle of the Author as Friend

Perhaps you have had the opportunity to meet and develop a personal relationship with an author. Or maybe a longstanding friend has written a book and given you a copy. We tend to read books written by our friends differently from books written by those we have never met. The principle of the author as friend suggests that our approach to personal Bible reading and study is enhanced by our personal relationship with the Holy Spirit.

First, when we view the Bible as a book written by our Friend, we will plan to read some of it every day, and all of it eventually. Some people just read parts of the Bible, but the Christian should study the whole Bible from Genesis to Revelation. The whole Bible has something to teach us about the Person and work of Jesus and how to live the Christian life (see Luke 24:27; 2 Tim. 3:16-17). Jesus taught from the whole Bible and urged His disciples to do the same (see Matt. 5:17-19). The whole Bible was written by our Friend the Holy Spirit, so we will want to read all of it.

Second, we will want to read our Friend's book systematically to ensure that we complete it and understand what is written. The early Christians read the Scriptures daily, setting a good example for Christians today (see Acts 17:11). Reading the Bible systematically implies reading the Bible every day, reading at the same time every day, and following the same pattern or reading schedule every day.

Third, when we read the Bible as a book authored by a Friend, we tend to read it by allowing our own intimate knowledge of our

Friend to color what we are reading. Perhaps a certain expression might pass unnoticed before you had a relationship with the author, but now it leaps off the page, having special meaning to you. As we grow in our relationship with the Holy Spirit, we will find ourselves increasing in our understanding of our Friend's book.

4. The Principle of the Author as Helper

Sometimes we have opportunity to attend a seminar, workshop or conference in which we receive help from an author-speaker. When that occurs, it is not unusual to want to purchase the author's books, particularly those books that he or she has written that deal with the problem area in which we have already received some help. Then, when we read that book, we read it not as we read other books but rather to gain additional insights that can be applied to our lives.

The principle of the author as helper suggests that as we experience the helping ministry of the Holy Spirit in our lives, we should be motivated to read the Bible to apply it to life. James urged the Early Church, "Be doers of the word, and not hearers only, deceiving yourselves" (Jas. 1:22, *NKJV*). As you read the Scriptures, ask yourself the following questions:

- Is there some command to obey?
- Is there some promise to claim?
- Is there some sin to avoid?
- Is there some prayer to pray?
- Is there some challenge to accept?

An author writes a book, hoping that it will be read. A reader reads a book, allowing knowledge of the author to influence his or her understanding of the book. The Holy Spirit wrote the Bible, intending for it to affect our lives. As you read the Bible this week, allow your growing knowledge of its divine Author to improve your understanding of and your response to its message.

10

The Creation Names
of the Holy Spirit

Creation Names for the Spirit

The Holy Spirit as Creator	
1. The Brooding Dove	His constant attention to creation
2. The Finger of God	His creative expression of beauty
3. The Voice of the Lord	His power in creation
4. The Breath of Life	His life in creation

The Spirit's Work in Creation	
1. The result of His work:	The creation of order
	The creation of design
	The creation of beauty
	The creation of life
	The preservation of creation
	The renewal of creation

When God created the heavens and the earth, the Holy Spirit was involved in the creation process. Sometimes, the activity of the Holy Spirit in creation is described wrongly as a passive work. The first mention of the Holy Spirit in Scripture describes His work by using a word normally used to describe a bird brooding over its nest of eggs or young chicks: "The Spirit of God was hovering over the face of the waters" (Gen. 1:2, *NKJV*). But other statements in

Scripture concerning the Holy Spirit's creative work make it clear that He was more active than passive in creation. In his counsel to Job, Elihu attributed the work of the creation of life directly to the Holy Spirit: "The Spirit of God has made me, and the breath of the Almighty gives me life" (Job 33:4, *NKJV*).

The Scriptures use a number of metaphors in reference to the creative work of the Holy Spirit. These names include the Breath names, "the Dove," "the Finger of God," the Life names and the Voice names of the Holy Spirit. Merely because other Scriptures identify the involvement of another member of the Trinity in the same creative function does not minimize the role of the Holy Spirit. It merely illustrates the cooperative work of the Trinity in the act of creation.

In this chapter we will consider several of these creation names of the Holy Spirit to better understand and appreciate His specific work in creation. This important teaching of Scripture has significant implications for our lives today.

The Holy Spirit as Creator

As noted above, several names of the Holy Spirit imply His work in the creation of the world, including such names as "the Spirit of God" (Gen. 1:2). Although all the names of the Holy Spirit imply His actions as Creator, four names in particular may be viewed as summary names emphasizing His creative work.

The Creative Names of God

1. The Brooding Dove
2. The Finger of God
3. The Voice of the Lord
4. The Breath of Life

The Brooding Dove
The first description of the Holy Spirit in Scripture describes Him in the context of a brooding dove. Although the emblem of a dove is not specifically mentioned in the context of creation (see Matt.

3:16), His presence as a dove in creation is implied by the use of a particular Hebrew verb in Genesis 1:2. The verb *merachepheth*, translated "was hovering," pictures the brooding action of a dove that gently nestles its eggs and keeps them warm until they hatch, then continues to hover over its young until they can fly and find food for themselves.

This picture of the Holy Spirit as the Brooding Dove describes His work in parenting the new world into existence. The first mention of the Holy Spirit in the New Testament also describes the work of the Holy Spirit in the context of parenting. There the Scriptures describe Mary as being "found with child of the Holy Spirit" (Matt. 1:18, *NKJV*). Some similarities between these two references of the Holy Spirit may be found, but the Holy Spirit's work in creation extended beyond what is normally considered in the context of parenting.

The Finger of God

Jesus used the expression "the finger of God" (Luke 11:20) to alert us to another way that the Scriptures describe the work of the Holy Spirit. David described the world God created as both "the work of Your fingers" and "the works of Your hands" (Ps. 8:3,6, *NKJV*). Other names of the Holy Spirit related to this creative name include "the hand of God" (2 Chron. 30:12), "the hand of the LORD" (Job 12:9), and "the hand of the Lord GOD" (Ezek. 8:1).

Just as an artist uses hands or fingers in creating a painting or a beautiful piece of pottery, so too the finger of God or the hand of God is a reference to the creative nature of the Holy Spirit that adds beauty, scope and dimension to the world. The Holy Spirit is at work to make creation attractive, appealing and pleasing to mankind.

This is "anthropomorphic" language—describing the divine in terms of the human. Scripture uses several such word pictures, speaking of the Holy Spirit creating life (see Job 12:9), bringing matter into existence (see Ps. 102:25), shaping the stellar heavens (see 8:3), gathering the physical land mass (see 95:5), creating man (see 119:73), and arranging the physical geography of the world (see Isa. 41:18-20). An understanding of the Holy Spirit's work in creation in this context should encourage a sense of celebration (see Ps. 92:4) and a humbling of oneself before the hand of God (see 1 Pet. 5:6).

The Voice of the Lord

Various voice names of the Holy Spirit also imply the Spirit's involvement in creation, not so much in the phrases themselves as in other statements concerning creation. An appreciation of the creative work of the voice of the LORD is foundational to a healthy and growing faith in God. "By faith we understand that the worlds were framed by the word of God, so that the things which are seen were not made of things which are visible" (Heb. 11:3, *NKJV*).

This implies the involvement of the Holy Spirit in the creation of the world out of nothing (that is, bringing matter into existence). It is significant in this regard how often the various voice names of the Holy Spirit are linked to physical manifestations in nature (see Pss. 18:13; 29:3-9; 77:18). When we hear the Holy Spirit's voice directing our lives today, our response should be that of obedience rather than rebellion (see Ps. 95:7-8; Heb. 3:7-8).

The Breath of Life

The Holy Spirit is described as "the Breath" (see Ezek. 37:9, *NKJV*), "the Breath of the Almighty" (see Job 33:4), "the Breath of God" (see 27:3, *NKJV*), "the Breath of life" (see Rev. 11:11, *NKJV*), "the Breath of the LORD" (see Isa. 40:7, *NKJV*), and "the Breath of Your nostrils" (see Ps. 18:15, *NKJV*). He is also described as "the Spirit of Life" (see Rom. 8:2) and by other names emphasizing His life-giving and life-sustaining ability.

All these names draw attention to that moment in history when "the LORD God formed man of the dust of the ground, and breathed into his nostrils the breath of life; and man became a living being" (Gen. 2:7, *NKJV*). The relationship between the Breath names of the Holy Spirit and the beginning of human life was specifically identified by Elihu when he said, "The Spirit of God has made me, and the breath of the Almighty gives me life" (Job 33:4, *NKJV*).

The Work of the Holy Spirit in Creation

As noted previously, the Holy Spirit was actively involved in several aspects of the creation of the world. A comparison of the biblical teaching concerning this ministry of the Holy Spirit reveals His direct responsibility for at least six aspects of the creation, preservation and renewal of this world. His involvement in creation resulted in the order, design, beauty and life of creation itself. His continuing creative role ensures both the present preservation and future renewal of creation.

Creation of Order

As we have noticed, the first mention of the Holy Spirit in Scripture describes His hovering over the primeval chaos and bringing a sense of order to the world (see Gen. 1:2). Isaiah described the Spirit of the Lord as measuring, calculating and weighing parts of the world as He brought it into existence (see Isa. 40:12-14). Also, the Holy Spirit is described as Creator of the heavens, which perhaps more than any other aspect of creation demonstrates the order of the universe (see Ps. 33:6).

Creation of Design

The Holy Spirit is also apparently responsible for the design in creation: "By His Spirit He adorned the heavens; His hand pierced the fleeing serpent" (Job 26:13, *NKJV*). Many Bible teachers believe that Job used the descriptive title "the fleeing serpent" as a reference to the Milky Way. If this conclusion is accurate, the creation of design in the heavens is attributed to the Holy Spirit. Although design is attributed to all three members of the Trinity, the Holy Spirit apparently shared in the planning of the creation much as an engineering team might share in the design of a bridge or a building.

When an engineer designs a structure, he or she does so with a particular object in mind. The engineer intends that structure to accomplish the purpose for which it was designed. The purpose of the Holy Spirit is to bring glory to God (see John 16:14). The Holy Spirit accomplished His purpose in the design of creation in that "the heavens declare the glory of God" (Ps. 19:1, *NKJV*).

Creation of Beauty

The statement by Job in Job 26:13 also implies the Holy Spirit's responsibility for the beauty of creation. In this sense the work of the Holy Spirit goes beyond that of a design engineer to that of an architect. When an engineer designs a building or other structure, he or she is primarily concerned with function. When an architect designs a building, he or she is also concerned with form. By applying certain building-code regulations to the design of a building, an engineer can draw four walls and a roof and prepare blueprints for a functional building. The architect may use those same regulations to design a similar building, but by the arrangements of doors and windows, the assignment of specific building materials, the shaping of the surrounding landscapes and the selection of specific colors, the architect turns that functional building into a work of art. As the one responsible for the beauty of creation, the Holy Spirit has made a functional universe beautiful.

Creation of Life

As noted in the above discussion of the Holy Spirit as the Breath of Life, the Spirit is also responsible for the creation of human life (see Job 33:4). It is not inconsistent to consider the Holy Spirit as the One who shaped that lump of clay in the Garden of Eden much as a potter shapes clay. The work of a human potter will ever remain inanimate. But the Holy Spirit breathed the breath of life into the first man, and he became a living soul.

Preservation of Creation

The involvement of the Holy Spirit in creation reaches beyond the original creation to include the preservation of creation. The psalmist affirmed, "You take away their breath, they die and return to their dust. You send forth Your Spirit, they are created; and You renew the face of the earth" (Ps. 104:29-30, *NKJV*). This implies the work of the Holy Spirit in sustaining life on Earth today. If the Holy Spirit ceased in this work, death and corruption would immediately set in. Because of the Holy Spirit's work in the preservation of creation, a continual renewing and sustaining of life on Earth is taking place.

Renewal of Creation

The final aspect of the Holy Spirit's work in creation involves the eventual renewal of creation at the return of Christ (see Rom. 8:21). In a certain sense the Holy Spirit is presently involved in this renewal process in transforming people into a new creation at conversion (see 2 Cor. 5:17) and in the continuing transformation of the converted (see Phil. 1:6). Yet in a more specialized sense, the Holy Spirit will be involved in the renewal of creation when it is released from the bondage of sin and sin's corruption and is restored to its original character. This renewal of creation is part of the hope of the Christian that is tied to the victorious return of Christ.

The Re-creative Work of the Spirit in Our Lives

When a person becomes a Christian, "he is a new creation; old things have passed away; behold, all things have become new" (2 Cor. 5:17, *NKJV*). This re-creative work of the Holy Spirit in our lives is based upon the work of the Holy Spirit in creation. Several principles derived from the creation names of the Holy Spirit help us understand how the Holy Spirit accomplishes His work of re-creation in our life with God.

The Principle of Spiritual Renewal

The first principle is that of spiritual renewal. The re-created spiritual life of the Christian is a result of the Breath of Life communicating that life to us. Just as the Holy Spirit was able to turn lifeless clay into a living soul, so only the Holy Spirit is able to transform a repentant and believing sinner into a Christian who possesses spiritual life.

This principle is also implied by the picture of the Brooding Dove. A fertile egg will not hatch into a baby chick unless the parent bird keeps the eggs evenly warmed during the incubation period. By way of application, one who has heard the gospel and is willing to repent of sin and trust Christ for salvation can only be brought to that point through the ministry of the Holy Spirit. Although other factors may encourage people to trust Christ as Savior, ultimately it is the Holy Spirit who makes people new creations in Christ.

Understanding this principle of spiritual renewal should affect the way we pray for others and ourselves. First, we should pray that the Holy Spirit will work through us and our efforts in reaching our friends with the gospel so that our outreach efforts will prove effective. Second, we should ask the Holy Spirit to use our Bible reading, fellowship with other Christians and exercise of other spiritual disciplines, such as worship, giving and so on, in His continuing work of re-creation in our lives. Only then can we be certain that these practices are helping rather than hindering our spiritual growth.

The Principle of Spiritual Standards

The term "Finger of God" implies the principle of spiritual standards that also influence our Christian lives. Although many references to the finger or hand of God in Scripture tend to emphasize the miraculous power of the Holy Spirit, at least two remind us of this principle of spiritual standards. First, the Law of God (the Ten Commandments) was originally written by the "finger of God" (Exod. 31:18; Deut. 9:10). Second, when God judged Babylon, He first caused His message of judgment to be written upon a wall with His finger (see Dan. 5:5). One of D. L. Moody's most famous sermons compared these two events and called upon the listener to realize that the judgment of God was based upon the standards in His law.

The principle of spiritual standards recognizes that the same Finger of God that fashioned the heavens has recorded a spiritual standard by which we should govern our lives. Usually, the manufacturer of a major appliance will publish a manual, directing the owner as to how to care for and maintain the appliance. Similarly, our Creator has also placed in the Scriptures the information and directions necessary for "operating" our lives—rising to our highest potential and experiencing our greatest sense of fulfillment.

The Principle of the Sword of the Spirit

A third principle arising out of the creation names of the Holy Spirit is the principle of the Sword of the Spirit. If we believe that the world was created by the Word of God, we will take advantage of "the sword of the Spirit, which is the word of God" (Eph. 6:17) and use it as an effective tool in both our personal spiritual growth and in our battles for the Lord.

The Greek word *rhema,* which is here translated "word," refers to a specific word that God brings to our mind in a specific context. Sometimes, as we read our Bible, a specific verse seems to jump off the page, having meaning that addresses a particular need in our life. At other times, as we struggle to make a decision, the Holy Spirit may bring a verse to mind that helps us clarify the issues and make the right decision. These are examples of the Sword of the Spirit, which is the Word (*rhema*) of God (see Rom. 10:8).

As we recognize the value of this principle at work in our lives, we should be motivated in our personal Bible reading and memorizing. The Holy Spirit is able to bring a verse to mind only if we are already familiar with that verse through our Bible reading and have committed that verse to memory. It is therefore reasonable to conclude that our faithfulness in Bible reading and Scripture memorizing will help ensure a greater effectiveness of the Sword of the Spirit in the re-creation process of our lives.

The Principle of the Leading of the Spirit

Another principle rising out of the creation names is that of the leading of the Spirit. This principle is an extension of the two mentioned previously. If we recognize the principles of spiritual standards and the Sword of the Spirit, we will want to follow the leading of the Spirit in our lives through His witness within and through the clear teaching of the Bible. Also, the Holy Spirit can and does use spiritual counsel from others, unique circumstances in which we find ourselves and other means of leading in our lives.

The Principle of Spiritual Intervention

The final principle arising out of the creation names of the Holy Spirit is that of spiritual intervention. It is logical to assume that there would have never been a world apart from its having been spoken into existence by God. Also, it appears that the world would have remained in chaos apart from the work of the Holy Spirit in creation. As God has intervened in the past to accomplish His will, so too He is at liberty to intervene in the future. The principle of spiritual intervention recognizes that there have been and will continue to be times when God intervenes to accomplish what only He can accomplish.

When a person becomes a Christian, sometimes a significant change occurs in life that cannot be explained apart from the intervention of God. Also, Christians often experience changes in their circumstances that are beyond their control but are not beyond the control of the Holy Spirit (see Prov. 21:1). Third, sometimes the intervention of the Holy Spirit is so subtle that it may not be recognized as divine intervention but merely as the next logical step in a series of events (see Acts 15:28). Recognizing the principle of spiritual intervention should make us more open to allowing God to make changes in our lives.

11

The Balanced Ministry of the Holy Spirit

The Balanced Ministry of the Holy Spirit

Seven General Descriptions	
1. The Spirit of Access	His role in helping us to pray
2. The Spirit of Indwelling	His presence in the believer
3. The Spirit of Power	His helping us accomplish His will
4. The Spirit of Unity	His role in bringing unity to believers
5. The Spirit of Fruitfulness	His role in making believers effective
6. The Spirit of Fullness	His role in giving us ability in our service
7. The Spirit of Victory	His role in helping us overcome

Grieving the Holy Spirit	
1. Blaspheming the Holy Spirit	Rejecting Jesus Christ
2. Lying to the Holy Spirit	Deceiving God
3. Insulting the Holy Spirit	Delaying salvation
4. Resisting the Holy Spirit	Rejecting the will of God
5. Quenching the Holy Spirit	Putting the Spirit's influence out of your life

The Holy Spirit is the Spirit of Christ (see Acts 16:7; Rom. 8:9; Gal. 4:6; Phil. 1:19; 1 Pet. 1:11). The Spirit therefore glorifies Christ.

Whatever attention is given to the Holy Spirit in Scripture glorifies Christ. Jesus told His disciples that the thrust of the Holy Spirit's ministry was to glorify the Son: "He will glorify Me, for He will take of what is Mine and declare it to you" (John 16:14, *NKJV*). As a result, an abundance of biblical material and songs exalt the name of Jesus. On the other hand, some feel that comparatively less attention is given to the Person and work of the Holy Spirit, though Scripture frequently calls attention to His work (see Matt. 10:19-20; Luke 2:25-29; 12:11-12; John 7:39; 14:26; 16:13; Acts 2:2-4; 5:3-4; 10:9,13-15,19,44-46; 11:5,7-8,12; 13:2; 15:28; 19:6; Rom. 8:5,16,26-27; 1 Cor. 2:13; 12:7-11; Gal. 4:6; 5:16-25; 6:8; 1 John 2:27). As a result, Christians often do not give the Holy Spirit His rightful place.

In the Holy Spirit's book, the Bible, we are more likely to read about the accomplishments of the first or second Persons of the Trinity than of the third Person of the Trinity. This does not mean the Holy Spirit is less important than others in the Godhead. Rather, it reflects His intent to exalt Christ and to bring glory to the Father. It seems the Holy Spirit only mentions Himself in His book when it brings glory to Christ.

The book of Ephesians places more emphasis on the practical work and ministry of the Holy Spirit to the believer than perhaps any other place in Scripture. (The book of Acts is descriptive, and Romans 8 is theological.) The book of Ephesians contains perhaps the most comprehensive scriptural discussion on the growth and maturity of the believer through the balanced ministry of the Holy Spirit. Here Paul describes the Christian's new position "in the heavenlies," which is only possible through the ministry of the Holy Spirit.

In what may be the apostle Paul's most complete discussion of the ministry of the Holy Spirit, a number of descriptive terms for the Holy Spirit are stated or implied in Ephesians. These include "the Spirit of Promise," "the Spirit of Wisdom," "the Spirit of Access," "the Spirit of Indwelling," "the Spirit of Revelation," "the Spirit of Power," "the Spirit of Unity," "the Spirit of Feeling," "the Spirit of Sealing," "the Spirit of Fruitfulness," "the Spirit of Fullness," "the Spirit of Victory" and "the Spirit of Prayer." Some of these descriptive terms have already been discussed. In this chapter, seven titles that have additional truths to teach us will be discussed in the context of the Spirit's work in balancing and undergirding the maturing process in the Christian life.

The Holy Spirit's Undergirding Ministry

In many respects Paul's discussion of the Holy Spirit in Ephesians amounts to a summary of His ministry in the Christian life. Following are seven names or titles of the Spirit that are implied in this summary.

Seven Implied Names of the Spirit

1. The Spirit of Access
2. The Spirit of Indwelling
3. The Spirit of Power
4. The Spirit of Unity
5. The Spirit of Fruitfulness
6. The Spirit of Fullness
7. The Spirit of Victory

The Spirit of Access

To give balance to the earthly life of the Christian, the Holy Spirit provides us entrance "into the heavenlies." His implied name in this respect is "the Spirit of Access" (see Eph. 2:18). Through the Holy Spirit, Christians have access to the family of God in salvation and access to God by prayer. When we pray, we do so because of the ministry of "the Spirit of grace and supplication" (Zech. 12:10, NKJV) in our lives. Again, enjoying fellowship with other Christians is possible because of the Holy Spirit's role in giving us new life when we are born again (see John 3:5). Therefore, the Holy Spirit may be described as the Spirit of Access.

The Spirit of Indwelling

The Holy Spirit may also be described as the Spirit of Indwelling (see Eph. 2:22). When a person becomes a Christian, he or she is immediately indwelt by the Holy Spirit. The biblical teaching concerning the indwelling of the Holy Spirit should motivate us to personal holiness (see 1 Cor. 6:15-20). But this teaching also reveals how it is possible for the Christian to live a holy life. The Christian life is the life of God living through us (see Gal. 2:20). Having the Holy Spirit indwelling every Christian makes it possible for every Christian to live a holy life.

What does the Holy Spirit do when He comes into our lives? Some think that the effect is mere feeling or excitement. It is true that the Spirit brings great joy and peace into our lives (see Gal. 5:22). But Christians should never seek an experience or a feeling for its own sake. The Christian life is not emotional hysteria. Instead of seeking a feeling, we should seek Jesus Himself, asking Him to enter our lives (see John 14:23; Rom. 8:9; Gal. 2:20). Feelings and excitement are not wrong. They are the inevitable byproduct of the Holy Spirit's work in our hearts. We should enjoy the experiences that the Holy Spirit brings but not seek them apart from Him.

What does the Holy Spirit bring when He indwells our lives? He gives us all that is good and spiritual.

What the Indwelling Spirit Gives

1. Eternal life
2. A new nature
3. Spiritual life
4. New desires
5. The fruit of the Spirit
6. Love and assurance

The Spirit of Power

Paul implied that the Holy Spirit could be described as the Spirit of Power when he prayed, "I bow my knees to the Father. . . that He would grant you, according to the riches of His glory, to be strengthened with might through His Spirit in the inner man" (Eph. 3:14-16, *NKJV*). Because the Christian life involves God living through us, the Holy Spirit is the source of all spiritual power that we need both to live for and to serve God. Just as an electric motor will not run if it is not plugged in, so too Christians will fail in their Christian lives if they are not plugged into the Holy Spirit, filled with His power and allowing Him to live through their lives.

The Spirit of Unity

Another implied title of the Holy Spirit in Ephesians is "the Spirit of Unity" (see Eph. 4:3). The Holy Spirit makes unity among Christians possible in at least two ways. First, He is the same Holy Spirit indwelling each Christian, empowering each to live a Christian life. This gives all Christians something in common, a basis for unity. Second, He is the one who has placed every Christian into a single body, the Body of Christ: "There is one body, and one Spirit" (Eph. 4:4). In this way the Holy Spirit has established the conditions by which unity can be enjoyed. When a sense of unity is absent in a group of Christians, the Holy Spirit is being hindered. In such cases, believers may be fighting God or simply refusing to allow the Holy Spirit to control their lives.

The Spirit of Fruitfulness

It has been suggested that the Holy Spirit could also be called the Spirit of Fruitfulness because He produces spiritual fruit in our lives. In Ephesians 5:9 we read, "The fruit of the Spirit is in all goodness and righteousness and truth." Just as fruit on a tree is the result of growth within the tree, so fruit in the Christian life is the result of the Holy Spirit working in and through us. How the Holy Spirit produces this spiritual fruit is discussed more fully in the chapter on the maturing names of the Holy Spirit (chapter 3).

The Spirit of Fullness

The description of the Holy Spirit as the Spirit of Fullness is based on the apostle's command, "Be filled with the Spirit" (Eph. 5:18). The fullness of the Holy Spirit is vital to the experience of living the normal Christian life. The tense of the Greek verb translated "be filled" carries the meaning of "be *continually* filled," demonstrating that experiencing the fullness of the Holy Spirit is a repeated experience for Christians. Rather than being controlled by the influence of the "spirits" of alcohol, Paul urged the Ephesians to allow God to control their lives through His Holy Spirit: "Do not be drunk with wine, in which is dissipation; but be filled with the Spirit" (Eph. 5:18,

NKJV). Notice the contrast between being drunk with the spirits of the bottle and the filling of the Spirit. The Christian does not get more of the Holy Spirit; rather, the Holy Spirit gets more of the Christian. Christians are filled with the Holy Spirit as they confess their sins to God (see 1 John 1:9) and yield completely to Him (see Rom. 6:13). Being filled with the Holy Spirit is an aspect of God's will for every Christian today.

The Filling of the Spirit Is:

1. Repeated
2. For service and holy living
3. Experiential
4. Available to all believers
5. For power in service and living

The Spirit of Victory

"The Spirit of Victory" is a title of the Holy Spirit implied in Ephesians 6:17-18. In Paul's discussion of the Christian armor, the Holy Spirit is mentioned twice in ways that are most likely to contribute to victory in spiritual warfare. First, the Word of God is described as the Sword of the Spirit. This means that the Bible is the instrument that the Holy Spirit uses to give believers victory. The sword of the Spirit is the only offensive weapon mentioned—most of the equipment described here is for the believer's defense. Yet no army experiences victory in a defensive mode. Hence, the necessity of the Sword of the Spirit.

Second, Paul concludes his illustration with an appeal to pray "in the Spirit." Paul returns to his theme of spiritual struggle, and praying in the Spirit is spiritual warfare. "We do not wrestle against flesh and blood, but against principalities, against powers, against the rulers of the darkness of this age, against spiritual hosts of wickedness in the heavenly places" (Eph. 6:12, *NKJV*).

Grieving the Holy Spirit

In light of the undergirding ministry of the Holy Spirit in the Christian life, it is important for the Christian to maintain a healthy relationship with the Spirit. Paul warned the Ephesians of the danger of grieving the Holy Spirit and urged them not to commit this sin. The believer is told, "Do not grieve the Holy Spirit of God, by whom you were sealed for the day of redemption" (Eph. 4:30, NKJV). Grieving the Holy Spirit means a believer allowing sin to remain in his or her life. This may be a hidden sin (to others but not to God) or what we consider a small sin (all sin is serious to God). A small sin may be a habit that is acceptable to others, so we do not feel convicted over it. But when the habit is wrong, it grieves the Holy Spirit.

In a sense, all sin grieves the Holy Spirit, but five sins in one way or another especially grieve the Holy Spirit.

Grieving the Holy Spirit

- Blaspheming the Spirit
- Lying to the Spirit
- Insulting the Spirit
- Resisting the Spirit
- Quenching the Spirit

Blaspheming the Holy Spirit

The most serious sin against the Holy Spirit mentioned in the New Testament is described as blaspheming Him (see Matt. 12:31-32; Luke 12:10). This sin is more popularly described as "the unpardonable sin" or "the unforgivable sin." Not all Bible teachers agree on the specific nature of this sin, but one clue as to its meaning may be that it is first referred to when the Jews who witnessed the power of the Holy Spirit in the miracles of Jesus ascribed those miracles to Satan.

Historically the sin of blaspheming the Holy Spirit involved the unbelief of those who rejected the miracles of God as well as the message of Jesus that the miracles substantiated. The unforgivable sin today is the final rejection of Christ as Savior during this life. God can forgive any sin, but He cannot forgive unbelief, because belief is necessary for salvation.

Lying to the Holy Spirit

A second sin against the Holy Spirit is described as lying to, or testing, the Holy Spirit (see Acts 5:4,9). In the Early Church a couple sold their land and made a significant financial contribution to the church from their profit. But in giving their money to the church, they attempted to convey the impression that they were giving all the sales money to God, when in fact they had kept back part of it for themselves. They were guilty of greed, fraud and lying to God. When confronted with their sin, both of them dropped dead. This event caused others to take seriously their relationship with God. It serves as a warning even to this day against attempting to deceive the Holy Spirit.

Insulting the Holy Spirit

A third sin against the Holy Spirit is described as insulting the Holy Spirit. The Hebrew writer asked,

> Of how much worse punishment, do you suppose, will he be thought worthy who has trampled the Son of God underfoot, counted the blood of the covenant by which he was sanctified a common thing, and insulted the Spirit of grace? (10:29, *NKJV*).

This sin is identified in one of the five warning passages of Hebrews. Many Bible teachers believe that these passages were specifically directed to unsaved persons who had become a part of the Early Church yet had not entered into a personal relationship with God through Christ. This teaching serves as a warning of the consequences of continued delay in responding to the gospel. Therefore, insulting the Holy Spirit may involve unnecessary delay in receiving the gospel once one has realized his or her need and been drawn to Christ by the Holy Spirit.

Resisting the Holy Spirit

A fourth way people grieve the Holy Spirit is through the sin of striving with, or resisting, the Holy Spirit. God warned the generation before Noah's flood, "My Spirit shall not strive with man forever, for he is indeed flesh" (Gen. 6:3, *NKJV*). In the New Testament, Stephen accused the Sanhedrin, "You stiff-necked and uncircumcised in heart and ears! You always resist the Holy Spirit; as your fathers did, so do you" (Acts 7:51, *NKJV*). This is a step beyond insulting the Holy Spirit and involves some degree of active opposition to the Spirit's leading in a person's life. When God makes His will known to His people and they refuse to accept it, or they challenge and reject it, they are resisting the Holy Spirit.

Quenching the Holy Spirit

When a believer allows sin to remain in his or her life, it grieves the Holy Spirit. When a believer allows sin to control his or her life and extinguish his or her testimony to others, it is called quenching the Holy Spirit. Paul warned, "Do not quench the Spirit" (1 Thess. 5:19, *NKJV*). The word "quench" means to put out, as in "quenching one's thirst" or putting out a fire. Because the Holy Spirit is God, in one sense He can never be quenched or put out of a person's life. God is everywhere. But people can minimize the influence of the Holy Spirit in their lives. Just as we can pour water on a fire until it no longer burns, so too we can gradually extinguish God's influence in our lives. This is usually symptomatic of other problems in our lives, such as sin that is hindering our relationship with God or indifference to things that will strengthen us. As a result, the leading of the Holy Spirit is not as significant in our lives as it once was.

How to Avoid Sinning Against the Holy Spirit

In Paul's appeal for us not to grieve the Holy Spirit, he also suggested several specific things that can be done to keep from committing such sins against the Holy Spirit:

> Let all bitterness, wrath, anger, clamor, and evil speaking be put away from you, with all malice. And be kind to one another, tenderhearted, forgiving one another, even as God in Christ forgave you (Eph. 4:31-32, *NKJV*).

The Principle of Actively Searching for Barriers

The first principle that will help us avoid sinning against the Holy Spirit is that we should actively examine our lives for things that would destroy us. Sins against the Holy Spirit are rarely committed in isolation from other sins. Most often Christians tend to grieve the Holy Spirit in their abusive treatment of other Christians. Therefore, Paul realizes that our first step in restoring our previous intimacy with the Holy Spirit is searching out sin in our lives and repenting of it—particularly any sin that has also hindered our relationship with other Christians.

The Principle of Applied Kindness

We should seek to be kind toward others, both toward those with whom we have a good relationship and those who have in some way offended us. This kindness was illustrated by Jesus on the cross in His dealing with the repentant thief. Earlier that day, the repentant thief had joined the other thief in mocking Jesus as He suffered on the cross. Then, when the thief repented, Jesus responded to him with kindness of the sort that we might think to be reflective of a relationship between two old friends. He was kind to the thief in spite of the way He must have felt at the time and in spite of the thief's previous comments.

The Principle of Tenderheartedness

Our response to others should also be characterized by tenderheartedness. The word "tenderhearted" suggests the idea of a heart full of compassion for others. Compassion for others was a motivating factor in the life of Jesus (see Matt. 9:36), and it should also motivate His followers in our dealings with others. When we begin to recognize hurting people and to help them, it will change our attitude toward those who offend us and help us to avoid sinning against the Holy Spirit.

The Principle of Forgiveness

The principle of forgiveness will help us overcome the tendency to grieve the Holy Spirit. We ought to forgive others, "even as God in Christ forgave [us]" (Eph. 4:32, *NKJV*). Only as we come to understand just how offensive sin is to God can we begin to understand the immensity of His love in forgiving us. "God demonstrates His own love toward us, in that while we were still sinners, Christ died for us" (Rom. 5:8, *NKJV*). Then, as we begin to understand God's love, we will realize that the Holy Spirit has poured out that same love of God in our hearts (see Rom. 5:5). Therefore, we also ought to express that love by forgiving others who have wronged us.

The Principle of Deliberate Steps

How can we do all these things? The key is found in our walk with God: "Be imitators of God as dear children" (Eph. 5:1, *NKJV*). Young children often desire to be like their parents or some other important person in their lives. They will deliberately imitate the unique mannerisms of their hero or role model. As Christians in the family of God, we too ought to desire to be like our Father in heaven and seek to imitate Him. Only as we yield and allow Him to live through us can we overcome the old nature and apply these principles to avoid sinning against the Holy Spirit.

The Principle of Building Up Others

The final principle implied in Paul's appeal is nurturing others. When problems take place between Christians, it is too often characteristic for them to engage in subtle attacks against each other. But Paul's appeal is that Christians should engage in nurturing one another, having a view of building each other up in the faith.

Because it is the nature of sin to attack that which offends sin, we realize that our old nature will attack anyone who offends that old nature. It is the new nature of a Christian to forgive that which attacks our new nature. If we as Christians want to ensure against grieving the Holy Spirit, the focus of our energies should be directed toward nurturing others, including those who have offended us.

The description of the Holy Spirit in the Epistle to the Ephesians portrays the Spirit's balanced ministry and emphasizes the important role He has in the Christian life. Therefore, we should be careful not to grieve Him by sinning against Him. Applying these principles to our lives will help us avoid falling into these sins.

12

Revival Names for the Holy Spirit

The Spirit of Revival

Revival Names	
1. My Blessing	His role in pouring out God's blessings upon believers
2. The Fullness of God	His role in making believers aware of God's presence
3. The Glory of the Lord	His role in making believers increasingly like God
4. The Spirit of Life	His role in revitalizing the waning spiritual life
5. The Spirit of Power	His role in energizing believers for ministry

Outpouring Names	
1. Rain names	His outpouring upon a group
2. The Anointing	His outpouring upon an individual

I was converted in a revival that moved through the Presbyterian churches of Savannah, Georgia, in the summer of 1950. Two Bible college students were pastoring a mission church during the summer. They met for prayer on a screened porch of a garage apartment at five o'clock every morning. A little church that seated 200 had more than 300 in attendance evening after evening. Electricity was in the air when people started gathering each evening. They expected people to come to Christ, and it happened. I was converted July 25, 1950, at approximately 11:15 P.M., while praying by my bed at home.

Today observers would call what happened then an "atmospheric revival," yet it had a deep influence, because the change in my heart is still effective 43 years later. What happened was not just an emotional experience but the anointing of the Holy Spirit on individuals and the outpouring of the Holy Spirit on a group of people. The word "revive" means to live again, and at this revival I felt that New Testament Christianity was alive again.

An evangelical revival is an extraordinary work of God in which first, Christians repent of their sins as they become intensely aware of God's presence, and second, people give a positive response to God in renewed obedience to His will. This results in both a deepening of their individual and corporate experience with God and an increased concern for the spiritual welfare of both themselves and others within their community.

The Holy Spirit is the agent of new spiritual life, or revival, so it is not surprising that several of the terms that Scripture uses to describe Him emphasize His work in revival. These names include "the Anointing" (the contemporary term for the filling of the Holy Spirit), "My Blessing," "the Breath of Life," "the Dew," "the Enduement of Power," "Floods upon the Dry Ground," "the Fullness of God," "the Glory of the Lord," "the Oil of Gladness," "the Power of the Highest," "Rain," "Rivers of Living Water," "Showers that Water the Earth," "the Spirit of Glory," "the Spirit of Life" and "the Spirit of Power."

The Holy Spirit and Revival

Although each of these ways of describing the Holy Spirit contributes to an understanding of revival, five of them may be considered as representative in describing His role in shaping the character of revival. These "names" are "My blessing" (Isa. 44:3, *NKJV*), "the fullness of God" (Eph. 3:19, *NKJV*), "the glory of the Lord" (2 Cor. 3:18), "the Spirit of life" (Rom. 8:2), and "the spirit . . . of power" (2 Tim. 1:7).

Revival Terms for the Holy Spirit

1. My Blessing
2. The Fullness of God

Revival Terms for the Holy Spirit (Continued)

3. The Glory of the Lord
4. The Spirit of Life
5. The Spirit of Power

My Blessing

The Spirit's name "My Blessing" is implied throughout the Scriptures in describing revival (see Pss. 24:5; 133:3; Mal. 3:10). The expression "blessing of God" is often used by Christians to describe the benefits that God pours out on His people, but ultimately the blessing of God is God Himself. During times of revival, Christians often have a renewed appreciation of who God is and the various blessings associated with His Person and work. This is a result of the Holy Spirit's work in revival as God's Blessing.

The Fullness of God

When those who experience revival attempt to describe their experience to others, it is not uncommon for them to confess, "The place seemed filled with the presence of God," or, "I sensed being filled with God until it seemed as if I could not contain any more." As the Fullness of God, the Holy Spirit makes Christians intensely aware of God's presence during times of revival. Contemporary observers call this "atmospheric revival."

Paul prayed that the Ephesians would "be filled with all the fullness of God" (Eph. 3:19, *NKJV*). In a sense God is present everywhere and at all times. But it is easy for Christians to believe in His omnipresence yet fail to recognize His presence in their daily lives. In revival it is as though the Holy Spirit opens our eyes so that we can see God's presence in our midst and allow Him to change our lives.

Results of God's Presence in Revival

1. Believers expect God to work (faith).
2. They are stirred to pray more.
3. They are motivated to good works.
4. They search themselves for sin.

5. They repent and cleanse themselves.
6. They offer praise to God.

The Glory of the Lord

Another revival expression for the Holy Spirit often used to describe revival is "the Glory of the Lord." Paul wrote,

> But we all, with unveiled face, beholding as in a mirror the glory of the Lord, are being transformed into the same image from glory to glory, just as by the Spirit of the Lord (2 Cor. 3:18, *NKJV*).

The Glory of the Lord is based on the Old Testament Shekinah, an actual manifestation of the glory of God to Israel during the wilderness wanderings and in Solomon's Temple.

During revival Christians once more gain a renewed vision of God in His glory and majesty through the ministry of the Holy Spirit. They sense being in the presence of God in all His splendor. They respond as did Isaiah (see Isa. 6:5) or John (see Rev. 1:17) in recognizing their complete unworthiness in His presence. When they view God in His glory, they begin to see just how far short they have fallen (see Rom. 3:23), and they repent of their sin. Perhaps the phrase "glory to glory" is an actual description of a revival when God continues to pour His blessings (or His presence) upon those who wait for revival.

The Spirit of Life

As the Spirit of Life, the Holy Spirit is the agent of revival, because He gives new life to the revived. "For the law of the Spirit of life in Christ Jesus has made me free from the law of sin and death" (Rom. 8:2, *NKJV*). The word "revival" is derived from two Latin words that mean "to live again," and it has two applications. First, revival is the return of New Testament Christianity to a group of people. Second, revival is a believer returning to his "first love" (Rev. 2:4)—the time when he was first converted.

One of the Hebrew words translated "revival" in the Old Testament is *chayah*, which is most often translated "living." Revival involves God's granting new life to dead or dying Christians and churches. This granting of life is a ministry of the Spirit of Life. Many Christians experience this revived life as they understand that the Holy Spirit has placed them "in Christ" so that He can live the Christian life through them.

The Spirit of Power

We have noted that although the phrase "spirit of power" found in 2 Timothy 1:7 may refer to the Christian's spirit, the *source* of this power is the Holy Spirit. This term would have caused Timothy to recall the revival in Ephesus when "the word of the Lord grew mightily and prevailed" (Acts 19:20, *NKJV*). During times of revival, Christians and churches are energized to do the work of God in a much more intense manner than may be the case normally. That is one reason churches often experience numerical growth during revivals. When the energy of revival is channeled into productive ministry, God often blesses our efforts in evangelism by giving extraordinary results. The key to this success in ministry is the Spirit of Power at work in our lives.

Revival and the Outpouring of the Holy Spirit

Two terms are used in revivalist literature to describe the experience of revival: "the outpouring of the Holy Spirit" and "the anointing of the Holy Spirit." Although experiences of revival are described in many ways, the expression "outpouring of the Holy Spirit" is usually a reference to the corporate spirit of revival in an area or among a group of Christians. In contrast, when revival comes to an individual, it is often described as an "anointing of the Holy Spirit."

The Outpouring of the Holy Spirit	The Anointing of the Holy Spirit
Revival of a group	Revival of a person

The terms "outpouring" and "anointing" refer to different degrees of the same ministry of the Holy Spirit. When the Holy Spirit comes upon one person, it is an anointing. When the Holy Spirit comes upon many people, it constitutes an outpouring. Both of these phrases find their origin in the Scriptures and are consistently used in revivalistic literature to describe an intense experience with the Holy Spirit. Both expressions are also tied to the revival names of the Holy Spirit.

Outpouring Names of the Holy Spirit

1. Rain names
2. The Anointing

Rain Names

Several of the revival terms for the Holy Spirit are tied to the picture of the Spirit watering the ground. These descriptive terms include "the dew" (Hos. 14:5), "floods upon the dry ground" (Isa. 44:3), "a fountain of water" (John 4:14, *NKJV*), "rain upon the mown grass" (Ps. 72:6), "rivers of living water" (John 7:38), "showers that water the earth" (Ps. 72:6), and "water" (Isa. 44:3).

In each case the Holy Spirit is described symbolically as the means by which God pours out His blessing to revive and refresh Christians, much as rain is the means by which the earth is refreshed. These revival names should not be taken as denials of the personality of the Holy Spirit but rather as descriptions that picture His influence in refreshing people who are spiritually thirsty, wilted or dying.

The Anointing

Another revival name of the Holy Spirit is "the anointing" (1 John 2:27), another term we considered earlier. Some view this name exclusively as a saving name of the Holy Spirit because they feel that the anointing causes people to understand spiritual truth. As such, the term refers to the illumination of the Holy Spirit.

But the Anointing can also be considered a revival name. The anointing of the Holy Spirit is not just a salvation experience but also a post-conversion experience suggested by the contrast of the nature and effects of the anointing and regeneration.

Because the Holy Spirit is the agent of regeneration, it is to be expected that similarities are found between regeneration and other ministries of the same Spirit. The differences serve to distinguish these various works.

Under the Levitical law, two anointings were practiced: the anointing of blood and the anointing of oil. This was practiced at the cleansing of a leper (see Lev. 14) and the consecration of a priest (see Lev. 8). Both have typical application for the Christian life. The cleansed leper is a type of one who is cleansed from sin. And the New Testament identifies the believer as part of "a royal priesthood" (1 Pet. 2:9). This dual anointing represents the twofold experience of believers. They are first anointed with the blood of Christ (that is, in regeneration), and then with the "oil" of the Holy Spirit in revival. David's desire to be "anointed with fresh oil" (Ps. 92:10) suggests that the anointing is a repeatable experience with the Holy Spirit.

Seven Steps Toward an Outpouring of the Holy Spirit

What can be done to encourage an outpouring of the Holy Spirit so that we might experience His revival names? Some Bible teachers believe that we will never experience another great outpouring of the Holy Spirit, or, if a worldwide revival takes place, it will come from God alone and cannot be the result of seeking God through prayer.

Others, however, realize that God responds to the prayers of His people, governs His activities by certain laws and will honor the promises of Scripture if we meet those conditions. Perhaps God will send a massive revival when His conditions are met (see 2 Chron. 7:14).

A survey of the biblical references to an outpouring of the Holy Spirit, or the pouring out of a blessing of God on His people, suggests seven principles associated with these promises. When an individual Christian meets these conditions, he or she may experience the anointing of the Holy Spirit. When a group of Christians together meet these conditions, then God will pour out His Holy Spirit on them.

1. The Principle of Desire

The first precondition for revival is desire. God's people must want it. God has promised, "I will pour water on him who is thirsty, and floods on the dry ground; I will pour My Spirit on your descendants, and My blessing on your offspring" (Isa. 44:3, *NKJV*). Here, as in other places in Scripture, God uses the imagery of thirst to identify an intense desire on the part of people for revival. God never sent revival to any people who did not first *want* a revival or the fruits of revival.

2. The Principle of Prayer
Prevailing and believing prayer is often mentioned as a precondition of revival in Scripture. Zechariah the prophet used the imagery of rain to describe the outpouring of the Holy Spirit, urging the people, "Ask the Lord for rain in the time of the latter rain. The Lord will make flashing clouds; He will give them showers of rain, grass in the field for everyone" (Zech. 10:1, *NKJV*; see also Joel 2:23; Jas. 5:7).

Prevailing prayer has been so much a part of historical revivals that some writers regard revival as a prayer movement. The kind of prayer that is essential to produce revival blessing is that which prevails, and this may be characterized as the prayer of faith.

3. The Principle of Repentance
Repentance of all known sin, which involves the humbling of the believer, is another essential precondition of revival. "Turn at my rebuke; surely I will pour out my spirit on you; I will make my words known to you" (Prov. 1:23, *NKJV*). The Scriptures also declare,

> For thus says the High and Lofty One who inhabits eternity, whose name is Holy: "I dwell in the high and holy place, with him who has a contrite and humble spirit, to revive the spirit of the humble, and to revive the heart of the contrite ones" (Isa. 57:15, *NKJV*).

4. The Principle of Yielding
Perhaps the most frequently mentioned precondition of revival in Scripture is that of a recognition of the Lordship, or Kingship, of Christ. Many of the prophetic statements concerning the outpouring of the Holy Spirit refer to a time when the people recognize

Christ as He returns to establish His kingdom (see Isa. 32:15; Joel 2:27,29; Acts 2:17-18). On the Day of Pentecost, Peter affirmed the Lordship of Christ as he concluded his sermon: "Let all the house of Israel know assuredly that God has made this Jesus, whom you crucified, both Lord and Christ" (Acts 2:36, *NKJV*).

Recognizing the Lordship of Christ usually involves the practice of seeking God, surrendering to His will and repenting of known sin. In the Old Testament people engaged in seeking God to obtain His blessing, as one might seek to obtain a request from a king.

5. The Principle of Fellowship

The unity of the brethren is identified as a precondition of revival blessing in Psalm 133. God commands His blessing in the presence of a united people. Also, both the anointing of Aaron and the dew of Hermon in this psalm are emblems of the outpouring of the Holy Spirit in Scripture. The expression "with one accord" is often used to characterize the united fellowship of the revived Church in the book of Acts (see Acts 1:14; 2:1).

6. The Principle of Worship

Praise is associated with the blessing of God. According to the *Peshitta* (an ancient Syriac translation of the Scriptures), the psalmist writes, "Whosoever offers the sacrifice of thanksgiving glorifies me; and to him will I show the way of the salvation of our God" (Ps. 50:23). This was also the way the verse was translated in both the *Septuagint* and *Vulgate* translations of the Old Testament. More recent English translations such as the *New International Version* also translate the verse in a similar way: "He who sacrifices thank offerings honors me, and he prepares the way so that I may show him the salvation of God" (Ps. 50:23, *NIV*). This means that God sends His revival blessing to those who properly worship Him.

If this reading of the verse is correct, it seems to teach that the "sacrifice of thanksgiving" (praise) is a precondition to God's manifesting His salvation. The word "salvation" should not be restricted to its soteriological sense but, as is often the case in the Old Testament, probably refers to a broader blessing of God, including that of revival. This emphasis is consistent with an earlier statement in the psalms: "But You are holy, enthroned in the praises of Israel" (22:3, *NKJV*).

Notice that God lives in the presence of a worshiping people. Their praises invite the presence of God in a unique way. At the dedication of Solomon's Temple, the praises of God's people ushered in the presence of God in a most unique way:

> Indeed it came to pass, when the trumpeters and singers were as one, to make one sound to be heard in praising and thanking the LORD, and when they lifted up their voice with the trumpets and cymbals and instruments of music, and praised the LORD, saying: "For He is good, For His mercy endures forever," that the house, the house of the LORD, was filled with a cloud, so that the priests could not continue ministering because of the cloud; for the glory of the LORD filled the house of God (2 Chron. 5:13-14, *NKJV*).

7. The Principle of Giving to God

Scripture also associates the promise that God will pour out His blessing with the practice of His people giving to Him:

> "Bring all the tithes into the storehouse, that there may be food in My house, and try Me now in this," says the LORD of hosts, "If I will not open for you the windows of heaven and pour out for you such blessing that there will not be room enough to receive it" (Mal. 3:10, *NKJV*).

Although the concept of tithing (giving 10 percent of our income to God) is interpreted differently among evangelical Christians today, sacrificial giving is an essential condition to be met in preparing for an outpouring of the Holy Spirit.

One reason some Christians do not properly give of their means to God is that they fail to understand the spiritual nature of biblical stewardship. The taking of an offering in church is not just a means used by churches to raise money, although that is one purpose. The Scriptures identify several essential principles of financial stewardship. First, giving is a spiritual matter, not just a financial one (see v. 7). Second, failure to give money to God is a personal affront to Him (see v. 8). And third, God will withhold many blessings from His people if they do not give to Him (see v. 9).

God encourages His people to prove Him, or test Him, in the financial area of their lives (see v. 10). When they do so, they discover that God rewards them abundantly. First, He rewards their faith (see v. 10). Second, they are protected (see v. 11). Third, God gives them fruit in their lives (see v. 12).

From time to time, Christians ask God for revival. They seek renewed meaning to their faith. These seven principles make believers revival friendly so that it is possible for them to experience the fullness of the revival terms for the Holy Spirit. As we meet these conditions in our lives, God will anoint us with the Holy Spirit, which will result in personal revival. If others join us in our effort to encourage revival, God will pour out His Holy Spirit on a larger group and effect a revival. If we want to experience revival in our personal lives, we can do something specific about it.

13

The Pictorial Names of the Holy Spirit

Portraits of the Holy Spirit

The Gallery of Religious Art	
1. The Anointing	His role in setting us apart to God
2. My Blessing	His role in blessing us with all spiritual blessings
3. Fire	His role in presenting our worship to God
4. Oil	His role in consecrating us to God
The Gallery of Social Customs	
1. A Deposit	His role in guaranteeing our salvation
2. The Doorkeeper	His role in bringing us to the Good Shepherd
3. The Enduement	His role in clothing us for ministry
The Gallery of Nature	
1. The Dew	His role in daily refreshing us
2. A Dove	His role in bringing fruition
3. Rivers	His role in filling us to overflowing
4. Wind and Water	His role in regeneration

Some of the names of the Holy Spirit are highly symbolic in nature. These terms may be described as pictures that illustrate different truths about the Holy Spirit. These portraits of the Holy Spirit are hung throughout the Scriptures to help us understand a little about the nature of both His Person and His work. When considering these picture names of the Holy Spirit, we should be careful not to come to conclusions that may be contrary to the clear teaching of Scripture. For example, pictures of the Holy Spirit as the Anointing Oil must not lead to the idea that He is actually a substance instead of a Person.

Despite their limitations, the picture names of the Holy Spirit contribute to our understanding of the third Person of the Trinity. These names describe the Holy Spirit in a context that is more familiar to us than such abstract concepts as grace, love and holiness.

Among the various pictorial names of the Holy Spirit are "the Anointing," "My Blessing," "a Deposit," "the Dew," "the Doorkeeper," "a Dove," "an Enduement" (clothing), "the Finger of God," "Fire," "Fountain," "the Guarantee," "the Oil," "Rain," "Rivers," "Water" and "Wind." Each of these names is ascribed to the Holy Spirit in Scripture in a specific context. To this list some Bible teachers would also add Eliezer, Abraham's servant, who went out from Abraham the father to find a bride for his son Isaac (see Gen. 24). They see a parallel between Abraham's servant and the work of the Holy Spirit in gathering the Church, which is described as the Bride of Christ during this age.

Perhaps the best way to consider the various pictorial names of the Holy Spirit is to do so in the context of a museum or art gallery. In a large art gallery, various artifacts may be arranged in different groupings around a common theme. As we enter this museum devoted to the Holy Spirit, we will be viewing 11 portraits that are arranged in three separate galleries.

The Pictorial Names of the Holy Spirit

The Gallery of Religious Art	The Gallery of Social Customs	The Gallery of Nature
1. The Anointing	1. A Deposit	1. The Dew
2. My Blessing	2. The Doorkeeper	2. A Dove
3. Fire	3. The Enduement	3. Rivers
4. Oil		4. Wind and Water

A Gallery of Religious Art

The first gallery in this museum may be described as the gallery of religious art. Some of the pictorial names of the Holy Spirit are drawn from the religious setting of Israel's national religion. Four of these religious picture names are "the Anointing," "My Blessing," "Fire" and "Oil."

The Anointing

It was customary in the religion of the Jews to set someone or something apart for God by an anointing with oil. The furnishings of the Tabernacle were anointed as were people who were set apart for such roles as prophet, priest or king. In each situation the anointing signified that the person or thing being anointed was set apart for the special service of God.

In the Old Testament context, only a few believers were filled with the Spirit for service. In the New Testament, in a certain sense, every Christian has "the anointing" (1 John 2:27). This means that every Christian today has been set apart for God for some special service. You can do something for God that only you can do for God. Christians should yield to the leading of the Anointing in their lives and use their spiritual gifts in the unique ministry opportunities prepared for them.

My Blessing

The second portrait in this gallery shows the priest with arms raised as he blesses the nation. This blessing is also a picture of the Holy Spirit (see Isa. 44:3). Many pastors today conclude their worship service by lifting their hands and reciting a benediction or blessing. When the priest offered his blessing on the people, it was not merely to conclude some aspect of worship but also to tell the people of God's favor upon them. Even when this blessing occurred at the end of a religious ceremony, the granting of this blessing upon the people was often the beginning of the heartfelt celebration and worship of God from the people themselves.

Perhaps this would be a good point in our tour of the gallery to pause and consider the many blessings God has granted us in addition to His Blessing, the Holy Spirit. An old hymn urges

Christians to "count [our] blessings, name them one by one."
When Christians follow the advice of this hymn writer and begin
listing all the good things that God has done for them, recalling
these blessings is often the beginning of spontaneous thanksgiving
to God for what He has done.

Fire

The third portrait of the Holy Spirit in this gallery is a picture
of fire burning on the sacrificial altar. At first it appears to be an
Old Testament altar for offering sacrifices to God. But on the Day
of Pentecost, tongues of fire appeared over those gathered in the
Upper Room as the Holy Spirit was poured out on them. The fire
of God upon the altar was the means by which all that was offered
to God ascended up to God and became "a sweet aroma to the
LORD" (Lev. 1:9, NKJV).

This too has an application in the Christian life. Christians
may attempt to serve God in two ways. When they serve Him in the
flesh, the fruit that results from those efforts may be described as
corrupted: "fruit unto death" (Rom. 7:5). But when we serve God
in the Spirit, then His Holy Fire will cause our efforts to ascend
before God, and we will worship and please Him.

Oil

The final portrait we shall consider in this gallery is that of a huge
vat of oil. This was the freshly mixed holy anointing oil. This too
is a picture of the Holy Spirit (see Heb. 1:9). When the Holy Spirit
is compared to this anointing oil, several similarities immediately become apparent. First, both the anointing oil and the Holy
Spirit are unique. The mixture of perfumes and spices used in the
anointing oil were prohibited from any other use. So also the Holy
Spirit is unique.

Second, notice the size of the vat holding the oil. This anointing oil was never mixed in small amounts. More oil was always
available than one might expect would be necessary. The Holy
Spirit is also unlimited in His supply.

Third, the damp puddles we can imagine lying in the corner of the picture indicate that the mixture has just been made.

The anointing oil was always prepared as needed and was there-fore always fresh when used. So also a freshness is evident in the ministry of the Holy Spirit in our lives.

A Gallery of Social Customs

As we leave the gallery of religious art, we come to a second gallery containing portraits of the Holy Spirit drawn from social customs. Three of the pictures hanging on the walls of this room deserve special attention as we continue our tour. These portray the Holy Spirit as a Deposit, a Doorkeeper and an Enduement, or Clothing.

A Deposit

The first picture in this gallery portrays two people sitting at a table, one passing the other a document and a bag of coins. It was customary in the first century to offer a deposit as a guarantee of the person's commitment to honor a contractual agreement. The apostle Paul drew on this cultural practice when he described "the Spirit in our hearts as a guarantee" (2 Cor. 1:22, *NKJV*). At the moment a person is converted, the Holy Spirit is given as "the guarantee of our inheritance until the redemption of the purchased possession, to the praise of His glory" (Eph. 1:14, *NKJV*). The ministry of the Holy Spirit in our lives is a constant reminder (guarantee) of future blessings that God also intends to bestow upon us.

The Doorkeeper

The next picture is that of a Doorkeeper at the gate of a sheep-fold: "To [the shepherd] the doorkeeper opens, and the sheep hear his voice; and he calls his own sheep by name and leads them out" (John 10:3, *NKJV*). Jesus is the Shepherd calling His sheep. The Doorkeeper is the Holy Spirit who opens the door of salvation so that people can become Christians then opens doors of service so that Christians can lead others to Christ. Concerning Lydia, the Bible says, "The Lord opened her heart to heed the things spoken by Paul" (Acts 16:14, *NKJV*). This portrait also illustrates the similar work of Jesus as "He who opens and no one shuts, and shuts and no one opens" (Rev. 3:7, *NKJV*).

An Eluement

The final picture in this gallery is that of a wardrobe filled with various styles of clothing. Jesus implied that the Holy Spirit was the Erement of Clothing when He told His disciples, "But tarry in the city of Jerusalem until you are endued with power from on high" (Luke 24:49, *NKJV*).

Just as one dresses in a certain way prior to taking on a certain role, so too Christians should be clothed in the power of the Holy Spirit before attempting to serve God. One would not expect a mechanic to wear a three-piece suit as he goes to the garage to work on a car or a bank manager to address his board wearing bib overalls. Today special wear is available for tennis, golf or bike riding. People dress in appropriate clothes to help rather than hinder them in their tasks. Perhaps the large number of garments portrayed in this picture serves as a reminder of how few Christians have taken seriously the need to be clothed in the Holy Spirit.

A Gallery of Nature

The third and final gallery of this museum is a gallery of nature. This gallery includes several landscapes and pictures portraying the wonders of nature around us. These pictures also have something to tell us about the Holy Spirit.

The Dew

The first picture in this gallery is a landscape. It is a morning scene of a grassy meadow on the side of a mountain. As you look closely, you can see the large drops of dew still clinging to the blades of grass and flower petals in the meadow. That dew is a picture of the Holy Spirit. The Holy Spirit wrote, "I will be like the dew to Israel" (Hos. 14:5, *NKJV*). Just as the morning dew symbolizes the freshness of the morning, so too the Holy Spirit makes all things fresh and new in our lives.

A Dove

The next picture is set in the branches of a tree. If we look closely, we can see a dove sitting in its nest. Although the eggs are hidden from view, it is obvious that the mother dove is waiting for those eggs to hatch.

The Holy Spirit was described as a Dove at the baptism of Jesus: "Immediately, coming up from the water, He saw the heavens parting and the Spirit descending upon Him like a dove" (Mark 1:10, *NKJV*). The Dove, symbolic of the Holy Spirit, gently came upon the Savior. Long before this scene the Bible portrayed the Holy Spirit brooding over the waters of the newly created Earth: "The Spirit of God was hovering over the face of the waters" (Gen. 1:2, *NKJV*). This portrait of the Dove serves to remind us of His role in creation, His beauty and His gentle character.

Rivers

The third picture in this gallery is another landscape. It portrays a winding river across a dry field. The vegetation on the banks of that river appear healthy and green, although the rest of the field seems to be suffering the effects of drought.

Jesus promised that the Holy Spirit would be like Rivers of Living Water: "He who believes in Me, as the Scripture has said, out of his heart will flow rivers of living water" (John 7:38, *NKJV*). This picture serves to remind us that the source of life is the Holy Spirit, who will constantly spring up within us.

Wind and Water

The final picture is that of a storm. As we ponder this picture, we see large trees bending in the wind and rain pelting to the ground from the clouds above. The Wind and Water portrayed in this picture are portraits of the Holy Spirit. The wind is not seen, but its effects are evident. We cannot see the Holy Spirit in the salvation experience, but His effects are evident. "So is everyone who is born of the Spirit" (John 3:8, *NKJV*). The rain that is falling upon the earth in this scene is the means by which the dry earth is refreshed, just as the Holy Spirit refreshes Christians: "He shall come down like rain upon the grass before mowing, like showers that water the earth" (Ps. 72:6, *NKJV*).

Arranging a Personal Gallery of Holy Spirit Portraits

Many people today have hobbies that involve collecting and displaying things that are important to them. These collections may

390 The Ultimate Guide to the Names of God

include such things as stamps, coins, baseball cards, antiques, salt and pepper shakers, or porcelain dolls. Other people collect art, such as oil paintings, prints or carvings. Still others collect slides or pictures of the family. Collecting and displaying such items are governed by certain principles that may also be applied to arranging a personal gallery of Holy Spirit portraits in your life.

The Principle of Authenticity

Nothing is more frustrating to a collector than to acquire something, only to learn later that the item is not genuine. This can have devastating effects as we arrange our personal gallery of portraits of the Holy Spirit. We need to be careful that all that is evident in our lives is the product of the Holy Spirit rather than of some other spirit. Our Christianity needs to be genuine. John's advice for first-century Christians is good advice for today as well: "Beloved, do not believe every spirit, but test the spirits, whether they are of God; because many false prophets have gone out into the world" (1 John 4:1, *NKJV*). That which is authentic of the Holy Spirit will affirm the Lordship of Jesus in our life and cause others to have a higher regard for Him.

The Principle of Balanced Arrangement

As is apparent from the study of the various names of the Holy Spirit, many different ministries of the Holy Spirit are evident in our lives. Just as a collector arranges art objects, considering an eye to balance and positioning that befits the art, so too Christians should give thoughtful attention to balancing these ministries of the Spirit. Sometimes Christians become so excited about one aspect of the Holy Spirit's ministry that they neglect other areas that are just as important. As you consider the various ministries of the Holy Spirit, be sure to let Him work in every area of your life. This is a part of Christian maturity. The word "maturity" means "complete" or "well rounded." The Christian should be complete or balanced in doctrine, character, service, giving, worship and Bible study.

The Principle of Visibility

The principle of visibility recognizes the desire of collectors to display their collection so that others can see it. As you consider your personal relationship with God, much of the Spirit's work is no doubt recognizable to you. The question is, What has the Holy Spirit done in your life that is evident to others? As we gather portraits of the Holy Spirit in our lives, we need to live in such a way that those portraits become visible to others.

The Principle of a Growing Collection

The one consistent thing about collectors is that they all collect. Something inside them keeps them searching for more. This means that they make occasional additions to the collection, resulting in periodic rearrangements of the display.

This will also take place in our gallery of the Holy Spirit. The Holy Spirit is still working in our lives, helping us become like Jesus (see Phil 1:6). Therefore, new portraits will always be added as long as we continue to allow the Holy Spirit to maintain control and as long as we continue growing in Christ.

What does your gallery of the Holy Spirit look like? Paul described his converts as "an epistle of Christ, ministered by us, written not with ink but by the Spirit of the living God, not on tablets of stone but on tablets of flesh, that is, of the heart" (2 Cor. 3:3, *NKJV*).

These studies have focused on the names of the Holy Spirit recorded in the written Word of God, the Bible. Had they been based upon that which the Holy Spirit Himself has written into your life, how might it have been different? May God help each of us as we develop our own unique galleries of the Holy Spirit.

ABOUT THE AUTHOR

ELMER L. TOWNS is Dean Emeritus of the School of Religion and Theological Seminary at Liberty University, which he cofounded in 1971 with Jerry Falwell. He continues to teach the Pastor's Bible Class at Thomas Road Baptist Church each Sunday, which is televised on a local network and Angel One. Elmer is a Gold Medallion Award-winning author, and his books include *Fasting with the Lord's Prayer, Fasting for Spiritual Breakthrough, Fasting for Financial Breakthrough, The Daniel Fast for Spiritual Breakthrough, God Laughs, How to Pray When You Don't Know What to Say* and *What's Right with the Church.*

For more information, visit:
WWW. ELMERTOWNS.COM

A LIFE TRANSFORMED BY A FAITHFUL GOD

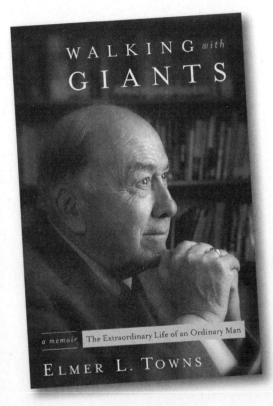

Walking with Giants
Elmer L. Towns
ISBN 978-0-8307-6382-5
ISBN 0-8307-6382-1

The ministry of Elmer Towns has spanned more than half a century and is well known to many in the Church. But what events and encounters in his early years shaped and prepared him for the extraordinary opportunities to come? *Walking with Giants* is Elmer Towns's story, in his own words, from his struggles as an adolescent to accepting salvation to pastoring his first congregation at the age of 19. You will read about the doors God opened for Elmer and his friend Jerry Falwell to found Liberty University and about the school's incredible growth over the past 40 years. Above all, you will see the faithful hand of God at work for His glory in the life of an ordinary man—and know without a doubt that He can work in you, too.

Three Bestselling Titles from
ELMER L. TOWNS
in One Volume

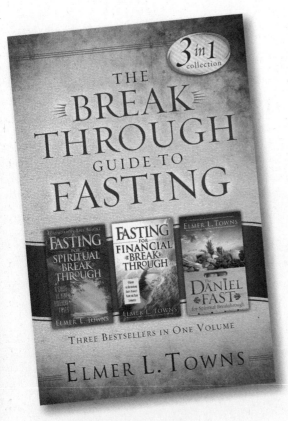

The Breakthrough Guide to Fasting
Elmer L. Towns
ISBN: 978.08307.67069

Access the wisdom and biblical knowledge of fasting in this three-in-one collection. Book one of this volume, *Fasting for Spiritual Breakthrough*, will show you the biblical reasons for fasting and how it can strengthen your faith, draw you closer to God, and enable you to truly overcome in Christ. This book will also introduce you to the nine fasts presented in the Bible—each designed for a specific physical and spiritual outcome. Book two, *Fasting for Financial Breakthrough*, reveals practical steps you can take to break the bonds of financial dependence and become a good steward of the resources God provides. Book three, *The Daniel Fast for Spiritual Breakthrough*, will coach you through a 10-day or 21-day fast based specifically on the Daniel Fast. This book includes 21 daily readings and recipes from executive chef John P. Perkins.

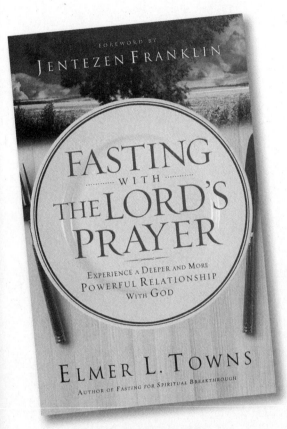